Just an Ordinary Decent Criminal

by
Paul Walmsley

Just an Ordinary Decent Criminal

© Paul Walmsley 2017

All rights reserved

The moral right of the author has been asserted

No part of this book may be reproduced or transmitted in any form or by any means without permission, except by a reviewer who wishes to quote brief passages in connection with a review written for insertion in a newspaper, magazine or broadcast.

All photographs from the Author's private collection

Introduction

For one reason and another, writing my life story has taken over five years. Putting pen to paper brought back memories which triggered other recollections buried so deeply, I couldn't speak a word the day I finally finished reading it as a complete story.

There are certain people who'll think they deserve a mention and others dreading picking it up in case I spill the beans; don't panic folks, I've been sensitive. Obviously we've all grown older and tried to move on in life, so I've changed names, been unspecific in true-life events and protected those I love dearly.

I haven't intended to hurt or annoy anybody as we all have families, established new relationships, earned respect in different aspects of our lives and even geographically relocated to avoid detection from the past. I believe some people need to know how I felt at the time and what my recollections, perceptions and opinions are. I never meaningfully set out to harm another person but sometimes, things just happen and you have to deal with it. So, to those who think I've been unfair, snide or just an idiot; I'm truly sorry.

Originally, this was written for my mum to help her understand how the secretive aspects of my life had panned out and was never meant for publication. It wasn't until I was ushered into a creative writing group in prison and began to type my handwritten, 130 000-word manuscript, that things began to change direction.

That turned out to be another life-changing moment which gave me the strength to side-step crime and head down the academic route.

To this day, I can't believe I've actually written something that may help just one person to change their path or behaviour for the better. And if it serves its purpose, then we've both won.

Acknowledgments

I'd like to thank the people who've helped to make this book happen. All my true friends past and present, my lovers and most of all, my unwavering Walmsley Clan.

Here's my list, in no order, of who I need to acknowledge:

Paul McGee, Annette Hennessey, Jo Liddy, The Jamie Carragher Sports and Learning Academy, The 23 Foundation, the lads on Spur 8 in HMP Lindholme, Doncaster, the lads in HMP Kirkham, Sharon Moss (Shelter), UCLAN, Becky Tallentire, the lads from HMP Kennet, Grace Robinson, Joy Mc, The Brunny, Cooked Meats, PSS, Dr. Lorna Brookes, SALT, ASSESS Tuition, the Koestler Trust, (Tom), Tim and Paul Speed, Gary Murphy, Dave McCabe, George Williams, Tony Husband (front cover), Sharon Sartain, Ste G, Barbara Travis, the Lanes, the Grants, my sisters (Shirley, Pat, Sue, Kathy, Lynn and Kim), my brothers (Bob and Stephen), my nieces and nephews, Ste Hill, Andy Molloy, Jackie Scott, Big Mo, Dessie, Roy, Ste H, 'Shark Bite', Lisa, Andrea, Josephine, my children: Dayne, Emilly, Paul and Lizzie and granddaughter Esmae.

Towards completion of this book, Gery Ganka Carragher passed away. She was a solid rock of help, support, creativity and boundless energy towards me completing this book and I would like to give her and Philly a special acknowledgement for guiding me with honesty, integrity and love.

Rest peacefully, Gery.

Scouse Glossary

Beaut – a form of human lowlife; often greedy, smelly, badly dressed, thick, snidey and with an extremely low moral code. A frequently-lamented pain in the arse. Often found in a bar, annoying the life out of everybody.

Bizzies – anybody who works for the police or acts like they work for them.

Blag – to use charm, cheek or any other methods possible to get your own way or gain entrance into a place, venue or event - usually without paying

Gouching – the unsavoury facial and bodily expressions exhibited by heroin addicts in small groups.

Graft/grafting - any criminal activity that could involve drugs, money and general skullduggery.

Hot knife – a method of burning solid cannabis using two heated knives

Keks – Scouse trousers.

Leg it - scarpering from a crime scene or having to leave the country urgently and without notice to loved ones.

Mooch – to hang about or loiter with intent to commit a crime. To assess the surrounding area for potential danger on the off-chance of monetary or material gain

Nasty – heroin also known as smack, bobby, the horrible or brown.

Off your/my barnet – out of control on drugs; usually ecstasy, cocaine or skunk.

On top – when the police know what you're doing

Plotted up – in a safe place and out of harm's way (usually hiding from the police or waiting for graft to arrive).

Screw – a male or female officer working for Her Majesty's Prison Service

Sitting off – waiting for graft to arrive or generally keeping your head down.

Tackle – any form of illegal drug.

The only photo of my entire family; clad in the unfortunate fashions of the 1980s

Just an Ordinary Decent Criminal

Foreword

This is the story of my life growing up on a Council Estate in Norris Green, North Liverpool.

With family, adventure, football, nostalgia, drugs and laughter as its backdrop, the book has lifted my spirit and shaken it so much that a future of integrity will put me back on the path I spectacularly veered off once my father died in 1984.

Heysel and Hillsborough; two of the world's worst footballing tragedies, have physically and emotionally challenged my soul to the extent of altering my personality and behaviour. I'm not saying that outside influences are responsible for my life, actions and reactions – far from it – it's all my own doing, but I believe things happen for a reason.

This is a record of my journey starting in childhood; you could say the foundation of my future crime-and-punishment era, and is what lead me to put pen to paper and leave a legacy of a cloaked, singular perception of a Scouse drug dealer – or as the police described me, *'just an ordinary, decent criminal'* for all to learn from and view me, laid bare.

Contents

Introduction	5
Acknowledgments	7
Scouse Glossary	8
Foreword	11
The Catalyst	15
Gay Paris	31
My Short Football Career	61
School	83
Checking My DNA	89
Sparrow Hall Boxing	93
Giz a Job	107
Flats, Trips and Cars	123
Norris Green on Magic Mushrooms	129
Landford Avenue	135
Rome and Heysel	151
Dad's Stash	155
King Kenny	173
Seeing Things	185
The State	199
Ecstasy Explosion	211
Strictly Business	219
London and Amsterdam	229
Away Days	253
Single-Cell Mentality	261
The Zoo	277
1995 – 2000	285
Cast Away	295
C-Section Day	309
The Smell of Petrol	315
Back to Graft	327

Music To The Rescue	333
Dead For One Minute	359
Istanbul - The Best Night of My Life	367
Six Minutes of Sheer Joy	383
Hero Worship	393
A Flight to Treasure	397
Charity Begins at Home	401
My Oasis	407
Star Struck	413
Another Chance to Escape the Drug Game	417
Domino Effect (Tumbling Down)	421
The Shit Hits The Fan	425
Hiding Out	435
On The Move	439
Back to the Dam – Keep Moving	443
My Greek Reunion	449
Chaos	459
Back to You, Fuckers	467
Where Do I Go?	471
Family Time	475
Charity on Your Toes	487
Sky News	491
Gone Fishing	495
The Final Goodbye	497
Decision time	501
Final Bender	507
The Court Process	511
Prison Life	517
Out of Place	523
Back to Court	525
Get On With It	533

Moving On 537
The Truth 539
Epilogue 543

The Catalyst

The best journeys are rarely planned, and walking out of a shop in Maghull, north Liverpool holding an ice-cold can of Dr Pepper, I was about to discover the price of life itself.

It was spring 2000, my two pals had picked me up in their car and proceeded to drive down the country lanes in Melling towards Southport. The plan was to view a working farm which had barn space available for rent. It was apparently perfect for cultivating skunk and we could have a large, growing farm up and running in no time.

The mood was great in the car as we chuckled and swapped stories about street life in Liverpool. I remember singing the catchy jingle from the Dr Pepper advert; *'Dr Pepper what's the worst thing that can happen?'* as I quenched my thirst.

We arrived at the farm, drove into the cobbled courtyard and parked up next to a white van beside two blue, barn doors. As we got out of the car, I could hear walkie-talkies in the background and felt a bit uneasy. In a flash, the huge doors flew open and I was knocked to the ground by a blow to the back of my head. A feeling of impending doom started to course through my veins.

Another blow to my head and I was grabbed by my coat collar and pistol whipped to the side of my forehead. Blood splattered all over my face and I could taste the salt as I tried to make sense of what the fuck was happening. My face was burning and I could taste the petrol that was being poured on me, then I knew it was time to start praying.

'This is the beginning of the end' I thought, as my life literally flashed in front of my eyes at warp speed. I reverted to a child and the moment I watched my beloved Liverpool FC just before my 5th birthday.

Dreaming of glory at our Norris Green garden gate

It was May 1974 in downtown Moscow… well, you might have thought so, looking around at the grey, drab, Norris Green council estate in North Liverpool. It looked like radical Communist groups had been waging pitch battles with the long-haired, flared-trouser-wearing Scouse militia. It was battle scarred in places, but in a far distant, corner was a rainbow of hope which shone for half of the masses; Liverpool Football Club and in particular, Bill Shankly.

This is my hometown; where my roots were down and the place that would mould and punch me into the person I am today.

I was sitting watching my mum put the Liverpool Echo's broadsheet pull-out section into our front living-room window. I couldn't make out what it said as it was only coming through backwards from inside the house, so I went into the front garden by the rows of red rose bushes which lined the path and flowerbed in front of the window. I gazed up to read, *'Come on you Reds - Good Luck Liverpool'.*

I looked into next door's window and noticed they had the same sign but with red and white crepe paper strips which had been twisted to decorate the inside of the window frame, but it didn't look that good as their net curtains seemed dirty and had the hue of off-white chewing gum. I compared our gleaming, vinegar-smelling pristine, decorated window to our neighbour's and was filled with delight as ours looked far superior. Two huge rosettes with massive silver FA Cups on either side of the Echo pull-out made ours look great.

It was FA Cup final day and Liverpool were playing Newcastle United. Mum began to tell me that Stephen and Robert, my two older brothers, had gone to the match and we could watch it on the telly a bit later on. My nearly-five-year-old brain started to engage in weird and magical thoughts as mum switched on the huge D.E.R rented set.

"So they're in the telly... now?" I asked, tentatively.

"No, not yet, they should be there in about an hour."

This got me thinking, so I went round to the back of the TV and started to figure out how my brothers would get in this four-legged box. I was amazed and intrigued.

"So they're gonna be in that telly... in an hour, Mum?" I needed to clarify this information so I could try and make an acceptable assumption as to what was actually happening.

"Yeah," replied mum, as she began to vacuum the living room with the upright Hoover.

I stood frowning at the cable coming from the TV into the hole in the outside wall and asked mum, while pointing to a specific spot on the cable.

"So if they're gonna be in that telly in an hour ..." I paused. "They should be about there right now…"

My mind had shrunk my brothers and somehow I pictured a microscopic coach travelling down the cable into the back of the television with thousands of other Liverpool supporters doing the same thing. This truly baffled me but my mum thought it funny and mentioned it to my dad when he came into the living room. They both had me at it, asking me every five minutes where I thought my brothers would be. Inevitably, I would be guessing the position of my shrunken-to-a-speck-of dust-sized siblings by pointing ever-so closer to the cable. I really believed my brothers were in there somehow, much to my parents' delight.

I was glued to the screen for five or six hours trying to catch a glimpse of them every time the spectators came onto the bulbous screen, but to no avail.

That is my first recollection of a family occasion, the 3-0 victory was the icing on the cake and gave me the football bug. It was like somebody had injected me with everlasting passion and I loved it. I was hooked.

I was the youngest of nine kids; I had six sisters and two brothers: Shirley, Robert, Patricia, Kim, Stephen, Kathy, Suzanne and Lynn. My mum's name is Kathy and Dad, Robert, but everybody knew him as Bobby. We weren't the only ones who lived in our house; my Dad's mum and the occasional friend of one of my siblings would stay with us too, so at any given time in our three-up, three-down, end-terrace house with a front and back garden, there could be 14 people living, breathing, sweating, farting, laughing and eating. It was hectic but colourful and entertaining, with never a dull moment.

Everybody under our roof always had music playing but my sisters' was the loudest. Diana Ross, Stevie Wonder, Bay City Rollers, Chic, Rose Royce, Earth, Wind and Fire, BA Robertson,

Supertramp, Wishbone Ash, Gerry Rafferty ... I could go on forever but I'll only mention two more, Glen Campbell and John Denver, who Dad would have blaring out most Sunday mornings from about 11am on our Waltham Stereo in the parlour.

I went to my first football match in the 1975/6 season – when I said I went, I mean my sisters took me in at three-quarter time. This was when the gates opened to let the crowd out with 15 minutes remaining which would give the stragglers outside a chance to catch the end of the game. It was Liverpool v Manchester City and the colours were amazing. The grass looked like the green baize of a snooker table under the brightest white lights, high up in the sky. It was as if it was painted green and the Man City kit was the bluest of summer skies you could ever imagine. The contrast of red, sky blue and the green grass was stunning and vivid. The noise of the crowd would sway like the wind as they followed the ball with *'Ooooohs* and *aaaaaaaaahs'* and gasps of anticipation when it was glued to Kevin Keegan's boots as he advanced, turning one way then the next like a ballroom dancer. It was dreamlike and that feeling, sound and sight, combined with the smell of piss will never leave me.

Football, family and friends always played a major role in the early development of my life. My dad was a docker: he drove a fork-lift truck and controlled cranes and other machinery on Liverpool docks at different stages of his life. There were times when I would wake up and open my bedroom door to find boxes, couches, car parts, shelled peanuts and almost anything else you can imagine blocking my route downstairs. I'd have to clamber over stuff to make my way to school or football training, then I'd look around for police cars or any other signs as to why our home had become a storage warehouse overnight.

On one occasion, I found myself having to zigzag my way around Talbot Horizon car doors and hatchback windows just so I could eat my breakfast. Using a Talbot Horizon rear window as a lap tray one Monday morning was strange but it seemed the accepted thing at the time.

No questions were ever asked regarding these strange occurrences, I knew better than that from an early age. The sight of me having to squeeze through my front door to get to my mates who were waiting for me to come and play football was nothing new. I couldn't let them know what goodies were behind the door.

Dad was a stern father but did let his guard down on occasions and have a laugh with us. It must have been difficult for him having to be a father to nine kids – hats off to him for that.

With all those children, obviously, there had to be vices and there were two of them: whisky and birds. By birds, I mean budgies, zebra finches and canaries, not strippers or ladies of the night (I think). He had his own retreat at the bottom of the back garden; an aviary and workshop, just for him.

Dad would go out every night at about 9 o'clock, walk over to his watering hole, *The Crown* on the East Lancashire Road and return a couple of hours later. Most nights, mum would have us on lookout from our bedroom windows. The reason being that when dad returned, a bit tipsy, he would *always* change the channel on the telly - regardless of what was on. To counteract this, Mum would always turn over from what she was watching, knowing that Dad would turn it back when he got home. We used to sit there on school-holiday nights and giggle with Mum knowing he was en route. She'd put his glasses on and mimic him half-pissed changing channels. He always thought he was in control, but more often than not, Mum had the last laugh.

There were some nerve-racking moments in our house too. Mum would have dad's meal ready and in front of him the second he walked through the door after work. Every night, bang on cue. Once, I was sitting on the couch with my tea on my lap when he came in and sat down to be greeted by Mum who put his plate on the coffee table in front of his chair. He took one forkful of his food and flipped. The plate was launched and smashed against the wall behind my head, I shat myself and froze.

"KATHLEEN!" he bellowed. Now if you got your full title, it spelt trouble. Mum rushed into the room and started to flap and fuss over dad.

"What's up, Love?"

"What's up? Don't you ever, ever, EVER put salt on my omelette!" He barked with venom.

'Oh, my God.' I thought, then I started to giggle to myself. I couldn't believe he was so pissed off because she'd put salt on his eggs. Was he serious? Did I really just witness that?

I looked at Mum who was a bit flustered, grabbed my plate and fled to my bedroom. I hated them fighting, it scared me and Mum noticed this. About 20 minutes later, she came to my room, shuffling through the door with her finger on her lips telling me to be quiet, then she whispered.

"Son, the top fell off the salt and it went all over Dad's tea. I tried to wipe it off but mustn't have got rid of it all." She started to giggle at Dad's antics from earlier on.

"Don't you ever, ever, EVER put salt on my omelette!" she chuckled. We both started to do it, still whispering because if Dad had heard us ... He did have a temper and if any one of his kids got out of line, they would face the wrath of Bobby the Hollywood Docker (his nickname on the docks). He'd come down on you like a ton of sharp bricks, so you'd definitely feel it.

Mum would do the weekly shop for the household on a Saturday afternoon and by Monday there'd be nothing to eat, food didn't last long in our house. Dad's favourite was the Sayer's Victoria sponge cake which Mum guarded with her life. Dad would often line us up like the Von Trapp family and interrogate us.

"Who's taken the cream out of the cake?" he'd demand, Gestapo-like, obviously not in a German accent as that would be weird, but it would be accompanied by a look that could cut you in half.

The cream never lasted as long as the sponge because we would all run our fingers round the edge of the cake at different times, taking a finger-full of fresh cream. We'd then press down the top layer to push the cream to the edge again so Dad wouldn't notice. But when nine people did it in the space of three hours, the cake ended up looking like a pointless pancake. That fresh cream was worth the ID parade we all undertook with our hands outstretched for examination.

There were times when Dad was nowhere to be found, sometimes for as long as 10 days at a time. Mum never raised an eyebrow and I knew I'd get a treat when he eventually came home, stinking of whisky.

This was because, three times a year the docks provided him with the opportunity of nearly drinking himself to death or getting enough extra money to feed the family for the year. He did them both with one clean sweep when this particular boat came in.

The whisky boat would provide him and his workmates a place to pilfer and live for a week or even longer if needed. The hold would contain enough cases of whisky to drown a couple of whales and preserve them forever. They would take the cases from the centre of the stack and make a passage to the middle, then unload enough cases to make room for living quarters for six men for a week, right in the middle of the cargo hold. They would then have the cases on hand to fill the passageway and entrance giving the illusion that it hadn't been touched. That's when a Union meeting would be called and all the stevedores would go on strike for a week. Bingo! Nobody would go near the boat and the six dockers sat tight in the hold with just whisky for a pillow. In the meantime, the bottles would be getting moved and sold around every nook and cranny the dockers could stagger to.

After a week or so, Dad would appear stinking of whisky and start to hand out £5 notes to all the finger-licking Von Trapp children. Mum would also get a nice bundle of cash to spend before Dad would traipse to bed and sleep, usually for two days or more.

Mum always looked her best at these times, I suppose it could be a case of absence makes the heart grow fonder or more likely 'whisky just got me a new hairdo, coat and five more tickets for the Bingo that night'. She was happy and that made me happy, plus I had extra money to go and spend on my beloved Liverpool Football Club. So it was win, win for all of us when the whisky boat came in.

Norris Green was a predominantly Catholic area and I was christened Catholic, but for whatever reason, I ended up going to a Church of England school; Ranworth Square Primary. The headmaster, Mr. Parry was Everton crazy; in fact, he was on the board in some capacity or other. He would often arrange for some Everton first-team players to come and visit and give us a talk. Mick Lyons showed up once and I remember his head was massive and he looked like a giant in his royal blue tracksuit as he stood in the assembly hall in the middle of our school.

There were two famous footballers who went to Ranworth Square and their pictures hung with pride outside the headmaster's office; Joe Royle and Steve Coppell. I always thought my picture would end up hanging alongside the two England internationals one day, in fact I dreamt about it on many occasions.

My secondary school was Ellergreen Comprehensive on Abbottsford Road, about half a mile away from our house. All my mates went to St Philomena's in Sparrow Hall; this was a rough-as-toast Catholic school. I'd asked my mum to arrange for me to go there with my friends but it just never happened. I was gutted but had to settle for my lot.

My first few days in high school were strange as I didn't know anybody so I didn't trust a soul. I bought myself a red pocket book and wrote all the lads names out of my class and one girl, Joanne Terry, she was a proper buzz, plus I fancied her.

Each day I would mark my classmates out of 10 and stash my book under my mattress. At the end of each week, I'd write how I felt about each of them, obviously taking into account the recent points they'd earned from my scoring system. I eventually whittled it down to four lads and Joanne Terry. This went on for about six weeks until Dad called me downstairs one Saturday morning in a very stern manner.

I trundled down to find him sitting in his favourite chair with my red note book in his hand.

"What the fuck is this?" he asked, swinging the book from side to side between his thumb and forefinger.

"Why?" I whispered, nervously. I was shitting myself by this time because although I knew I'd done nothing wrong, it just felt like I had. I explained the rating system and my reasoning behind it and was greeted by a huge grin on his face by the time I'd stopped talking.

"Come and sit here, Son," he said, lovingly. He began to tell me he thought the red book was some sort of gambling racket and gave me advice on that first. He told me the best way to double your money is not to gamble but fold it in half and put it back in your pocket. Then he ran his finger slowly down the list and said knowingly,

"So it looks like you've got four lads who you're classing as your proper friends".

"Yeah, yeah." I replied.

"Well, get rid of two of them, Son, because you already have two brothers and it only takes four people to carry your coffin."

Fucking hell! I'm 11 years old and my Dad's talking about my coffin. Is he serious?

To be fair, it took about another 20 years before I understood the implications of that wise statement and it still resonates with me today.

There were some situations which required a certain skill and mum taught me how to handle these moments without even knowing. Dad could be a grumpy bastard at times, especially when he woke up from a nap in his comfy chair. We decided the best strategy was to let him sleep as long as possible. As soon as he began to snore gently; Mum would instruct us to 'muffle the knocker'. There would be a silent panic to find a rogue sock which we'd tie around the brass knocker to deaden the sharp rap, should anybody call round.

Another occasion I can recall involved him coming from work a little worse for drink and falling asleep as mum was putting his tea in front of him. The now-lukewarm meal was returned to the oven to be kept warm. A few hours later, Mum was looking worried as she's left the oven on high and his food was cremated. Dad was still fast asleep but she knew when he woke up, he'd be starving and demanding his dinner.

She quickly made a mixture of water, flour, lard and Oxo and heated it up in a pan. I was wondering what she was going to do until she took a teaspoon of the gloopy liquid and started to drip it down his shirt and onto his drunken, sleepy face. She shuffled out of the room stealthily and waited for him to wake up.

I stood by the living room door looking at his legs as they started to move about restlessly then in an instant, he was awake.

"Kathy! Where's my tea?" He barked in his usual, tyrannical fashion.

Mum burst through the door confidently, moved towards his chair and bent down to get eye level with him.

"Love, you had your tea when you came home". She said in a matter-of-fact kind of way.

"Have I fuck."

"Look Love, you came in half pissed, sat there and had your tea and fell asleep." Mum paused for effect. "Look, it's on your shirt and round your mouth."

He put his hand to his mouth to reveal the drops of greasy brown gravy. After a quick sniff and look at the drips on his shirt he looked up at Mum and said,

"Alright, Kath, I'm still hungry. Can I have some cheese and crackers?"

"Yeah, I'll sort it now." Mum said cheekily with a conspiratorial glance in my direction.

If there was a book of *'Moves to Fool Your Partner',* then that would be in Chapter 1. I loved every good and bad minute I spent around my family, friends and football, it was the start of my mind-bending, brain-sharpening, eye-popping adventure called life.

Enjoy the ride.

Gay Paris

A bewildering kaleidoscope of patterns and colours confirms I'm a product of the 70s

It's 11th April 1981, just 90 minutes before the European Cup semi-final first leg at Anfield. I'm with my brothers, Stephen, Robert and his girlfriend Pam, heading to the match in Robert's cream Dolomite Sprint. This was no big deal back then; it was a regular occurrence for Liverpool, my beloved football team, to be at the dizzy heights of European football's elite competition.

We were playing the massively-talented, physical and muscular German-champions, Bayern Munich, who came with a huge pedigree and the prolific international striker; Karl-Heinz Rummenigge, as their target man.

The journey to the stadium was filled with talk of the final in Paris, obviously this was utmost in Pam's mind as she was dreaming of the possibility of a few days' window shopping in Gay Paris (well that's what I presumed, being the youngest brother of six girls who never stopped talking about shopping, waspy belts, pencil skirts and good-looking fellas).

The match itself was a tense, tit-for-tat affair ending in a 0-0 draw. Graeme Souness, our harder-than-nails, midfield string-puller was injured and had to sit this one out. All the Liverpool fans feared the worst but as it happens, it turned out to be a great result as away goals counted double and at least the Germans had to score to make any strides into getting to the final on May 27th in Paris. 'We only need one goal and they need to score two,' I thought while walking away from the throbbing, sweating, magical place they call Anfield Road.

"One goal and we'll go through." I said excitedly.

Because I got no reply, I repeated it, twice as loud as the first time.

"One goal and we'll go through."

"Do you reckon, Kidda?" asked Stephen.

"Yeah, we'll do the Germans you know." I insisted – fighting talk from an 11¾-year-old, crazed football fan who thought Liverpool was the centre of the universe – because in my developing brain, it was. We had The Beatles, Liverpool, Everton, the two cathedrals, the Docks and Meccano, so in my mind, the universe revolved around the actual spot I was standing on at any given time. I imagine everybody I knew thought the same, too. Looking back, it was one of life's given things – a mental strength and the belief that the universe did orbit me.

"Well, if we get through to the final, you can go." Stephen replied.

"WHAT?" I said, looking at him with an intense feeling of elation starting to course through my veins. "Deffo? Can I deffo go, Ste?"

"Yeah, not a problem, I'll sort it with Mum and Dad."

"Get in there!" I shouted as I jumped in the air, clenching my fists. My hands were throbbing from all the clapping I'd been doing for two solid hours at the match and were red raw.

"Honestly? Honestly?" I asked again but now I was looking at my other brother for some reason, I think because I'd jumped and spun in the air like a performing mongrel on a cheap talent show and landed the opposite way.

"Yeah, you can go if we get through, Paul,' said Robert.

Result! I'd had two yeses from two brothers, so in the mind of an 11-year-old, crazed, football fan; that was 100% confirmation. I was going, cut and dried.

I should have taken into account the six or seven pints of lager they'd both had before and during the match, but that hadn't entered my head.

The next morning I was up early and out of the house like a flash with news of a possible trip to Paris for my second European Cup final. The second leg was a week later at the Olympic Stadium in Munich.

It couldn't come quickly enough for me now. I read every sports' section in any newspaper I could get my hands on to gather as much information about the location of the final. The Park du Princess National Stadium in the centre of Paris was the venue and it was likely to be against Real Madrid who'd already beaten their opponents in the first leg.

During that week, I must have slipped in the possibility of me going to the match at every possible opportunity or break in conversation. My mates all looked on in amazement and must have been envious at the time. Nobody ever questioned me or doubted for a minute that I would be going - if we eventually got through, that is.

The Wednesday morning of the second leg was the same as any other, except when I finished school I ran home in record time without breaking sweat. I was up the stairs in a flash and changed out of my school uniform and into my beloved red shirt with the number 7 on the back – my hero, Kenny Dalglish. This man gave me my purpose and my reason for living.

I know this sounds a bit dramatic for a child, so I'll explain. We've all had times when we were younger when the thought of death was running through our minds and we tried to make sense out of it. *'When will I die? Why does this happen?'* and so on...

These were serious issues to a youngster like me especially as I used to cry myself to sleep sometimes thinking that one day I would be dead – the end, kaput. I suppose you could say I was an earnest child as I thought everything through. The only way I could get my head around it was to think of my 100% hero, the one I looked up to and worshipped and that person was Kenny Dalglish.

He was 15 years older than me, so in my mind he would die before me and if it was good enough for him, it was certainly good enough for me. Football had given me my answers to life and what I was searching for, and much more too.

To be honest, I was only eight or nine when I had this epiphany as Dalglish had signed in June 1977 and I was seven at the time. You can understand how I felt about Kenny Dalglish and how I worshipped the number 7 on the back of my tiny, replica shirt.

It was the day of the semi-final second leg, the sun was cracking the flags and the blackbirds sang their heads off all day. The match was kicking off at 8pm as it was being played in Germany, which meant I could listen to it on the radio in the parlour where the Waltham stereo we had built into the cabinet, was situated. The quality of the commentary was like putting on an old, crackly, vinyl album; you could feel the warmth and genuine love that had gone into bringing that sound into your home. Very tinny but real, live and I loved it.

I tuned in about 7pm to get all the build-up – although to be fair, there wasn't that much of a build-up, most of it was in my mind.

I kept running my own imaginary commentary through my head where we would score an absolute belter in the last minute to reach the final – and who would score? Obviously, my hero, King Kenny.

The game kicked off on schedule with surprises in the Liverpool line up. Alan Kennedy and Phil Thompson were both injured and had been replaced by Colin Irwin and Richard Money, who were both steady stand-ins for Bob Paisley's tactical plans on the night, but I only had thoughts of Paris running through my mind.

The Germans had Dalglish down as Liverpool's focal point, so they made him a target man and at any given moment, kicked lumps out of him. It wasn't long before he was injured and had to be taken off; in fact it was nine minutes into the game. I was devastated; I thought my dreams had been shattered when King Kenny left the pitch.

I may have underestimated the resources of Liverpool Football Club though; we brought a virtual unknown onto the pitch. Howard Gayle was a black Scouser who ran the Germans ragged for an hour. He was as fast as light itself - or so it seemed by the tone of the commentator's voice. Our sub took that much of a battering; he had to be taken off on 70 minutes, not because he was injured but because he was starting to retaliate to the heavy-duty Germans.

Ten minutes to go in this tense occasion and my dad bounced into the room.

"Son, I need cigs and a half bottle of Bell's from the off-licence."

"But, Dad... I'm listening to the match..."

He gave me the look that said everything but actually nothing at all. I knew not to answer back but to take the money and do as I was told, I'd seen that look many times before.

Out the door, a quick left and left again onto the East Lancashire Road. Nearly every house had the match blaring from some sort of radio with their windows and doors wide open as it was a beautiful evening, so the match commentary was still freely available to me on my journey. I could just hear it in the distance as I sprinted to get Dad's luxuries. It felt like my feet never touched the ground for the ¼ mile trip.

If Jesus did walk on water, then this is how he felt, I thought – levitating on dreams, gliding on emotion as my breathing became heavy. I reached the off-licence to the roar of the fella who worked there and two others who were buying themselves some booze and cigs.

"Get in der!"

"Yeeeahhhhhh!" they all shouted jubilantly whilst looking at me with their eyes nearly popping out of their heads. I heard the commentator say,

'Ray Kennedy has bundled the ball over the line, he shouldn't even be on the pitch though, he's injured and hobbling around – amazing really.'

I roared all over the shop like a crazed lunatic, quickly asked for the cigs and half bottle of whisky and paid for them, while still bouncing around with these two unknown fellas. I bolted through the door at warp speed – down the East Lancs Road and back home in record time.

My heart was pounding out of my tiny chest; the celebrations in the off-licence had taken it out of me. I was exhausted and panting like mad. I burst into the house with my ears pricked up to the commentary – I could only hear my own breathing at first, then I was greeted by the words,

'Karl-Heinz Rummenigge has levelled the tie on the night.'

I paused before realising they'd equalised, the commentator could hardly be heard over the noise of 80 000 Bayern fans blowing horns in the background. I was shitting myself. They only needed one goal and it was curtains.

We seemed to have them stretched with our formation. The last few minutes felt like hours, I was walking around the parlour like a leopard in a pen taking the longest route around the smallest space while singing, *'You'll Never Walk Alone'* to myself.

The final whistle blew and I was going to Gay Paris. The song which our fans had been singing for the past few weeks came into my head.

'On the dole, drinking wine in Gay Pareeeeeee...' to the tune of 'Here We Go'.

I went and grabbed the Liverpool Echo to confirm that *'Midweek Match'* was on at 11pm. I had to ask my Dad if I could stay up to watch as it was a school night. By now, he was buzzing too and nodded as he gently tipped a single whisky down his throat.

The next week flew by; I was on a countdown to Paris. I was asking my brothers every day about getting a passport as the furthest I'd ever been was Wembley in 1978. That was when King Kenny scored the only goal against FC Brugge.

With 10 days to go to the final, I was lying on the living room floor watching Captain Pugwash beside our Robinson and Wiley Corporation standard gas fire, when Stephen came into the room with a bulging, white carrier bag. He stood in front of the TV so I couldn't see it, so I rolled onto my side to gain a full view of the Captain and Roger, the Cabin Boy caught at sea in a heavy storm. This sudden move almost made me burn my arse as I moved closer to the fire.

"Ouch!" I yelped as I looked up at my brother.

"I've got good and bad news for you." Stephen said as he put a carrier bag on the floor in front of me, "And that's your good news."

As I looked into the bag I noticed it was bulging with Panini football stickers. I immediately emptied the contents onto the floor in sheer delight and never gave the bad-news content of the initial announcement a second thought.

Panini football stickers were every boy's playground pastime back then. We'd trade and look in amazement at how many swaps you had or how big your elastic band was to keep them all neat, tidy and in mint condition. I began to tear the packets open, in the hope of maybe filling in a whole team page or even just get some Liverpool players – that was always an added buzz and bonus, plus these stickers had a special smell due to the adhesive on them, maybe that's got something to do with the massive amount of glue sniffers today.

My brother kicked the bottom of my foot,

"I can't take you to Paris, something's come up."

"What?? Aaah, you're messing with me, Ste." I gulped with my face screwed up. I could feel tears welling and just stared at him with my jaw almost on the floor. I couldn't believe what I'd just heard, my head clicked into gear and I said rapidly,

"But our Rob's going to take me then, because the two of you said I could go – didn't you? Didn't you?"

"You'll have to speak to Rob about that when he's home from work," Stephen said quietly, as he began to slip out the living room.

Thinking back, he was probably just relieved just to have got it out of the way. He must have had other plans with his mates and to deal with an 11-year-old might have cramped their style.

I grabbed the scattered Panini stickers off the maroon, wool carpet, clutched them to my chest and moved swiftly to my bedroom to plot my next move in this ever-changing saga.

It felt like I'd had terminal news, but there was a glimmer of hope with Robert still to be confronted. He wasn't due back until around

8.30pm, so I had a few hours to make contingency plans. (This time proved to be vital as you'll find out later on).

The long wait for my brother to arrive home from Bowyers, the local pie factory, was agonising and plot filled. Every two minutes I would jump on the bed right underneath the white-wooden-framed window in my bedroom and lean my head out like a giraffe, looking in both directions for his Dolomite Sprint to appear.

A trip to the toilet was needed and by the time I'd jumped off my bed and spent a penny, I heard his car pull up. I rushed downstairs, taking five steps at a time whilst holding onto the banister. In three movements, I was unlocking the front door to greet him, with an anguished look on my angelic face.

"Rob, can I go to the final with you and Pam? Ste has to go with his mates and there's no room for me but you *did say* I could go when we walked to the car after the first leg, remember? Remember?"

All of this was said in one breath and delivered like a Labrador awaiting his master's return with a ball in his mouth. I stood and waited for what seemed like forever for him to look at me and start talking.

"Let's go inside, Paul. I need to sit down and talk with mum and dad first and we'll sort this out now." He replied calmly.

I couldn't fathom what needed to be sorted out, I was either going or I wasn't – in my mind it was as simple as that, so what was to be sorted out?

I wasn't allowed in the living room for the conversation. I tried my best to listen at the door but with the TV blaring, I couldn't hear much. To be fair, I was none the wiser for my eaves-dropping experience and I waited to be summoned into the living room with a dry mouth and sweaty palms.

"Paul! Get in here," shouted Dad.

Whoosh! I was there rapidly and never said a word; I just stood by the fire and surveyed the room like a submarine's periscope.

"I'm sorry, but you can't go." Robert said with slumped shoulders and a face to match.

I was wounded, properly wounded. All the life drained out of me. I could see that look, the one my dad gave me that told me all I need to know. I knew then, that was that. They all tried to explain but it was as if somebody had turned the volume down because I couldn't hear them, their mouths were moving but I'd switched off and I was numb by now. This was the end of the world to me.

I did mention earlier that the 3½ hours I'd waited were put to good use and I'd already put together my own hare-brained, back-up plan into play, I wasn't going to let this stand in my way. I would go by myself. Yes, an 11-year-old, Scouse, mad-football fan planning to traipse across European borders to just see his dream come true. Alone. It seemed logical to me.

I had £25 of my own money put away; it was stashed under the carpet in the corner of my bedroom where only dust and huge spiders dared to tread. As a kid, I was Jack the Lad – the face of an angel but the mind of a revolutionary, planning to overthrow the Government on a daily basis.

I was often awoken in a hushed manner in the middle of the night by my brother, Stephen. He'd ask me to get dressed quickly and meet him downstairs by the front door where he'd be waiting with my snorkel parka coat held out like he was my own live-in butler. Along with his two pals, who shall remain nameless, we'd walk towards the industrial estate on the other side of Norris Green, obviously on the mooch.

This happened roughly every six weeks and coincided with the arrival of a ship at Liverpool docks from Canada. The ship would be full of John West tinned salmon and proved to be a fine bounty for us to get our thieving hands on. It was offloaded from the ship and transferred to freight trains that would transport it to a distribution warehouse on the outskirts of Liverpool. Somehow, Ste and his pals always knew when this would happen.

The industrial estate had the rail track running right through it and this is where we would make our move. The train would travel slowly as it passed by the residential estate. It would never make a racket or it would have woken everybody up, so it had to crawl through to keep the locals happy.

Because I was the only one who could fit between the railings, I would drag something combustible onto the line, like an old mattress. I'd listen for the oncoming train and as soon as I heard it, set fire to the mattress and the train would have to grind to a halt.

Once it had completely stopped, I would find the hole in the wooden cargo trailer where the salmon was stored and crawl through it. The reason my brother waited by the door with my snorkel parka now came into play. I could only fit one case of salmon through the gap but I could fit another case into my coat pockets and down the sleeves, once I'd tucked the cuffs into my gloves. This made me more efficient as time was of the essence. We usually had about 15 minutes and would end up with about 10 cases – 240 tins. Back in 1981, tinned salmon cost about £1 a tin as it was seen as a luxury item. We would get half price if we went from pub to pub.

They always paid me £10 the next day. I never said a word to anybody and never busted their balls over my cut - so they ended up with £55 each and I was delighted with my tenner.

That was one of the ways I had my stash of cash with the dust mites and spiders under my bedroom carpet. Now this money would be put to great use in getting me to Paris.

I needed a passport quickly. I'd already done my research; I could get a one-year passport from the local post office. This was the Black Bull branch in Walton, only a bus ride or 25-minute walk from my front door. I already had the forms and had blagged my mum to sign them – she never had a clue what I was up to, plus, the sun shone out of my arse at that time so she wouldn't question me.

My pal up the road, known as Bod, was 13 but he always looked about 17 or 18. He seemed to have had that beard since birth. He was tall enough and certainly looked old enough, so he fitted the bill perfectly.

He helped me out by accompanying me to the Post Office. We stood in the queue for about 10 minutes, nervous and conspicuous until it was all done and dusted. I had a passport; it was a three-fold cardboard version with what looked like huge dog hairs embedded into it. Step One of my mission was complete.

The next component of my plan was to convince my mum and dad I was going to be staying with my mate for a few days. I sometimes watched the match with him and his dad and was occasionally allowed to sleep over. That part was a piece of cake, completed in record time as I caught my parents when they'd just come back from the pub. They'd agree to (almost) anything after a few beers and Bell's whisky chasers.

I packed my Mitre football bag with my passport along with my beloved replica kit and some other bits of clothing for my few days' adventure. I'd heard loads of talk about everybody leaving from Lime Street Station on the Tuesday at 6.30am to London, Euston. This would eventually end up in Paris in the early hours of Wednesday, the morning of the match. Everything in between would have to be winged, but I was sure I could do it. I was adamant I would get the pot of gold at the end of my rainbow - the European Cup final.

The days flew by and before I knew it, it was Monday morning when my mum shouted me for school much earlier than usual. I traipsed downstairs to find Mum, Dad and Robert sitting down, eating toast while my sister was clinking away in the kitchen making a brew. The air was filled with the aroma of toast, butter and early-morning optimism.

"Do you wanna go to the match?" Robert asked.

I looked around the room to see smiling faces, especially my dad's. That was all the confirmation I needed, the look from my dad said it all.

"Yeah, yeah, YEAH! Can I go? Honestly?"

"Yes, go and get ready because I'm taking you for a passport at 8.30 as soon as the Post Office opens. I paused... sat down and thought.

Oh, shit! I was either going to have to go along with it and tell him at the last minute that I had another one. Or I'd say nothing and just have two passports. Yeah, that's what I'd do. I'll keep my gob shut and have two; as long as I was going the Final, nothing else mattered.

"When are we gonna go, Rob?" I asked, with a ridiculous grin on my face.

"As soon as we get back from the Post Office. Pam will be here in half an hour and we're going to Lime Street Station for the 10.30 to London."

I was already packed and ready to go as a result of my own contingency plan – yippee! This couldn't happen quickly enough for me and the bottom line was, I was legitimately going and that was that.

The train journey to London and then on to Folkestone was filled with Liverpool songs, massive *'party cans'* of bitter which had to be accessed with a tin opener – oh, and the obligatory smell of piss from the overflowing toilets. To be perfectly honest, I would have endured anything to get to Paris, so the piss just added another dimension to the adventure. Now I had a smell to remember which would accompany what I'd seen and heard on the journey.

From Folkestone to Calais, we took the hovercraft which was like an inflatable pub on water. It was a short walk to the platform once we'd made our way up the jetty. To me, it was amazing, I loved every minute of the journey across the Channel in the knowledge it was edging me closer to my first trip abroad and to the European Cup final in Paris. Scousers were all over the place, singing, drinking and dancing; and I was part of it.

We arrived at Central Station in the French capital at 1.30am on the Wednesday to be greeted by a line of the Parisian riot-squad police, dressed from top to toe in battle gear and wielding sub-machine guns. Most of the travelling fans had drunk so much that the atmosphere was really subdued and you could only hear the muted voices singing football songs in the distance. The sight of these men dressed in sinister riot gear really put the shits up me. It was a sobering sight; I'd only taken the occasional sip from my brother's beer, so I could only imagine how the bevvied mob of Scousers must have felt.

We made our way to the Metro station only to be told in 'sign language' that the station closed at 1am. I remember looking at the track and seeing a huge rat just walking about without a care in the world. I also remember thinking that this was a French rat and a totally different species from the English rat; it had a different agenda, a French agenda.

It took us about 45 minutes to find the Hotel Diana on the edge of a park somewhere in a suburb of Paris. It was more of a hostel then a hotel. The sign was lit up in bright, white neon and reminded me of Lady Diana Spencer who was being mentioned a lot in the Press at the time.

Once we'd woken up the landlord and scurried up some tight, stone steps, we made our way up beautiful wooden stairs to our room for the next two nights. It was shabby but still seemed exotic to me. The smell of cigarettes and coffee had permanently stained the air and gave me the impression that I was on the film set of *The Day of the Jackal* - I liked it though. We plonked our bags on the floor and did the obligatory *stick-your-head-out-of-the-window* routine to survey the surroundings and soak up the atmosphere. I noticed it was weirdly warm and raining at the same time and that the cars parked on the streets had strange-looking number plates which reflected off the yellow street lights, like cats' eyes.

As I tried to go to sleep, I noticed a pink light in the window of the building opposite, which was so bright it kept me awake, it reflected onto our window when we switched our lights off. I asked Rob and Pam about the bright light and they both giggled and told me to go to sleep and they'd tell me in the morning. I drifted off to sleep with Parisian dreams and strange-coloured lights beaming into the room.

I awoke to the beautiful smell of strong coffee and what I now know to be freshly-baked croissants drenched in raspberry and blackcurrant jam. The smell was wonderful and had my nose twitching and my taste buds dripping. Suddenly, I realised it was the morning of the European Cup final and I was in Paris. Excitement surged through my body and in record time, I jumped into the shower, washed, dried and then put on my beloved number-7 shirt.

I couldn't wait to get down those stairs and let everybody know I was going to watch the Mighty Reds. I knew that just wearing the kit on that day and speaking a foreign language would announce my intentions to all and sundry. I was proud just to be part of the occasion and it showed on my face as confidence and belief oozed out of me – this was my local club, playing on foreign soil in a European Cup final. Things could only get better if we lifted the trophy, good old 'Big Ears' as it was known, and brought it back to Liverpool for the third time.

I bounced down the stairs in world-record time, past the reception, nodding at the fella who sat by the pigeon-holes, and into the dining room to grab some breakfast.

"The fella at the reception desk just smiled at me and he's got the worst teeth I've ever seen," I said to Rob and Pam with a giggle at the back of my throat.

Rob and Pam chuckled like two lovers would and passed me some cereal. There were Sugar Puffs in the bowl and I picked a few up, put them in my mouth and smiled at them while laughing and trying to speak at the same time.

"Bonjour...Do I look like the fella on reception?" I asked with a mouth like a row of bombed houses. It was so funny, we couldn't stop looking at this fella's teeth and mimicking him with the Sugar Puffs in our mouths. Once we'd all been fed and watered, it was time to head off on the next stage of our adventure.

Pam wanted to do some window shopping, so we had about half an hour around the Champs d'Elysee. I noticed another pink light in a massive window of a beautiful house. Remembering the giggling from the night before, I nudged Robert and asked him about it again. He leaned down and whispered in my ear,

"That's a sign for prostitutes."

I was amazed by this, as it was my first ever encounter with the seedy world of the red-light district. Everywhere I looked now, pink lights would register in my brain. There were also loads of pink flamingos lit up in windows, too. These lights now popped up like a mass-advertising campaign for the Parisian sex trade. We eventually walked out of that area and the lights seemed to disappear as quickly as they came. For the next few hours we wandered from shop to bar on the now-Scouse-filled streets.

It was about 3pm and Rob and Pam seemed drunk to me, so I decided to ask if we could get closer to the stadium. They looked at their watches and simultaneously said,

"Oh shit! We need to get tickets."

"What? We've not got tickets?" I said horrified.

"It's no problem, we'll bunk in if we don't get any," said Robert, half pissed and with red-stained lips from the wine he'd been knocking back en route.

I was starting to panic a bit by now. I'd been to the final in 1978 at Wembley with my Uncle Ronnie without any tickets and it was touch and go. We all got in that year but there was 20 of us then. It was brilliant, the bouncing sensation would never leave me, you could feel the concrete terraces shaking beneath your feet as we celebrated King Kenny's winning goal.

Compared to that incredible night at Wembley, this felt very different, for loads of reasons: the French riot police with their sub-machine guns, the language barrier and fewer people than in London, although there were plenty of Liverpool fans roaming the streets.

With all of this on my young, attentive mind, I urged Robert and Pam to get to the Parc-de-Princess stadium pronto so we could make inroads to gaining access to the ground. By hook or by crook I was going to get into this game with time to spare.

They both agreed and we hopped onto the nearest Metro heading to the stadium. It took about 30 minutes to make the journey with hordes of singing Liverpool fans heading the same way. I couldn't believe how many had travelled – in all, it was around 40 000. I kept thinking the ground capacity was 60 000 and I'd only seen five Real Madrid fans all day. Yeah, honestly, only five, but they did look really cool in their silky, white, replica Madrid kits.

As soon as we came up the Metro steps, you could see the stadium, but the Riot Police Squad that was gathered in groups of about 20 were as visible as the stadium itself. This was starting to look daunting and I was feeling intimidated by the Police presence.

At any major inner city event there's always an open public square which attracts the masses, so we made our way to the nearest one. Rob and Pam started to ask for tickets, but they all seemed to be owned by some French person and far too expensive for our budget. Walking around on the mooch for tickets I ended up bumping into a kid from our estate whose name was Phil, he was two years older than me and was there with his dad.

I didn't know him that well, but there weren't many kids in sight so his company was welcome. Robert knew Phil's dad and they allowed me to spend an hour or so with them. A rendezvous was arranged for 6pm, two hours before the kick off. To be honest I wanted to get away from Rob and Pam as they were pissed and holding hands solidly, plus I was still on the hunt for a ticket, or even the scent of one, as were Rob and Pam in another location not too far away by now (I hoped).

Ten minutes into my wander with Phil and his dad, I bumped into my brother Stephen, and his posse of scoundrel friends. We were buzzing at the chance encounter and I must have had about 30 rubs of the head from everybody in his company. He was chuffed to see me and asked who I was with, as he had left on the Saturday and knew nothing about me going to the match.

"Have you got a ticket, Ste?' I said anxiously, but also knowing our Ste's boundaries knew no limits.

"Fuck no! We're all bunking in."

"I want a ticket, Ste – can you get me one?" I asked quickly.

All Stephen's mates started to laugh and rubbed my head again. I pushed them away with a huge frown, growing ever-so angry but also cute at the same time.

"Come with me, Paul," said Tony, one of our Ste's pals.

Tony walked me away from all the singing fans, holding my hand and we weaved through the riot police and into a nearby park, where there seemed to be thousands of French ticket touts

"Just watch that large mob over there and follow me when I say, OK?" Tony whispered into my ear.

"What for?"

"I'm gonna create a crowd, then cause a scene and I'll point to the pocket of a spiv who's got tickets in it. But don't worry because I'll have hold of him so he won't know you're in his pocket."

"Are you joking?" I was bemused and slightly terrified.

"No, just practice on me now and tell me what you think."

And so began my first lesson in pick-pocketing etiquette. The rehearsal lasted about five minutes then he turned around and said in a cocky, confident tone,

"Right, let's do it."

There was no time to think, I was shitting myself but the thought of getting a ticket or possibly not getting to see the match far outweighed things in my mind. He grabbed my hand and we went for the biggest crowd where loads of people were trying to sort tickets out. This was it.

With a few French francs in his hand, Tony started to gesticulate and speak louder and louder to this fella who was overweight, sweating like a seal in a sauna and smelling like one too. The spiv grabbed a ticket out of his back pocket while shouting something in French. There was a big reel of tickets and he peeled one off and put the rest in his back pocket. I couldn't keep my eyes of this cluster of tickets.

Tony gave me the signal to move closer as he started to push the spiv into other unsuspecting fans. This was my time to move in and grab what I could and scarper. Swiftly but accurately, I got my palm into his back pocket and put my scissor-like fingers together and pulled upwards to grab two triangular perforated edges of tickets. I put them into the waistband of my shorts and Tony and I moved on quickly leaving the spiv none the wiser. I was elated with my first successful pick pocket.

"Let's have a look, Paul." Tony said quietly as he crouched down to my eye level.

"Wait a sec, they're down my waistband." I pulled out these two small triangles of paper to roars of laughter from Tony.

"What are you laughing at?"

"That's the tear-off portion you get when you enter the stadium," he said with a huge grin on his face.

I was wounded, gutted, livid and buzzing all at the same time.

"So they're no good then...? Let's do it again!" I said, enthusiastically.

"Come on, let's sort it and don't worry, you're a natural. Wait till I tell your kid, he'll be made up."

With those words of encouragement, Tony and I had a half hour spree with a huge success rate and ended up with 23 tickets, yes, 23. We got 15 from one unsuspecting fella who we took to the cleaners.

The five-minute walk back to the square was amazing; the singing, the elation and the colours. I felt like I was Neil Armstrong landing on the moon. I seemed to glide back to that square on a cushion of French-perfumed air.

When we eventually found Stephen, Phil and his dad, our Robert and Pam had found them too, obviously in an even-more drunken state by now.

"Where've you been?" asked Rob, as his eyes seemed to wobble.

"Looking for tickets," I replied.

"But you've got no money," he slurred.

As he stopped speaking, I smiled at him and pulled 14 tickets out of my waistband.

"Fuck me, Paul! Where are they from?"

"I found them when I went to the shop to buy some chewing gum with Tony." I looked over Rob's shoulder to see Tony and Ste winking at me both holding open bottles of red wine in the air.

"Is that right, Tony?" Robert asked, adjusting his balance.

"Yeah, we found a bunch of them. Look, I've got errr... nine.' Tony had a huge grin on his chubby, red face and we all burst into song...

'On the dole, drinking wine in Gay Pareeeeeeeeeee'. It was hilarious and seemed to lift the occasion to stratospheric levels. I was on top of the world at that moment; believe me – on top of the fucking world. The universal pivot point had shifted and began to revolve around me again.

We ended up getting into the stadium about an hour before the kick off and our newly-acquired seats were directly behind the goal where most of the Liverpool fans were seated. I remember just about hearing the Real Madrid mariachi band in the distance playing tunes in the rafters behind the opposite goal.

The next hour was spent singing and taking in the atmosphere with every breath and glance; more than three quarters of the ground was packed with Liverpool fans – as the centre of the universe had moved to Paris for the night. It made my experience palpable... and I was there, living it.

There was an added bonus as King Kenny had passed a late fitness test and we had Graeme Souness back in the middle of the park. The match kicked off and the nerves kicked in, as did the alcohol consumption of the Scouse contingency who'd been on it all day. Real Madrid didn't really have the skill, although they did have Laurie Cunningham the silky-skilled English winger, Vincent Del Bosque and Uli Stielike, the ex-Borussia Mönchengladbach midfielder who played against us in the 1977 final, which helped bolster their power on the day.

They didn't have the mental strength to match the Mighty Reds, although they managed to keep the game level until the last 10 minutes, when Alan 'Barney Rubble' Kennedy burst through the left hand side of the penalty area to score a belting goal; especially for a left-back. With both arms in the air, he ran behind the goal, where we were going absolutely crazy. There was a tidal wave of emotion as we all crowd surfed from row to row and seat to seat, roaring at the top of our voices.

By the time we'd calmed down and stopped sweating like crazy, the final whistle was only seconds away. I stared at the clock in the far corner ticking away wishing time passed quicker. Finally, the whistle blew.

We burst into, *You'll Never Walk Alone* followed by *'On the dole, drinking wine in Gay Paris...'* over and over again until Phil Thompson, a local lad, finally lifted the European Cup for the third time. We partied and celebrated through the night on the streets of Paris, even the French Riot Police joined in. Our sheer numbers and jubilant behaviour was infectious. Viva la Scouse revolucion!

We headed back to Hotel Diana with Stephen and Tony in tow, so they could stay the night with us. This was due to them being stinking, rotten drunk and they didn't know where their hotel was. They had to sleep on the floor of our room but at least we all stayed together on that wonderful night. I spent my last night in Paris with thoughts of the last few hours bouncing around my brain like a pinball machine on autopilot. I kept pinching myself just to see if this had really happened. Oh yes, it was true.

The next morning was an early start, especially as Rob and Pam had lost their passports - oh and mine too - the red wine had seen to that. They said they had them when they were in the match, but they were panicking now and looking at me in disbelief. They said they would have to go to the British Embassy to report them missing and get issued with a temporary one to get them home. I started to panic for a minute, too.

They rushed around the room and started to push me out of the door and told me to go and have some breakfast with Ste and Tony downstairs. I bounced down the stairs and sat and enjoyed my first milky foreign coffee. The creamy, frothy cloud-like drink tasted and looked magical.

Suddenly it dawned on me that I had my other passport at the bottom of my bag, the one I got with Bod. I found my bag, delved in and there it was; my three-fold, cardboard passport was pulled out like a magic trick. I rushed back upstairs to Rob and Pam who were still rummaging round in their clothes

"What the fuck are you doing with that?" Rob asked, in a voice two octaves higher than usual, as he noticed the passport in my hand.

"You gave it to me yesterday morning." I lied instantly.

"I thought your passport was with ours." Pam squeaked out as she reached for her toothbrush.

"Looks like I'm going home with Ste and Tony then, hey?" I said, as an unmasked smile began to appear on my fresh face.

"Go on then." Rob reluctantly agreed, as he looked at Pam and shrugged his shoulders.

I flew down the stairs with my five-step routine, holding onto the banisters. Rob and Pam were running behind me until I reached the dining room where Ste and Tony were trying to make sense of the sports' section in the French newspaper.

"Ste, we've lost our passports and we need to shoot to the Embassy, so can you take Paul home with you?"

"No problem." Ste gave a sly wink in my direction. Tony also nodded in agreement. So Rob and Pam said their goodbyes and headed off as I finished my magical, frothy drink.

The journey home was absolutely fantastic with Ste, Tony and all the lads they hung around with. The story about the up-and-coming pup on the firm who'd picked a pocket or two for 23 tickets was on everybody's lips. This made me a sort of 'Artful Dodger' character but with the face of an angel. I loved every bit of attention that came with it too. I even had some full match tickets to prove my story, along with the pictures of glory imprinted on my soul forever.

My Short Football Career

With my spoils of victory in Duisburg

I've always thought that I was a half-decent football player but just never got the breaks in life to become one, full-time. I told the career's officer in secondary school that I'd be a professional one day. I was adamant; in fact I was a bit cocky about it.

Jamie Carragher's dad, Philly, once told me he's sick of hearing hard-luck stories about kids who would/should/could have made it only for one reason or another getting in the way. In his opinion, you've either got that mental strength or you ain't - simple really. He never said it quite like that; there was a host of more explicit adjectives within this short-but-stern statement.

To be honest, I have to agree with him. I suppose it helps having good advice from loved ones and professional people, but only if you're willing to listen and learn from it.

The Crown pub on the East Lancashire Road was the first Sunday League team I played for. My Uncle Ronnie managed the team, with a little help from some locals who used to prop up the back-bar.

Uncle Ronnie was also one of my Dad's drinking buddies, so it was an obvious choice really – plus, he was a crazy Liverpool fan who took me to the European Cup final at Wembley in 1978. I'll never forget that day for as long as I live and the other 20 who travelled down with me in the back of that Luton van will never forget it either.

All the kids who played for *The Crown Under-11's* in the Walton and Kirkdale League came from Norris Green or Sparrow Hall, in fact, I think everybody's dad drank in *The Crown*. It wasn't a bad team but it wasn't a good one either. With me thinking I was one of the best players around, it was a shock to me when I was dropped to sub for the third game of the season. This wasn't due to my lack of footballing skills, more to do with me falling out with another player, Mick the Ming.

He was a rubbish footballer and I told him so every chance I had. I often just stood on the pitch with my hands on my hips shouting,

"What the fuck is he doing on the pitch? He's shite!" to the roars of laughter from the few dads who'd be watching.

My dad never came to watch me play so I thought I could get away with swearing – he never mentioned it to me, so I guess that Uncle Ronnie and the other dads never told him.

We came up with a solution to the problem of my dislike for Mick the Ming. I would go sub for the first half and Mick would be brought off at half time. This would give the team a better chance of getting a result as I would always come on like a whirling dervish, causing havoc and more often than not, score. I was still miffed that Mick had to play at all, but one day, it was explained to me that his dad was also Uncle Ronnie's mate, so what could I do?

It wasn't too long before a few better teams asked me to sign for them. *Pacific* had a great team and their manager, Peter Edwards, always made me feel 10-feet tall. He was a great fella and sometimes invited me to go and train with them; obviously Dad wouldn't let me go.

Eddie Hewitt managed *East Villa* and he always had time for me and would chat for what seemed like ages about Liverpool FC outside the gates of the Jeffrey Humble Playing Field on Long Lane, where all the matches were played. We called it the LBA for some reason. I remember there was live, televised American Baseball from there back in the 70s. I was amazed with the TV crew and trucks being on our downtrodden estate. As a kid, it seemed like I spent all my Saturday and Sunday mornings at the LBA doing something or other; it was a magical place to me.

I ended up finishing the season with *The Crown* and was looking forward to the next season as I wouldn't be playing with Mick the Ming. To be fair, Mick was a laugh a minute and would be the first one to take the piss out of somebody else's misfortune or cause havoc if he was left out of any social gatherings or parties.

On one occasion, we were invited to a mate's house in Faversham Road for a Sunday night get together because his mum and dad had gone out for the evening. They wouldn't allow Mick in because he would take the piss out of the girls and ruin the chance of anyone pulling a bird.

He was prowling around outside the house until about 9.30pm and once he realised he wasn't getting in, he decided to loiter outside The Crown. He went inside to see his dad and noticed the party-lad's parents sitting in the corner having a quiet drink; he didn't miss a trick and began to plot his revenge for not getting into the house.

By now, the party was in full swing, due to them having found the stash of ale in the cupboard. Now girls, plus alcohol usually ends in tears and trouble, so by the time Mick had summonsed the fire brigade and the police to the house, it was all just kicking off. By this time, Mick had also told his dad to pass on the message to the unsuspecting couple in the corner that all hell had broken loose at their home. With this news they ran back to find screaming, drunken girls falling all over the place surrounded by the emergency services, who by now were scattered on the floor, comforting drunken kids.

There were no more parties at that particular address for a long time and Mick had the last laugh – well, that's what he thought anyhow.

After one season, Uncle Ronnie gave up managing the team and it quickly folded, but it was re-jigged a while later under the new name of *Sparrow Hall*. Another of Dad's drinking pals took over and my dad made me sign for them again, to my great disappointment. So it was another season with the same team mates plus one or two new faces, including Mick the Ming. I begged my dad to let me play for another team but he just gave me that look. I knew not to ask him again, well, not that season, anyway.

The new manager was Bobby Savage, his eldest son played for Liverpool, so I was buzzing. I imagined he had some sort of Midas touch when it came to football just because his son was a professional. I'd learned quickly not to say nothing on the pitch about Mick being shite, as the manager had a word with me and said he wouldn't put up with me swearing – especially at a team-mate. He didn't realise he wasn't really my mate. I didn't say much off the pitch so no-one really knew what I thought.

That season was just like the one before (minus the swearing) and this time I played all the games. We reached the semi-finals of the cup and it was played on a Thursday night at 5.30pm on the LBA pitches. My father had never watched me before but he turned up for this one, thanks to his barfly pals telling him I'd been playing well. I scored a back-heel from a corner in the first half and was buzzing coming off at half time knowing my dad was there, watching.

The usual squash and orange segments were on offer; I obliged of course. Just as I was about to go back on the pitch for the second half, I farted and followed through and couldn't get to the toilet as the ref was waiting to kick off. I was in limbo but had to make a quick decision to start the match with shit running down my leg. I was devastated. I waited for the earliest opportunity to make a slide tackle to try and blend the shite with the mud. What else could I do? I could really smell it by now and it stank, so I obviously thought everyone else could too.

Embarrassment set in, I hid in my shell that half and we ended up losing 2-1. I was mortified and my dad wasn't too impressed either, I didn't have the nerve to tell him what had happened as the embarrassment was still uppermost in my mind.

That was more-or-less the high point for that season and I was still being asked to sign for other teams. I knew I was a decent player but I knew my shit stank, too. I dreamed of dad letting me change teams.

I trained with East Villa that summer and was all set to sign for them. I brought the form home which had to be signed by both my parents. Mum signed it no problem and I waited to pick my moment to ask my dad. Obviously terrified of his unpredictable reaction, I caught him one day when I thought he was in a good mood.

"What's this?"

"My signing-on form for this season," I was clenching my hands in anticipation and fear.

"This is saying you're signing-on for East Villa... You're not - you're signing for Bobby's team."

"But Dad, I've said I'll sign for them, my two mates are signing too." I pleaded.

"You glory-hunting bastard." He bellowed in a tone that shook me to my core. I wasn't going to back down this time though; I'd spent two seasons doing what he wanted. This time I was doing what I wanted, which was to play with better players under a better manager – or so I thought. Dad threw the form onto the coffee table in the living room and said,

"You've got no fuckin' chance, Lad." He staked out, slamming the door in fury.

Mum came in and asked what was happening as I was in turmoil. I explained and she told me not to worry, she would have a word with him later on. She ended up talking him round somehow and a few days later, the form was behind the carriage clock on the mantelpiece, signed and waiting to be grabbed with both hands. So now it was on; I was signing for a better team with better players and I was buzzing.

I loved training with East Villa and especially Eddie Hewitt, the manager. He was an absolute gent who showed me the utmost respect at every moment. I always arrived first at training and was last to leave. Every race, shuttle task and training exercise was completed to the best of my ability, and more often than not, I was first in all the races. Eddie loved me for this and during one half-time team-talk back in the dressing room; he asked me to stand up in front of everybody and said,

"If I had another 10 of him on the pitch right now, we'd be about 6-0 up instead of 0-0. I want you to all take a leaf out of his book and buck your ideas up."

It made me feel like a giant, as if I could slay anyone or anything by the dozen. Some of my mates weren't too happy with me but that wasn't my problem, I was just chuffed to be held in such high regard by Eddie. He certainly knew how to push my buttons and motivate me.

We ended up winning 2-0 and I was given Man of the Match by Eddie when we were getting changed. He always named his best player at this point so I would wait for some sort of praise or recognition. It didn't always come, but what did was the offer of a place in the *Walton and Kirkdale Under -13's Reps* for my progress and sheer endeavour. I was buzzing and it gave me one of my biggest boosts. If Google Earth had been around back then, you could have zoomed into the playing field on the day of my call up and seen my pride visibly swelling.

The Rep team played at Melwood; Liverpool's training ground, against the LFC schoolboy team and at Bellfield against Everton's juniors. It was wonderful to get the chance to play on those glorious pitches and have the chance to walk in the footsteps on my heroes for a few hours. The sight of that famous red shirt on the other side of the halfway line sent shivers down my spine – as did the Everton kit, but that was for a different reason. I always seemed to play better against Everton as I would have the rivalry coursing through my veins, but with Liverpool, I just seemed to sit back and admire them.

I made sure the staff at both clubs were aware that I'd love the chance to have trials with them – I was a bit like Yozzer Hughes in 'Boys from the Blackstuff'.

East Villa had a great team and it showed in the results that season. We were only beaten twice all year and that was by the team from Aigburth who went unbeaten and had six lads who played for Liverpool and Everton by the end of that season.

I loved every minute of our one-touch football. Eddie Hewitt would drill it into us about not keeping hold of the ball for too long, *'one touch and pass'* would be the mantra from the side lines. I learned a lot that season and became a more-rounded player.

The *East Villa Under-14's* conquered all before them the following year. A few players joined us and made us a bigger, more physical side. I was still tiny but had spent the summer in the gym doing plenty of weights and my thighs had gone massive. I was buzzing with my new physique and was a yard quicker than all of my team-mates, much to Eddie's delight, but not the defenders who I ran ragged in pre-season.

He moved me from right wing to left wing as I was mostly right footed and spent time on my left foot in training. It worked; we had a great team and the quality of football for a Sunday League junior team was being noticed. Talent scouts would regularly turn up and offer trials to all the high-quality players. I was always trying to impress, but when I say I was tiny, I'm not joking. Always 100% committed to the team and I was improving with each game, but I was still tiny.

The *Under-15's* weren't much different from the previous season except for a few injuries. This was due to me rapidly growing a few inches and my knees would play up, occasionally leaving me standing on the sidelines some weeks.

I wasn't a good substitute either; I would be on Eddie Hewitt's coat tails like Yozzer Hughes again when things weren't going well,

'Let me on, I'll score – I promise you.' I would plead. He must have thought I was a nuisance. We just got better and better that season and I ended up playing in most of the games towards the end. My left foot was now in constant use and I even scored some glorious goals with it – thanks, Eddie.

The summer break was spent working in the gym in Broadway swimming baths, five days a week. There was a boxing gym upstairs, I pounded the bags and was squatting heavy weight for my size all summer in preparation for the Under 16's season. Little did I know that doing heavy weights at such an age could stunt my growth.

I was sent on holiday to Ibiza this summer with my sister, Pat and her son Antony, who was like my little brother. When I say 'sent', I mean sent. My Dad became unwell earlier in the year and it wasn't looking good for him. The family decided that if Dad was going to die, then it was to be at home and I wasn't to witness it. This decision was mainly taken by my mum, but everyone agreed.

The morning of this so-called 'holiday', I sat in my bedroom trying to figure out what was going on while I packed my suitcase. I put pen to paper and wrote my mum and dad a letter trying to explain my thoughts. I was young, naive and void of emotion, but I knew changes were happening.

Three or four times I tried to start writing but for one reason or another I just couldn't do it. In the end, I wrote a short, but heartfelt note to my dying father and caring mother, but couldn't bring myself to give it to them. I tore it up into several pieces and threw it in the bin. That afternoon I left for Ibiza after kissing my dad on the forehead while he lay semi-conscious in his bed in the parlour. That was the last time I saw him.

A week into my trip in the blazing, summer heat, my sister came back from the phone in reception with tears rolling down her cheeks. I knew something was up and feared the worst without letting on. I don't think I wanted to know the truth. The following day we packed up and made our way back to the airport to catch a flight to Manchester. When we landed, a stewardess took us to a private room where my mum and sisters had been waiting to tell us the tragic news in person. Everything seemed to go silent and stayed that way for about a week. Dad was dead. He was getting buried the day after we landed so everything passed me by without me saying a word to anybody. I was stunned; I loved my dad.

I tried to get back to normal as quickly as possible and football was a major part of my life back then, so that seemed the most natural route to turn my thoughts away from personal matters. Eddie took me to one side and told me he was always there if I needed him. What a gentleman he was and he always went out of his way; he had become a father figure to me.

That season was brilliant for East Villa. I scored 22 goals from the left-wing position and started to play in centre midfield for the first time. I was offered trials at Oldham Athletic and Crewe Alexandra – things were looking up, I thought.

East Villa were also presented the opportunity to play in an international tournament in Duisburg, Germany with FC Rotterdam, Calais, Hadjuk Split, Duisburg, FC Köln and other teams I couldn't pronounce, never mind, remember.

This was the best experience of my short life. The flight to Dusseldorf and the journey to the MSV Duisburg Stadium for the welcoming ceremony was first class. We all had new tracksuits and thought we looked the dog's bollocks until we saw the other teams in their sponsored-to-the-eyeballs rigouts - they made us look like the Artful Dodger's firm on wash day – plus, everybody was 6 feet tall. My neck was hurting from constantly looking up on this meet-and-greet get together; but it was amazing.

Our living quarters were to be the local British Army base in Duisburg. They gave us our own dorm and two squaddies to look after us and keep us up to scratch about armed-forces living. They took the entire squad into Duisburg town centre, where we were treated like stars and frequently stopped for autographs and to pose for photos. It wasn't until we'd walked around for a while that we noticed the posters up all over the town billing us as FC Liverpool. Everyone thought we were famous, up-and-coming stars.

The attention from the young girls was unbelievable too; they turned up at all our training sessions and frequently followed us back to the barracks. They would wait outside for hours and me and the lads would duly oblige and make our way into town with the girls in tow – when the squaddies allowed us to.

We trained hard and prepared for the matches. We drew the first two games so we needed to win the third. We defeated Racing Calais 3-1 to go through to the semi-final against FC Köln. We fought hard but their physical presence and strength was just that step too far and we lost 2-0. I was gutted but had the consolation of winning Man of the Match and praise in the dressing room afterwards. I was the youngest and smallest player in the tournament by a mile.

There was a play-off for third place with the two semi-final losers: us and Duisburg to be played at MSV Duisburg training ground on the first-team pitch, which was like a crown-green bowling surface. It was a pleasure to run on, never mind play football.

There was a good crowd, as one side had a seated stand which held two thousand spectators and was jam-packed with fans and young girls, screaming. I felt like a superstar running onto the pitch before the game.

The match kicked off at a frantic pace and we had the upper hand as our work rate was on the money. Half time came and went and with 15 minutes remaining we scored a belter, to the delight of about 100 squaddies and 50 screaming teenage girls. Five minutes later we scored again from a misplaced back pass which I intercepted, rounded the keeper and slotted home on the second attempt.

I couldn't contain myself; running and ducking under team-mates just to get to Eddie and hug him.

"That was for Dad." I whispered in his ear. Ten minutes later the game was over and it took time for my heartbeat to return to normal as I was elated.

Celebrating with the pitch-invading squaddies was a great feeling; it was like we'd won the tournament, especially as they were all a year or more older than any of our team. One of the screaming girls spoke perfect English and invited me back to her house. I had to decline that night as I'd arranged to have a shandy with the marauding squaddies in the NAAFI Bar on the campus. I did, however, arrange to meet her the next day at noon as the flight back home wasn't until midnight, so I had four or five hours to spare.

Two bottles of Grolsch for 50p and loads of lemonade got me tipsy and an early night was on the cards due to NAAFI prices and my tender age catching up with me.

The following day I met up with the German school girl, Katrina. We took the 30-minute bus ride to her beautiful house in the Duisburg suburbs to be greeted by her most-welcoming mother. Katrina's father was a pilot for Lufthansa and was due home any minute from a few days' flying. This seemed to be a perfect family and Katrina's smile was so pretty and unforced. We listened to some music and swapped addresses before it was time to leave. A kiss was granted and indulged in, only for her father to interrupt proceedings by arriving home in his shiny, top-of-the-range Mercedes and that was the end of my first international romance; short and sweet.

Stephen bought me a pair of Diadora Zico pig-skin boots as I was about to have a trial for Oldham Athletic, I loved them.

My trip to Oldham was scheduled in August and a match was organised for the evening at their training ground. A freak storm appeared overhead and it battered the surface for two solid hours, I've never seen rain like it on that balmy summer's night. With about 20 minutes of the game gone, I noticed my new boots had ripped; in fact they were properly fucked. Usually, I'd have a spare pair but I'd forgotten to bring them in the melee – what a dickhead.

The walk to the dressing room was filled with shame and anger. The rain was still bouncing off the ground like a tin of spilt marbles hitting a stone floor. I was greeted by Big Head himself, Joe Royle, the Oldham manager who took one look at me and asked,

"How old are you, Son?"

"Sixteen."

"You need to go home and eat all your Sunday dinners, Son.' He said in what felt like a *sympathetic* fashion.

I felt deflated enough about my £70 Diadora Zico pig-skin boots, but this was like a dagger through my dreams. *'Go home and eat all your Sunday dinners, Son.'*

He might as well have said *'Fuck off you midget!'* because by the time it filtered through my head, that's what it sounded like.

Under 18's was the next step with East Villa and a new manager, Pat Smith. It was more or less the same, but with a better squad of players. Another tournament in Duisburg was on the cards and eagerly anticipated. I couldn't wait for it to happen again and built up to it with caution and excitement.

Our squad improved big time as did the average height in the team, except me. I was still Joe Royle's midget, but with a massive point to prove now.

Again, the Duisburg Army barracks was to be our home for a week. As we'd all grown up and matured, the NAAFI was on everybody's lips on our journey to Germany and was our first port of call once we'd settled into our dorm.

The same two squaddies became our guides and translators as we roamed the Army base and beyond. A friendly match was arranged with the battalion team for the next afternoon as part of our training, so the lads decided to have a stroll into Duisburg town centre that night to take in the local surroundings.

At about 10.30pm, we decided to have something to eat and bounced into the nearest pizza parlour. There were a few drunken squaddies who started to get a bit mouthy with us. Now most of us grew up on the street and wouldn't take shit from anybody, so when one of the squaddies turned their verbal onslaught into hay-making punches, it all turned a bit nasty.

One of our lads who played centre midfield was a knockout merchant and sparked the squaddie flat out. One punch was all it took and he was out cold. The other drunken soldiers did nothing other than pick their pal up from the floor and get him out of the way, rapidly.

We never gave the incident a second thought, until about midnight when we were back in the barracks trying to sleep. We were dragged out of our bunk beds by Military Police wielding pick-axe handles and sub machine guns, calling us all the Scouse civvy bastards under the sun. It hurt being dragged, semi-naked with a pick-axe handle shoved under my chin, across the parade yard. They locked six of us up, that's before they kicked fuck out of us and accused us of robbing and assaulting the soldier earlier on in the pizzeria.

They wouldn't listen to any of us as we were slung into the military cells, which were as shiny as a Sergeant Major's boots – you could see your reflection in the floor and this was the first thing I noticed when the Military Police forced my face down with their boots; my breath was making the floor's shiny surface cloud up.

They opened us up the following morning at 8am and put us all in one room to be spoken to by the Chief MP, our minders and two East Villa reps, who were beyond pissed off with the whole saga and threatened to send us home, until our minders spoke up on our behalf; thank fuck as it was becoming frightening.

The MPs took the meeting outside for about 10 minutes and when they returned we were told to stand up, quickly. We were given a stern telling off and escorted to our dorms, to be met by the guides. They explained that the drunken squaddie had made these kinds of accusations before and to shut him up we had to pay £200 and it would be forgotten. We paid up, pronto, but with an air of injustice as we didn't rob the soldier.

The match against the battalion was still going ahead that day to our severe disapproval, as we thought our cards were marked, but that wasn't the case. The handshakes and general mood was one of friendship. They told us later on in the NAAFI (after we'd beaten them 14-1) that the drunken squaddie was a wanker and they'd be right behind us for the forthcoming tournament; which was a relief as some of the soldiers were massive.

Needless to say we were spurred on by the events of the last few days ringing in our ears, along with the 200 soldiers draped in

Union Jacks, who cheered us along in the tournament. With this new-found fan base and belief, to our sheer delight, we reached the final.

We played FC Köln, who hadn't conceded a goal through the entire tournament. As we lined up to go out onto the pitch, I could hear the squaddies singing their heads off. I looked up at the Köln players who all seemed stern, huge and nervous. I started to leap as high as I could doing tuck jumps, screaming aggressively at the top of my voice,

"Let's have this, lads. Don't give them an inch and when you get a chance, kick fuck out of them!"

The entire Köln team looked stunned as 10 more Scousers joined in with this battle cry. I looked for the biggest one and made sure he caught my eye, I wasn't gonna lose. 'I will conquer and I'm not afraid to die trying' I thought as we began to walk out onto the pitch.

This is the attitude that makes or breaks you, it wasn't going to break me, not this day or any other day, I thought.

Guess what? We won 2-1 and I scored the first goal to break the deadlock. I was the first to knock down their defensive wall in this tournament. I was on cloud nine, ten and eleven for a while. The squaddies invaded the pitch again like marauding crusaders – it was absolutely wonderful, this time we'd gone one step further and actually won the trophy.

At the presentation I was also handed a 'Player of the Tournament' award to my sheer shock and delight. It couldn't get any better than this, could it?

During the celebrations, I heard somebody calling my name - it was Katrina and her father. I was in such a good mood at this point; I hugged and kissed her as if her father wasn't there – bad move. The firm tap on my shoulder and that same look my father often gave me was in his eye. Time to lay off, I thought, naturally.

To be fair, Katrina's dad was great afterwards and joined us back at the NAAFI as the Army had laid on a special party. Tracy Chapman songs and Taja Seville's *Love is Contagious* would be regulars on the NAAFI jukebox, as well as *Boys are Back in Town.* That was a great day and I stayed in touch with Katrina for a few years too... double result.

When I arrived home with my medals and stories, I was as proud as a home-coming soldier from battle. Mum was over the moon and kept telling me how proud Dad would have been. She even paraded me around our street to let all and sundry see my medals and huge trophy.

Directly opposite our house in Faversham Road lived a lady named Mrs. Saunders who was around 60 years old and lived with her 85-year-old mum. She was always nice to me, especially after dad had died. When mum took me to her front door she immediately took me into her living room, which looked like it was trapped in the 1940s, it was like a museum.

As I sat down on her couch she began to tell me how proud my dad would have been and how she cried when she read the letter I'd written to my father on his death bed.

As she stopped talking I asked her, "Which letter?"

"The one you wrote and ripped up and threw in the bin..." Mrs. Saunders said slowly, realising she'd let the cat out of the bag and said I'd better go and speak to my mum. I bounced over the road in double-quick time to find my mum on the phone. I waited patiently for her to finish and asked her about the letter.

"I'm sorry for not telling you, Son, but I was saving it for you." Mum rummaged around at the bottom of her bag to pull out her black, leather purse. She opened it up to reveal a sellotaped piece of white paper, folded twice. She unfolded it carefully and placed it in my palm like a treasured relic.

To this day that letter sends shivers down my spine.

The next time I saw her, Mrs. Saunders shouted me over to apologise for the misunderstanding.

"I know you look like a boy, but you were a man when you wrote that letter, and I'm proud of you."

I thanked her for her heartfelt words, turned and walked back to my house with a single tear running down my cheek. 'Was I a man?' I wondered as I wiped the tear away.

There were a few more years of sporadic football playing, but other priorities would take over in the end. After a one-season spell as

East Villa's youngest-ever manager, I managed the Under 11s in the Walton and Kirkdale League, until a three-way spiral fracture of my tibia and fibula put an end to it.

I still had my beloved Liverpool Football Club to follow around the country and over foreign borders to keep my football flames burning brightly, as well as the knowledge of the sellotaped letter in my mum's black leather purse.

School

Ellergreen Comprehensive School - or Clubmoor Community School as it was called during the Thatcher school reform years – was to be my school from the age of 11 -16. It was a mixed school, with kids from Norris Green and Croxteth. Our Headmaster was a crazed Evertonian, Mr. Bernicoff, better known as Leon (and June) from Gogglebox.

There wasn't much going on in terms of excitement, so we had to make our own fun and sometimes, break a few rules, laws and windows in the process.

It took me about two years to properly find my feet and realise I enjoyed school life. The teachers helped with that as a few of them seemed to take a bit of a liking to me.

My Form and History teacher for two years was Mr. Aughton and he was the first I struck a chord with. His tweed jacket with leather elbow patches and his polyvelt, tan shoes which looked like Cornish pasties always made him stand out; he was quite witty too.

There was the odd occasion when I got into mischief and 'three of the best' with the cane was the order of the day. With Mr. Aughton being my Form teacher, he would have to do the deed. He always said 'sorry' beforehand, so I felt no ill towards him.

PE was a subject I excelled in. I was captain of the school football team and was boxing at the time, too. Fitness was not a problem, either on the football pitch or in the boxing gym; it was an everyday occurrence in those days.

Mr. Davis, a small, rotund Welshman took the PE classes with his stern sidekick, Mr. Purvis. Mr. Davis was brilliant with me; he would turn up at the sports hall with his navy blue ironed-to-death nylon tracksuit and just tell me to pick the teams for football, 99.9% of the time.

The track suit was a belter - shiny and looking like it had been ironed on an anvil with a hammer. Mr. Purvis was a totally different piece of cake from the portly Welshman. He would often wear a really tight polo shirt with two naughty sweat stains under his armpits, a whistle on a bootlace and a huge stopwatch round his neck. He reminded me of a German Panzer tank commander with his pale-blue eyes and cropped light reddish hair. He sometimes acted like one, too.

I never let that put me off PE as Mr. Davies was a proper buzz when we played football. Imagine the school PE teacher from the Barry Hines book, Kes; add a few sprinkles of Smiffy from Gavin and Stacey and you've nailed it. That was Mr. Davies, I loved him – not in a gay way, but in an early-role-model way.

Geography was a good subject for me and I found it enjoyable – anything you enjoy you don't mind doing, do you?

Our teacher was Mr. Richardson; a tank-top-wearing, small fella who had massive glasses and a barnet like the arse-end of a bumble bee. As I enjoyed the subject, he was always pleasant and talkative with me, but there was a time when I hated him.

The homework task one weekend was to draw a free-hand map of the United Kingdom and plot the major towns, rivers and mountain areas. This was to be coloured in and presented the following Tuesday.

I would always do my homework as soon as it was issued as it would give me more time to do my own thing. That was my way then and it still is now.

Tuesday arrived and the Geography class was at 10.30 until lunch-time. I handed in my homework and thought nothing of it. At the end of the lesson, Mr. Richardson asked for our attention so he could show the whole class the UK maps. He began to hold each map in the air, reading everybody's names out. As mine was produced, everybody burst out laughing. Mr. Richardson read my name out and I could feel my face burning to the point where anger took over. I wanted to punch his teeth right down his throat, but I didn't know why. I got my breath back and asked my mate next to me why everybody was laughing.

"You've coloured the rivers and the sea in purple," he told me.

"No, it's not, its blue."

"Nah, it's definitely purple, that's why they're laughing." He nodded his head to reaffirm.

I was puzzled, embarrassed and humiliated to my core. That moment will never go away because it was the day I found out I was severely colour blind. I couldn't forgive Mr. Richardson for demeaning me in front of my classmates, ever.

A couple of weeks of having the piss taken out of me by my close mates passed and to our great delight, the snow arrived. I turned up for school thinking we'd be sent home, but that wasn't the case.

PE was the first lesson and Mr. Davies had been snowed in somewhere near North Wales, so couldn't make it. Mr. Purvis was off sick, so we waited for the stand-in teacher to appear. Who walked through the double wooden fire doors? Yes, Mr. Richardson. He asked everybody what usually happened and everybody pointed to me and said,

"We play football and he picks the teams."

With that, he asked me to go ahead while he put his shorts and trainers on in the staff changing room. He jogged into the cold sports hall and asked,

"Right then, lads, whose side am I on?"

"You're on that side," I replied, pointing to the opposite end of the hall. He blew the whistle and for one solid hour I kicked fuck out of him at every given opportunity. I made sure that if he was by the wall, I would slam him with full power against it, knocking his glasses off every time. I gave him a torrid time but also showed some great skills too. When he finally blew the whistle, he made a beeline for me with his hand out. I shook it firmly and he asked,

"Why did you just do that? Was it because of the map incident?" He'd obviously answered his own question with a question, but I replied anyway.

"Yeah, you made me look like a fool in front of my mates, Sir."

"Well, I apologise for that and would like to congratulate you for being a man and shaking my hand."

This made me feel 10-feet tall, I'd gained the respect of an elder for showing passion, skill and strength of character; a valuable lesson indeed.

Checking My DNA

Football and boxing played a major role in filling my spare time outside of school in the early 1980s but as I got older; I became more inquisitive and wanted answers to certain questions. I began to follow current affairs on the TV news and in the newspaper much to my parents' amazement or disbelief, take your pick.

I remember coming home from school having read about a conflict on some faraway shore in Mr. Aughton's copy of *The Times* and asking Dad if he thought a totalitarian regime was a fair one. He looked at me as if I'd sprouted two heads, surveyed the living room for signs of intelligence or breathing mammals and said,

"Are you fucking kidding me?"

My jaw began to drop in anticipation of an educated response. I started to think that I'd unearthed something in common with my dad. That emotion was short lived as his next response was,

"What the fuck does totalitarian mean? Kathy! Kathy! Have you heard what this fella's saying? Is he for real?"

Now Dad wasn't stupid, it was just that he knew nothing about politics, government or current affairs; if it wasn't on our doorstep, he didn't want to know. To be honest, I asked everyone in our house that question and they all gave a similar response. At that time, I thought that I was adopted and seriously started asking my close friends if I looked like my brothers and sisters. This was always greeted by roars of laughter.

At the end of the third year seniors, we could choose the subjects we wanted to study in our final two years. Government and Politics, Sociology, History, Maths, English Literature and PE were the subjects I enjoyed, so were obviously on my list of options.

The school year started and I took to the new teachers and they took to me. The Government and Politics teacher was a ringer for Art Garfunkel in every way. His name was Mr. Sutton and would later on arrange a trip to the House of Commons where we had tea and biscuits in David Alton's (Liberal) office. It was then that I wanted to be a politician, yeah, I know, how funny does that seem right now? I'd be the only real person anywhere near Black Rod or the Bar since Guy Fawkes.

Every class I was in, a kid called Thomas Farrelly seemed to be there too. He wore the school blazer and badge with pride. What was weird about that is no-one in the entire school wore a blazer back then, never mind a badge.

Thomas would turn up every day with polished shoes, blazer, satchel and his bright red, flaming hair, ready to take on all-comers in the race for the 'cleverest kid in the school'.

I always gave him credit for this, but the militant school masses would tear him to shreds anytime they got the chance. Boy! That kid and his family took some stick. To be fair, I felt sorry for him and wouldn't join in; I had my own beef with him though. I wanted to be the cleverest kid in the school, too.

I buried my head into my school work and did my best in the end-of-year exams. On the last day of term we would be given our school reports and exam results, so that day was eagerly awaited by Thomas and me.

The brown envelope arrived and was opened in record time. As I unfolded the two pristine pieces of white paper, my eyes quickly went down the list. I had to go over this three times to make sure I was reading it right.

Of the ten subjects, I had straight A+'s. Over and over again I checked as I walked out of the classroom onto the yard and out of the main school gates. As I walked down Abbotsford Road, I noticed the one-and-only blazer about 50 yards ahead of me – it stood out like an orange ball in the snow. I pushed past what seemed like a thousand grey V-neck jumpers and Farah trousers to catch up with Thomas Farrelly and his blazer.

'How many A's did you get?' I asked, rapidly.

He began to unpeel his brown envelope to reveal he only had 9A+'s. I was buzzing and noticed he only got a C for PE. Oh my God. I'm not only captain of the football team, but it's official that I'm now a straight-A student. I couldn't wait to tell my parents.

Sparrow Hall Boxing

Directly behind our house in Faversham Road was a predominantly Catholic housing estate called Sparrow Hall. This was an area of huge families, so in turn came an abundance of kids – that's Catholics for you. It seemed like thousands of kids, as most family's numbers swelled to around seven and eight.

Faversham Road seemed to be an overspill for Sparrow Hall and Bulford Road; at one stage our road had about 200 kids from the age of six to16. It was lively, to say the least.

The Sparrow Hall estate had their own community centre: disco, boxing club and playing fields which were controlled by a handful of community-spirited, local individuals.

I found myself attracted to the local boxing club as a thin-but-fit-as-a-fiddle 9-year-old. I was so fit back then, I remember being able to get from my bedroom to our living room without touching the floor or breaking sweat, on a regular basis.

I could jump out of my steel, gunmetal-grey bunk bed and cling onto the white, panelled door with the aid of the huge, round door knob, two thirds of the way down the right hand side. Then I would swing my right leg around the door and in one movement be on the other side. That took me to the upstairs landing with the hand-rail on my left side. With one swift jump I was on the banister with two options available; the fast route which was obviously just to slide down the banister or opt for the more skillful, tricky route. This involved clinging on to the picture rail with my fingertips; this rail was about a foot from the ceiling, but enabled me to shuffle my feet on the handrail which followed the angle of banister to the bottom of the stairs.

Once I was at the bottom of the stairs, I could leap onto the front door in the same fashion as my bedroom door routine. Then for the dangerous bit – the bark-design Artex that was the standard wall covering in 90% of Scouse houses back in the late 70s and early 80s, so obviously, it was daubed all over our house back then, too. One false move would have resulted in a serious graze or cut. Some of the edges were sharp, jagged and deadly. Standing barefoot on the top of the skirting board and holding onto the dado rail at waist height with my arse sticking out for balance was daring and hazardous, so I would shuffle along trying to avoid any Artex contact.

The hall was about 10 feet long and once that section was complete, it was a case of the door-leap-and-swing routine onto the living room door, which then usually resulted in a spectacular dive onto our couch (depending whether or not my dad was in the room) accompanied by a running commentary. This whole procedure usually took about a minute from start to couch dive. I loved it.

In retrospect, it all sounds a bit dangerous, but nobody ever warned me not to do it or took any notice of me, although there was usually only me and my mum in the house and she was always busy doing something. Bear in mind, I was the youngest of nine so by that time, my mum had seen, heard and done everything and I just got on with it. Later on in life, we worked out that Mum had been pregnant for a total of seven years; no wonder she turned a blind eye to my carrying on.

I was tiny at the time and probably only weighed a few stone. With this nimbleness I decided to follow a few of the older lads from my road to Sparrow Hall Boxing Club one night to see what all the fuss was about, as they frequently chatted about it.

I'll never forget that musty, stale, sweaty smell the first time I walked in. It seemed to absorb everything and anything that was in a 20-yard radius and it somehow immediately wallpapered itself to the back of my throat.

Billy Quinn was the local boxing trainer and just happened to be my Dad's drinking partner in The Crown. It didn't take too long before my dad started to ask questions and Billy began to show me a bit more one-on-one time than the others. In fact, it was only my second session when Billy asked me to spar with one of the older lads who'd been training for a while.

I wasn't frightened about getting hurt, it was the 14oz scuffed and battered gloves, which he pulled from the canvas Army rucksack he kept beneath the scaffold frame of the boxing ring, which terrified me. They were massive and laced up like a pair of knee-high Doc Martin boots; when I tried them on, they were up to my elbows. I could hardly move my arms as I tried to bounce around the creaking, bouncy boards of the ring. It felt like somebody had tied my neck to both my shoulders as when I tried to move my right hand, it would all move together as the glove came above my elbow by now, rendering me immobile.

The sparring rounds only lasted one minute, so the thought of another two rounds running around my brain terrorised my soul as I was getting hit full in the face every few seconds. This was due to me being unable to lift my heavily-weighted arms to defend myself.

It wasn't until we finished that Billy told me I should have worn a head-guard and the gloves were too big – thanks Billy, or was it my dad, teaching me a second-hand lesson?

Every Tuesday and Thursday night was spent learning how to skip, bob and weave, take a punch, give a punch and dance around the ring fighting my shadow. I started to enjoy it and had been going for a few months solid when Billy told us we were having an inter-boxing club match with Holy Name in Fazakerley.

Oh shit! What was my opponent going to be like? How big, strong or fast would he be? Thoughts started to fester into doubts and manifested into fear.

The evening arrived as quickly as it was mentioned and we all travelled to the Holy Name on the 17C bus. It was only four stops away, but six young boxers and their old trainer, all travelling together had a bit of camaraderie surrounding it.

It was labelled as an Exhibition Match but nobody had told us or our opponents as we all went at it like crazed lunatics, fighting for survival and pride. There were no winners or losers apparently and we all got medals at the end of it. It was amazing and frightening at the same time, but something that had captured my full attention.

My first boxing medal made the journey home with me, a good trip, plenty of banter and I was proud as Punch – excuse the pun.

The following morning, my Dad asked to see the medal and to my sheer disappointment he took it from me. I wanted to show it off to my schoolmates and the girls in my class too. Why had he pissed on my parade? I was wounded.

That same evening at teatime, Dad called me down to his aviary or his 'second home' as I called it, to reveal the medal with *Paul Joseph Walmsley* and the date engraved on the back. I was buzzing my little socks off; now everyone I showed it to would know it was mine - it said so on the back, it was etched into the metal.

Going to school the following day, I bumped into Robert Chadwick who lived in our road. He was two years older than me, but was loved by all the kids as the stories he told (which he convinced himself were true) were unbelievable.

I was only tiny and that two-year age difference and about a foot in height made him man-like to me, so for him to pull me to one side and ask about my recent boxing adventure was a doff of the cap from an elder.

That morning, the walk to school with Robert was filled with his new adventures, obviously, once he'd heard mine. My favourite was the story about him finding a robin's nest under some brambles in the woods. It was in an old paint tin and he got to it by crawling on his belly through the undergrowth, getting torn to shreds by thorns and nettles. When he eventually found it, the nest had two eggs. He said he took one for his collection and as he got up off the floor with his newly-acquired egg, he saw the bird on top of the paint can with a tear rolling down from its eye and on to its red breast. He automatically thought, in his own bizarre way, that he should put the egg back as the robin was clearly upset. I found this funny and couldn't stop laughing all day in school; in fact one teacher asked me to share my joke with the rest of the class as I kept putting my head in my hands and chuckling into my desk. I couldn't bring myself to tell the class, so my teacher punished me by making me stand in the corner of the room and say to a brick wall, repeatedly,

"You're a brick and I'm a brick and I'm as thick as you."

My classmates thought this was hysterical and every time I came to the end of a sentence, they all chuckled and highlighted the word *'you'* by shouting it out loud, until the teacher threatened the whole class with the same treatment. The crying-robin story was still a belter though and I still giggle about it today.

A few months later, it was all change in Faversham Road as the local council Works Department had taken over the street to begin to redevelop the whole dilapidated estate. It wasn't long before all our hide-outs and dens had been acquired by the council for storage of scaffold, building materials and what seemed like an island of sand.

They were giving us all new windows, tiled roofs, loft insulation and the entire house was to be rewired. You can imagine the influx of workers on a daily basis and new machinery started to pop up all over the estate; dropping pavement slabs, new kerb stones and the general mess that came with that sort of stuff, cluttered the space we used to play and hang out in.

The council workers used the two houses at the end of the road as their office and general meeting point for lunch and the likes. It was a corner plot with two triangular pieces of grass outside leading to the bus stop on Townsend Avenue.

After a week of wear and tear and two heavy nights of rain, the grass triangles turned into mud patches with deeply-gorged tipper-truck tyre tracks running through them, creating deep ruts where the rain gathered and sat.

One night when we were bored, we decided to have a mud fight and cause havoc on the corner of our road. I don't remember who came up with the idea but we all enjoyed the mudslinging episode and left some bus-stop dwellers running for cover a few times. At one point, a bus pulled up while we were in mid flow and somehow mud made its way onto the bus via an open window – much to the dismay and disgust of an unsuspecting female passenger who looked like she'd fallen head-first into a pig sty.

The bus driver was fuming, pushed the counter forwards and jumped off to shout at us, but we all cheered and jeered, waving mud balls at him. All of us were covered from head to foot in mud, it was mob-like and we must have looked like Zulu mud warriors in Norris Green, but somehow this triggered an idea.

The next night we walked up to the bus stop, two stops away from our new mud triangles and tossed coins to decide who would ride the bus the short distance. Whilst on the bus, the loser of the toss had to open all the sliding windows and sit at the back of the bus to have the best seat in the house to witness our amusing skullduggery. That part of the plan was all set and the rest of us, four in total, rapidly walked down Townsend Avenue to make mud balls and hide behind the bushes of the corner houses.

We knew the approximate time of the buses so the planning was good; we waited for five minutes until we heard the bus approaching in the distance. It pulled up at the bus stop and all the windows had been opened. Like Jack-in-the-boxes we sprang into action and pelted the bus, getting about four direct hits. The driver was livid and pulled off swiftly, as the barrage of mud balls was relentless. His passengers were up in arms with mud dripping inside and outside the windows. We thought this was hilarious as we legged it up the other end of the street, having found a new game that involved mud, running and ambushing.

The next few nights of mudslinging and laughter came and went but one thing had changed – the driver was on to us. On about the sixth consecutive night he was primed to race out of the traps and somehow ended up chasing me down Faversham Road, much to the amusement of my pals and by now, half the street, due to the racket of the chase and my mates shouting and laughing.

I was fast as lightning as I retreated, but covered in mud so I couldn't really say I wasn't there. As I ran at full pelt, I slipped near a car and the bus driver was now tight on my tail. I jumped up and placed both hands on the bonnet of a car and noticed a thin, wet driver with both hands on the boot of the car opposite me panting like mad. He looked directly into my eyes with rain dripping off his red face and panted,

"I'm gonna fucking kill you, you little cunt."

I glanced over the bus driver's shoulder and noticed my dad about 10-feet behind him approaching quickly in his boxer shorts looking livid. He was dripping wet as the rain was bouncing down by this time. He had *that* look in his eye, I knew I was in trouble, but I also knew how protective he was over his kids.

"You little cunt, I'm gonna fucking kill you," repeated the bus driver, panting profusely.

I took my hands off the bonnet as Dad shouted,

"I heard that mate and I'm his father... Paul, get home and get to bed NOW!"

As I moved past the bus driver I looked up at him, saying in a soft, scared, knowing way,

"I think my Dad's gonna smash your head in."

Bish, bash bosh, I heard as I sprinted home with my feet squelching, dripping and with mud oozing out with every step. Whoosh! I undressed and was in bed in record time knowing that I wouldn't be moving for at least a week – that meant my new schedule would be school and then straight home to my bedroom until dad said otherwise.

Dad never mentioned the outcome of the incident, but my mates told me in school that it was one punch from my dripping-wet, boxer-short-wearing father that ended the driver's ideas of laying a finger on me.

Who got off lightly? Me or the bus driver?

The week passed as slowly as an injured snail heading to A&E. The relief at my sudden release from my bedroom prison cell was greeted with cheers and plenty of jibes from my mudslinging mates. It took a few weeks to find a new hideout, as our previous ones has been taken over by the influx of council workmen.

By this time we'd bonded with some of the workers who'd pay us to go to the shops for them during our school holidays and weekends. This relationship worked both ways, as we seemed to leave them alone and not mooch around their metal, cargo containers dotted around the estate although we frequently tried to peek inside to see what goodies were waiting to be pilfered at some point along the way.

We settled for a back garden of an empty house where the council stored; equipment, tools, waste and a mound of sand in the front garden. We collected old doors and discarded wooden boxes to use as seats and looking back, built ourselves what amounted to a death trap; but we loved our own space and treated it like it was a palace.

THE NEW BOOK CLUB FODDER: FEMINIST DYSTOPIAS

Don't shoot the messenger, but pandemics are at the heart of some of the most buzzed-about fiction for 2021. *The End of Men* by Christina Sweeney-Baird (Borough Press, April 29) imagines a flu pandemic that targets only men. *Last One at the Party* by Bethany Clift (Hodder & Stoughton, February 4) follows the only woman left on Earth as she tries to survive after the human race has been wiped out by a virus — think *Fleabag* meets post-apocalyptic action thriller. And *Outlawed* by Anna North (Weidenfeld & Nicolson, January 28) is a feminist western, perfect for fans of Margaret Atwood, in which Ada, is forced to flee a town where it is every woman's duty to have a child to replace those that were lost in the Great Flu, and be hanged as witches if they fail to conceive. Some light reading then.

get close to the car and would come scurrying out like a hungry hippo, but with a snarling, rabid mouth.

Ricky was a reddish colour, with a glorious shiny coat and was well kept by his owners who were the butt of all the Faversham Road trampy jokes. Kids can be the worst kind of human beings; relentless and naive but we knew no better, we just took the piss at any opportunity.

One night we went to the chippy and got chips and buttered barm cakes and headed to our den. To our disbelief, the smell of the food attracted Ricky to the entrance. At first we were all terrified until he came right to the middle of the floor to pick up a dropped, dirty, hot chip. Then he sat down looking for more while we all looked at each other, open mouthed.

We couldn't believe he was just sitting there, in our den, peacefully. It was astonishing because he was usually snapping at our heels constantly. The heat from the Calor gas stove was warming us all up while Ricky just sat there for what seemed like ages until we coaxed him closer to us with a few chips.

One of my mates pushed me off the paint tin I was sitting on, picked it up and opened it with a discarded six-inch nail. As Ricky was being peacefully fed by the rest of the lads, my pal gently poured this thick gloopy gloss paint all over Ricky's auburn coat – starting at the tail and ending at his neck.

I couldn't stop laughing, Ricky never moved for about hour as we continued to feed him scraps of chips and by the time he decided to try and leave, the gloss paint had hardened and looked like it had been styled by a sports car company with its side skirts moulded and perfectly formed – it looked amazing – like an Andy Warhol sculpture.

Ricky did have some trouble adjusting to his new-found stiffness but we helped him on his way with much laughter all the way down the street that night. Watching Ricky with a glorious red head and the rest of his body looking like a styled Scottie dog was hilarious. If you did something like that today, you'd get an ASBO slapped on you and it would possibly make headline news.

From that day onwards though, Ricky never once bothered us playing football in the street and we never bothered him. You could say he got the message, although the owners held an inquest into what happened, obviously not finding out much. Well, now the cat's out of the bag.

Giz a Job

The next year was spent playing football, going to school and mooching around our newly-modernised estate.

I took my football skills, knowledge and fanaticism to another level too; by watching Liverpool Reserves as well as going to the First Team home games on a regular basis. I would wait by the players' entrance and try to meet some of my idols from the first team, who often made their comeback from injury in the reserves.

The amount of quality players Liverpool had in reserve was astounding at that time: Ronnie Whelan, Sammy Lee, Ian Rush, Alan Harper, Kevin Sheedy, Paul Jewel and Dave Watson, to name but a few.

With Roy Evans as their manager, they used to win the Central League title nearly every season. The quality was there for the small, devoted, enthusiastic crowd who turned up on Friday evenings or Saturday mornings to watch the reserves in the early 1980s.

My regular presence was now being acknowledged by a Scouse reserve player who'd just broken through from the youth ranks, by the name of Stiga Foley. He often gave me free tickets to get in. I thought I was the bollocks with my complimentary tickets. What a result. I would always ask for him when I got to the Players' Entrance.

Whilst watching these matches, I noticed kids in the empty parts of the ground as only the Main Stand was open for spectators. These kids seemed to be ball boys as they would scamper up the seat in the Kemlyn Road end when the ball was kicked up into the empty seated area. The kids behind the Anfield Road and the Kop Terrace used to watch the ball ricochet like a pinball machine off the stepped terrace and the white crowd-control barriers. It was funny watching the kids trying to judge the direction of the ball once it started to bounce on the angled terraces.

The First Team didn't have a ball boy, so I thought this was a privileged position for any kid who was a Liverpool Football Club supporter.

At the next Friday evening reserve match, I took up my position at 5.45 outside the players' entrance. I was waiting for the players to arrive with the anticipation of one of the First Team regulars to show up.

The fella who controlled and patrolled the door came over to me and asked if I would go to the shop and buy him some cigarettes – he must have trusted me but only because I'd been a regular at his door for the past few months. I ran to the shop by the Kop End and legged it back; buzzing that somebody who worked for the club had asked me to do them a favour.

When I got back, I noticed two of the young ball boys walking through the players' entrance.

'Oh my God' I thought, 'They actually get to walk in the players' entrance and into the underbelly of my beloved football club.' As I gave the old man on the door his cigs and change, he put his hand out to shake mine.

At this time, the Alan Bleasdale series about downtrodden Liverpool, *'Boys from the Blackstuff'* was on everybody's lips – especially mine at this moment. I was just about to say, *'Giz a job, I can do that.'* I thought this over and over again as did Yozzer Hughes' character, when looking for work. I looked up at his rotund, mature face and his red and grey Liverpool Football Club tie stood out

"My name's Fred," he said in a posh accent – well a posh, Scouse accent.

"I'm Paul Walmsley," I replied quickly.

"Do you want to be a ball-boy tonight?"

I couldn't believe my luck.

"Yeah! When? Now?"

"Yeah, follow me," Fred said, opening the red door with *'Players' Entrance'* written in black on a white plastic sign that was screwed to the top of the door.

I was now walking into the players' entrance of Liverpool Football Club; the smell hit me about six strides down the corridor – liniment and Ralgex – boy it was powerful. My eyes started watering as it grew stronger and stronger.

Fred walked me into a room which had a caged cell in one corner and a counter with a drop-down lid at the right hand side, acting as a divide which split the room in two. He asked me to sit down and started to explain that I would be paid 45p and could have a hot drink at half time in the Police Room. I couldn't believe my luck as I glanced up at the other lads who were sitting on their hands as it was chilly in there.

"The Police Room?" I queried.

"Where you're sitting now is the police area."

Now the cage in the corner made sense to me and the counter was for the desk sergeant on first-team match days. I would often hear the tannoy announce somebody needed to go to the police room ASAP and to ask their nearest steward for information and he would take them. I now knew where that room was and what it looked and smelled like.

Fred asked us all to leave and in a stern voice said, "Make sure you stay off the pitch."

There were seven other kids there by this time; they were brought in by the Chief Steward who wore a reflective, orange coat with writing on the back. He came towards me and said,

"You're new, what's your name?"

"Paul Walmsley." I don't know why I kept giving my full name, maybe it was just my good manners and I had them in abundance, or maybe I felt taken aback – awe-struck to a degree.

"Well, Paul Walmsley, follow me and I'll take you to your spec."

Later on somebody told me his name was Tom and he pointed to another ball-boy and told me that was his son, Craig.

I couldn't believe my luck as I was taken past the dressing rooms, down the famous steps with the *'This is Anfield'* sign overhead, then up a few steps to a pitch-black, empty stadium and headed to the Anfield Road end.

I first noticed the famous dugouts and immediately imagined Bob Paisley, Joe Fagan and Tom Saunders sitting there, wearing their overcoats. This was like my dream wonderland had come to life. Oh my God – I thought, nobody will believe me when I tell them. It was the stuff of dreams for any young Liverpool Fan.

Suddenly, the lights came on and illuminated the velvety, green pitch and the grey seats in the Kemlyn Road. Tom, the Chief Steward, told me to go behind the goal in the Anfield Road end. There was a massive tunnel behind there which led to the toilets, cafe and turnstiles - and that's where I stood waiting for the players to come out.

The wind was bitter that night but I never felt it at all; I was warmed with the excitement. Liverpool came out first to a hand clap and cheers from about 300 fans at most who'd gathered within the 10-minute wait I'd stoically endured. They ran towards the Kop End and about two minutes later, Manchester City followed and ran towards me.

The smell of liniment was powerful again and now balls were flying behind me at a rapid rate. This was a sign of things to come – Liverpool Reserves eventually won 3-1. I thought I did well for my first ball-boy role and was buzzing my little socks off going back down the tunnel to the Police Room for my 45p wages.

Fred was puffing heavily on a cigarette and Tom was giving the ball-boys their money as it was stacked up in piles on the navy blue Police Room counter.

"Where are you from?" He asked me.

"By The Crown, Nogsy." I replied as snotty residue escaped from my freezing nose.

"Well, I live by Broadway so if you wanna lift wait here and I'll drop you off."

I was buzzing again; I didn't even have to pay bus fare to get home. I used to walk or even run home when I watched the first team and reserves before so this was another bonus, a lift home.

Tom took me as far as Richard Kelly Drive on the East Lancs Road in his new white, but battered, Ford Transit van with plywood strapped to the roof rack and loads of tools and more plywood in the back. Craig was in the front and turned round to talk to me on the journey home.

"What school do you go to?' Do you play football?" Craig asked trying to make small talk. But the most important conversation came from his dad, when he said,

"Right Paul, I'll see you two weeks Friday, then?" as I jumped out of the sliding side door of the van. I couldn't believe I'd been asked back. I was over the moon and had a massive grin on my face as I rushed home to tell all and sundry my good fortune.

The next two weeks couldn't come fast enough and I think my entire family and my mates had enough of me chatting about my new job by this time too.

Four matches in and I'd finally established myself as a regular ball-boy and they even let me into the First Team matches for free and, yes, in the players' entrance and down the tunnel on match days. Unbelievable, I was actually walking in the footsteps of my idols.

I would turn up at 5pm for reserve matches and run errands for Fred, Billy Gamble (the dressing room attendant) and Peggy who worked in the main office. I could just walk about the place like it was home, and nobody batted an eyelid.

The Trophy Room, the players' lounge, the boot room, the dressing rooms and even the Ref's changing room were all fair game for me as I had an 'access all areas' pass. I was the luckiest boy alive.

I'd forged a great relationship with Craig and Tom by this time, too. Tom introduced me to a fella called Rocky and told me he was the first teams' bodyguard when they travelled to European matches. He had a tough look and a hairdo that resembled Doyle out of *The Professionals*. I was amazed by him and before too long I was friendly with Rocky too.

The next reserve match was against Blackburn Rovers and I'd turned up early because Rocky had asked me to help him with the dressing room area the week before. Any chance to get in there was taken with gusto and confident cheekiness. As I helped him wheel a huge metal bin into the home team dressing room, I heard a Scottish accent shout, 'Bobby!' (Rocky's real name)

I looked around and about six feet away from me with the huge smile on his face was my hero, Kenny Dalglish.

I froze solid with no facial expression and felt my jaw hit my neck in shock. Oh my God, what should I do? Should I say something?

I decided to stay mute because I didn't want to look like an idiot. I knew every statistic about this man, yet I couldn't utter a single word. As he stood next to me talking openly to Rocky, he reached out and rubbed the top of my head and ruffled my hair. I looked at him and smiled without showing my teeth as by now I had lockjaw with excitement. I made a sort of gesture but I still couldn't open my mouth.

"That's Paul, he's a good kid," Rocky said to my hero. I was jumping up and down inside thinking 'Kenny Dalglish knows my name, he's rubbed my head and he's standing next to me. Yeah!' I was numb with sheer delight and shock.

That reserve match was like another European Cup final to me. Every time I saw Dalglish on the pitch I thought, *he knows who I am – he knows my name.* I was the most complete 12-year-old in the world and nobody could tell me any different. What a wonderful emotion that was, I wanted to feel like this forever.

After the match, Rocky drove me home in his Alfa-Romeo sports' car and it wasn't long before I angled the conversation to King Kenny; how long have you known him? Is he your friend? Have you been to his house? Rocky laughed and quickly changed the subject to boxing. He only did that because he knew how much I worshiped this man.

I orbited myself that night with the knowledge that King Kenny knew my name.

Rocky was the chief steward in the Anfield Road End for the first team matches and I found later on that his real name was Bobby Stein. The name Rocky came from his obvious fighting skills, his seriously flat nose and his look of a hard bastard that was there for all to see.

A month or so into knowing him, he asked if I was interested in boxing. I told him I'd trained for about a year at Sparrow Hall Boxing Club and I'd had a few exhibition fights. Next thing I knew he was picking me up with Billy Gamble, the dressing room caretaker who was also caretaker for the Liverpool Stadium in the city centre. We would go to the boxing gym at the side of the stadium called Liverpool Star ABC. That familiar smell would be lingering as soon as the rickety, wooden door had been unlocked; must, stale sweat and leather would hit you and cling to the back of your throat until you eventually left the building. It wasn't pleasant but I loved it.

Rocky was a kickboxing champion and would travel all over the world to fight, but Liverpool ABC was his home training base. This was where I began to learn to defend myself properly, stay on my feet, never go down and always be fitter than the next man to gain the edge that a small lad needed.

I was tiny compared to the rest of my pals, school mates and football team mates. I was captain of Ellergreen Comprehensive as I was the best player by a long way back then. I was as fit as a fiddle due to the three-times-a-week football training and playing matches twice a week. I played football on Saturday morning for the school and on Sunday for Sparrow Hall – my Dad's mate's team.

Now everyone I knew was a livewire, but word must have got around that I was boxing as nobody ever picked a fight with me or did anything untoward. I wasn't a trouble-maker or unpopular but having the skills to defend yourself in Norris Green came in handy at times – especially being so small.

I would spar with Rocky all the time and he would put me through my paces on the pads in the ring. Occasionally he would burst into lightning-quick combinations whilst sparring, but at the last moment of contact he would freeze, as if to say, 'Look, I can do it'. I must point out that I was boxing and he would start to kick box so his foot would appear, as if by magic, two inches from my face. This would keep me on my little toes at all times.

I ended up having six schoolboy fights for Liverpool Star ABC that year. The final fight was against a lad from Willaston in Cheshire.

He was much taller than me and had loads more fights but that didn't bother me. I wasn't the best fighter but I was game as fuck - and fit - and that goes a long way in the boxing ring.

Due to the constant training with Rocky, the kick-boxing style was creeping into my psyche. I ended up getting disqualified for head butting him and kneeing him in the chest – the boos still ring in my head now. I thought no better at the time as I'd always fight like that when I was sparring with Rocky – it was good fun and terrifying at the same time. This, though, gave me certain skills and a mental attitude that has served me well through the years, so thanks, Bobby.

A couple of months after my last boxing bout, I was minding my own business eating a portion of chips outside The Crown, when a lad named Paul Johnson came over to me. Without saying a word he put his hand right into my bag of chips, took a handful and started eating them. Now, Paul was about 6ft tall and I was barely 5ft then. I never really spoke to him over the years, but noticed him when I was in our garden as his house backed onto ours. You know when you just don't like somebody because of the way they look? Well, this was the case with me towards him.

"What the fuck are you doing?"

"Shut it you, ya little squirt!" he replied, putting his hand back into the paper and taking another fistful of vinegar-soaked chips.

"Don't do that again. You big blurt." I said, firmly.

"Why? What are you gonna do, you little squirt…?" he said, laughing and eating my chips at the same time. I looked at my mate who'd shit himself and passed him the crumpled remains of my chips.

I bounced around this giant on my toes like Tigger from Winnie the Pooh and hit him full on the face with two powerful, rapid punches, then hit him with another two combinations on the side of the head. I could see his nose bleeding from the first few shots and I bounced up to hit him full in the face again only to feign it and stoop low and punch him full blast in the bollocks...OUCH!

He burst into tears instantly, legged it across the East Lancs Road and was never seen again – well, when I say never seen again – about 20 years after that I got my key stuck in the lock of my front door and needed a locksmith. I found one in the Yellow Pages and who should turn up? Yes, Paul Johnson, the lad who stole my chips. He didn't recognise me but I'd never forgotten him. Anyhow, he fixed my lock and gave me an £80 bill. I told him to 'go and get fucked' and this 'Little Squirt wouldn't be paying him'. The look of shock, disbelief and that chip-snatching-incident was brought back to him instantly, it was written all over his face for me to see once again. I love that key and lock now.

We still had our den in the back garden of the empty house in Faversham Road, but we had rivals now. The older lads, 14 and 15, had their own den and mob. Our mob split into two groups as some lads couldn't take the stick that was constantly flying about.

The Meanies and the Panthers – as we were now known – were now operational and we both tried our best to avoid The Flies; who were ruthless thugs who'd beat you up if you didn't do as you were told. Their den was beneath the railway bridge next to Walton Hall Park and they called it Fly Valley – in fact, I think it's still written on the bridge today, more than 35 years later. They'd back us up when needed and as people came through the estate we would tax or harass them in a nice way, no violence; more like wasps than vultures.

Igor, a local do-gooder who patrolled the streets on his bike was no longer a threat as our numbers swelled due to the backup of The Flies, who were just older lads from our estate. I knew all of them really well as my brother, Stephen, knew all their brothers and my six sisters knew their sisters.

We all got along but when it got serious we wouldn't be visible on the streets for example, a few years earlier when the Toxteth Riots kicked off, the police had the estate on lockdown – or so they thought. The Flies would be causing havoc under the cover of darkness and as Toxteth was diverting the attention of the Police, they were out earning a few quid.

By this time, I'd found myself a best mate, Dougie. We had loads in common and only lived 20 houses apart. We spent all our spare time together, he even joined the boxing club about a year earlier, I got him a job as a ball-boy too and we went everywhere together.

We both felt hard done by as we thought we'd been harshly treated by our parents so we hatched a harebrained plan to run away.

We both had a bit of money put aside and decided to buy a tent and survival kit from Wakefield Camping shop in Liverpool's town centre.

We made our way to the wooded area at the back of Fazakerley Hospital and across the road from the cemetery where we'd built our swing years before, wearing our Peter Storm waterproof coats – we set trends back then, as well as being self-sufficient and adventurous.

Our survival kit consisted of fuel blocks to cook food and boil water, freeze-dried ready meals in sealed foil bags, Kendal mint cake, a compass and a first aid kit.

The tent was yellow and green and just about fitted us both in with our bits and bobs. We thought we were set until it started to rain and the tent we'd bought was only shower proof. We got soaked and had an uncomfortable night, to say the least.

The next morning was spent trying to ignite the fuel blocks so we could have some hot food or drinks to warm us up. All our belongings and essentials got drenched, so the matches we had, proved useless in the end. We had to wait till about 11ish when we saw a man walking his dog and smoking a cigarette. He loaned us his lighter for a moment and we got cracking with the hot meals.

We'd eaten all our rations by tea time and started to think about going to the factories to have a mooch, when a lad from our road turned up walking his dog. His name was Stewie. He'd only moved into our road a few months earlier and we all fancied his sister, Karen, so we made him feel extra welcome on this occasion.

His arrival in the Annex that night sparked a different reaction though, we told him to sit in the tent and told him that we'd kidnapped him and he couldn't move or The Flies would come and do damage. We were only joking initially while showing a serious exterior, but he didn't see the funny side, so we played on that. We eventually got him to write a note, under duress;

We've got your son. If you don't give us two packets of Custard Creams, a packet of Wagon Wheels, two pints of milk and a box of Sugar Puffs, your son is getting it!

Earlier on, Stewie had told us what food they had in the cupboard and I quickly sprinted over the muddy field, through Sparrow Hall, across the East Lancs to Faversham Road to knock on Stewie's door to be greeted by his mum. I handed her the note, still out of breath and noticed her turning away once she'd read it. She was laughing her head off

"Are you for real?" she asked

"Oh yeah!" I replied, straight-faced. She started to laugh even more as she clung on to the wall to keep herself upright, she was borderline hysterical by now and I started to get worried. She walked into the kitchen and out of sight for a minute or so before appearing with a carrier bag full of our demands. Tears of laughter were rolling down her face as she came to the door.

"What time will Stewie be back then?"

"As soon as we've eaten this." I replied in a matter-of-fact way, turning to take the same route back to the Annex with my bag of goodies.

We only lasted till 10 o'clock that night as it started raining again. The funny thing was that when I got back home, nobody realised I hadn't been there the night before. So much for getting attention regarding my mistreatment issues – nobody gave a shit that I'd run away from home – well, not that time, anyway.

Flats, Trips and Cars

The East Lancashire Road runs from Walton, Liverpool to Manchester and was the main route for most of the skulduggery in North Liverpool in the mid-80s. This dual carriageway was a standing area and arena to view car chases, running pitch battles with rival gangs and home comings of my beloved football team, Liverpool, with many trophies (oh, and a few for Everton too. Mustn't annoy the neighbours, hey?)

There was a firm of lads who'd mastered the art of car theft and rally driving through the back streets of Sparrow Hall and Norris Green under the cover of darkness.

During the long, summer evenings, there would be hordes of teenagers awaiting the arrival of some kind of high-powered performance car to screech through the estate, on to the East Lancs Road to take chase from the on-looking police cars.

One particular evening, the masses had gathered due to extensive gossip that there would be thousands of teenagers from different, fractious parts of rival estates scattered in all four corners, awaiting these pursuits.

The atmosphere was intense and the balmy weather added to the occasion - as did the appearance of the full moon once daylight faded into night with an air of anticipation embedded into the revellers' psyche. The rumours were rife about which car had been stolen and from which corner of the estate it would appear. All eyes were peeled and ears pricked like under-threat meerkats.

Townsend Avenue ran into the East Lancs Road at a T-junction which gave you the advantage of viewing more than any other place as it sat strategically proud on the urban landscape. Landford Avenue was a great vantage point too, especially behind the barriers by the bus stop. This is where these four-wheeled-gladiator battles took place on a regular basis and I liked staying over my side of the East Lancs in case it all went tits up and I had to leg it.

You always had to be on your toes in the 80s as there were a few coppers who'd stitch you up or even give you a beating, given half a chance. While we waited for the arrival of the stolen car, the police arrived and tried to disperse the ever-increasing crowd with the haughty shouts of, *'There's nothing happening here, make your way home or you'll be arrested.'*

This was always greeted with a blag walk this way or that, but eventually we'd make our way back to our chosen vantage point.

After the third blag manoeuvre, we heard the screech of tyres in the distance and knew tarmac was being disintegrated by sheer engine power; the noise was deafening. As I turned for my night's excitement, I noticed my mum looking at me with her arms folded. "Paul, get 'ere... NOW!" she screeched over the noise of the hordes of reprobates heading towards the burning rubber.

I legged it towards her thinking I'd just give her a bullshit story and a cute little smile and I'd be back as part of the madding crowd.

"What's up, Mar?"

"Where the fuck do you think ya goin'?" She rolled her eyes at me and grabbed my arm.

"I'm... I'm just going to watch the robbed car with me mates, Mar." I tried to pull away and take her hand off my arm. She was in my face now and I could taste the Benson & Hedges she reeked of.

"Listen son, you're not going down that fuckin' road, you're coming home with me, now." She was dragging me. As she pulled on my arm, I somehow let my sweatshirt be dragged off and before I knew it, I'd wriggled out of it and broken free of her vice-like grip.

"Son, I told your father I'd keep an eye on ya ... and you're going down the wrong path." she said while holding on to my empty sweatshirt. This was a plea from deep in her soul, but I had other ideas and only wanted to be with my pals. I was following the crowd and that was that. Off I went with no regard for her. Selfish and stupid, but I'd had my shackles removed and I was running with the pack now.

As the crowd began to cheer and run towards the main road, there was a metallic-black Ford Capri 2.8 Injection in a cloud of fuel and burning-rubber smoke, turning circles in the middle of the three-lane, dual carriageway. The crowds went crazy and ran towards the car, as did the police. Once the police got to within 50 yards, it headed straight towards them at break-neck speed, in a game of chicken. The police got out of the way, spun round and gave chase to the cheers of the crowd, swelling by the minute due to the sirens roaring from every direction.

The Capri darted the wrong way down the East Lancs, turned right down Townsend Avenue, then left into Ranworth Road with three Fiesta 'fizz bomb' police cars in pursuit. Within 20 seconds, the sight of the Fiestas reversing out of the Ranworth, frantically performing reverse hand-brake turns to avoid being rammed off the road by the now-oncoming Capri, was amazing.

It turned into Ranworth Road and hand-braked a full turn, pointing the opposite way while switching its lights off. As soon as the police cars turned into the road, the Capri's lights were back on and it headed full pelt at the on-coming Fizz Bombs. The crowd went absolutely mad and started to taunt the police, so it wasn't long before the black Marias with riot roll bars - just like Mr. T and Hannibal knocked up in an old barn in the A-Team - turned up in numbers.

They'd block the roads and disperse the crowds by any means as they'd lost control on many occasions, and they didn't like that. These times became legendary across Liverpool and are still talked about today.

Over a period of a year, the cars got better while the crowds increased due to gossip, pillow talk, CB radios and the local press. Porsche, R5 Turbos, R5 Cosworths, 4x4 Sierras and many other chipped-to-death performance cars appeared on the East Lancs Road and Sparrow Hall Estate - to the great delight of the teenage masses.

Norris Green on Magic Mushrooms

Another focal point in bringing the youth of Norris Green together was at the opposite end of Townsend Avenue by Broadway; the Norris Green Youth Club. Many a night was spent playing pool, snooker, badminton and 5-a-side football with lads the same age and older. It was three, domed-shaped buildings that looked like half of an Aero chocolate bar, only this one didn't have bubbles in the middle of it. At times, this place was scary and helped to shape the person I became.

Music would always be blaring from the food kiosk as they allowed us to bring our own tapes in. Supertramp, Pink Floyd, Genesis, ELO, The Doors, The Specials, UB40 and Fleetwood Mac - *Rumours,* of course - were ever present. The smell of weed would always be strong and once the lads had settled into a competitive state of mind, the usual sounds of Jon and Vangelis, Friends of Mr Cairo and State of Independence would be put on so the troops could chill. My life at every stage had its own soundtrack which would stay with me through my future trials and tribulations. Every superhero needs a theme tune and mine was a mixed bag of musical treats.

The constant smell of the weed in the club made me inquisitive about finding out the effects of these mind-bending substances and opened my eyes to another dimension. This would be my first step into a world of deceit, greed, fair-weather friends, peer pressure, procrastination, bad choices, total-and-utter destruction, paranoia and excitement. You might be thinking that I smoked a joint or had a hot knife; oh no, I went for the natural buzz; magic mushrooms.

Queen Mary High School on Long Lane had the best playing fields on our estate by a country mile; it was like a bowling green in places. We'd often play football there on Sunday afternoon after we'd finished our league match on the LBA across the road earlier in the day.

Every time we played on the Queenie (that's what we called it) we would have to dodge around some older lads on their hands and knees picking tiny mushrooms from the plush, green grass. They'd put them in an empty cigarette box for safe keeping, then disappear like they'd fallen into sinkholes. One minute you saw them, the next minute they'd gone. You would never notice them going but would suddenly realise they'd vanished. It felt as if we had a delete button, we just switched it on and these pickers would blend into the velvet grass as if it were an unpublished scene from a Lewis Carroll novel.

I had just turned 13 and decided I would take an empty cigarette box over to the Queenie and pick myself a few of these tiny mushrooms and see what all the fuss was about. My young, inquisitive mind hadn't differentiated between weed and magic mushrooms; they were both the same to me. I couldn't have been more wrong.

A pal and I crawled around on our hands and knees gathering about 20 mushrooms each. As soon as we counted our harvested bounty, we decided to eat them on the spot. Bad move. They tasted awful, like slimy, chewy mud, but were washed down with a can of Lilt and a finger of a Twix, neither of which did much in the way of getting rid of the nasty aftertaste of Mother Nature's narcotics. It felt like a Romany Gypsy had moved into my mouth and set up camp for the night.

After about an hour, the effects of the mushrooms began to kick in. By this time we had taken up a position on top of the garage roofs that ran along the side of the Queenie.

We both lay motionless looking at the ever-changing sky, occasionally asking each other how we felt. There was a point on that roof when I became mute, but I could still communicate; there was no need for speech as my thoughts had become the dynamic colours in the sky. The clouds started to look like a mountainous region of a far-away land covering the peaks of the mountains. It was wonderful for a short time, as things would click into place then dismantle in a jagged way, until my mind mashed it up into a jigsaw puzzle. I had to force my brain to tell my mind that things were ok, but it wasn't working. My brain was broken and someone had stolen my mind and put a replacement in a different location.

Where had I gone? I started to wonder while trying to control my breathing. Before I knew it, darkness had fallen, the stars became flickering fairies and in a split second I realised I had to be home for 10.30pm. Oh shit! I thought, as my upper body jerked into life and I actually forgot for a few seconds that I was off my barnet. We both climbed down from the garage roofs walking gingerly, then floating towards home. It was only a short journey so we didn't have much time to think about anything other than arriving on time. It was like I'd travelled home on a conveyor belt.

The walk up my path to my front door was ok until I entered the hallway and looked into the gilt-framed, oblong mirror above the phone table and saw my huge eyes staring back at me like never before. They were as big and dark as baby seal.

If that wasn't bad enough, I heard my dad talking to my mum in the living room. As I walked in, I felt as if eyes were looking at me from every angle and it was 'on top' for me. I immediately slumped on the floor and began to watch the telly, stretched out like I always did, you know, trying to blend in. I couldn't stop thinking that mum and dad had noticed my huge eyes so I gave it another five minutes before saying goodnight and sheepishly made my exit to my bedroom. Phew! I'd gotten away with my magic mushroom experience and made it through the night, I thought. Oh no. This was not the end of my mind-bending adventure as the second burst of the mushrooms suddenly appeared in my mind and made my shabby bedroom look and feel like the cockpit of Sputnik on launch day.

I put my Waltham record player on, plugged in the headphones and lay on my bed with *Supertramp's Breakfast in America* ringing round my ears like never before. I heard every cymbal, hi-hat, triangle, tambourine and guitar riff like it was actually being played in my bedroom. Over and over again I listened to Supertramp with my brother's headphones tight to my head like they had become part of me. I learnt every word and it was about 2am when I tried to nod off.

I tried, tried and tried again to sleep, but these tiny mushrooms had a grip on me for a few more hours yet. The next morning wasn't a school day, thank God, as I felt like I'd been hit with a wheelbarrow full of bricks the minute I awoke. Rough as burnt toast. I couldn't remember what time I fell asleep, for some reason it felt like one huge, continuous far-reaching event. I was ok once I'd eventually come out of the other end.

That was my first drug experience and didn't really know what to make of it other than that it deffo fucked your mind and thought process right up. It would be a couple of years before I dipped my soul into that deep chasm again - and not by choice either.

Landford Avenue

Not long after my father passed away, I ended up moving to Sparrow Hall with my sister, Pat, and her son Antony. It was the only way my mum could deal with things at the time, so that's what was decided.

A two-bedroomed, ground-floor flat in Waresley Crescent was my new home. It was right next door to the Missionary Church and a stone's throw from Landford shops. In front of my new living room window there was only a square piece of grass between us and the row of shops. The chippy, chandlers, Co-op, chemist, Nigel's hairdressers, greengrocer, Sayers and the sweet shop were now all in eyeshot. Sayers was always my first choice as I'm a sucker for an egg custard, custard slice or cream slices. In fact, any cake really.

Landford Avenue was always lively and a source of never-ending entertainment. If it wasn't somebody stealing a JCB from the nearby industrial estate and ram raiding the Co-op to every onlooker's amazement; or the constant movement of smack heads selling anything they got their hands on, then the police would provide a constant atmosphere with their presence. This was a hotspot; a melting pot of mischief and money-making manoeuvres, spawned from Maggie Thatcher's privatisation plans that buggered the unions and tested solidarity to its limit. Now I'm not saying the Tory government put the drugs on the streets, but they did appear once the country revolted and rioted in protest to being downtrodden. In a short space of time it went from being underground and nocturnal, to packs of hunchbacks, gouching on street corners in broad daylight.

Even the lads who had great expectations put upon them by their families and peers turned to heroin. Up-and-coming footballers who'd captained England Schoolboys at Wembley in front of millions on live telly to university-bound students, were victims of this new endemic behaviour. What the fuck was happening? Whatever it was now was being viewed from my own cinema seat looking out of my new front window. It was hard not to watch as it was in your face, every day. *'Sparrow Hall - the Soap Opera'*. I'm sure this was happening on every council estate across Britain at that time: Manchester, Birmingham, London; take your pick.

There would often be knocks on our front door at all hours from someone who we knew being chased by the police and needed refuge, or the police looking for someone who'd been chased into the cut-through that ran past the Missionary Church from Landford Place to Waresley Crescent.

It was a local rat run; an escape route that would give you four or five options for a getaway from impending trouble. If it was somebody you knew well, they would be allowed to jump into bed with you as if they'd been there all night, as we'd curtain twitch to see what was happening outside.

The police weren't daft, if you didn't curtain twitch then you wouldn't be human, therefore making your front door a target. With that ingrained in my brain from an early age, it became a behavioural trait to look out of the window with inquisitive delight as the police searched the area, even if no one was in our flat. That was the art of curtain twitching, you had to be consistent in keeping up the façade and leaving the police guessing.

I was an integral part of Sparrow Hall life now and all the community Catholic spirit that came with it. There was a family on Long Lane that most of my family were close to, the Grants. They had three daughters around my age and a son who was about five years younger than me called Tony.

Pat and Tony Snr would always chat when they bumped into me as they used the cut-through next to our flat every day to walk to St. Philomena's Catholic School on Sparrow Hall Road. He would ask me about football, and now and again would turn up to watch me playing a match with young Tony in tow. With them having three daughters - who were really pretty - I'd often spend time on Long Lane waiting to catch a glimpse of the oldest daughter, Mandy, in her spotless Dash tracksuit or her sailor's dress she'd had specially made for her by a local dressmaker.

Needless to say, I would say fuck all and more or less shat my pants if she spoke to me. Lindsay was second sister and then there was Amy who was about six or seven and was constantly giggling and smiling. She was a cute kid and had a special way about her.

A few months into getting to know Tony Snr, he told me that young Tony was having trials at Everton and needed some moulded-sole football boots to borrow until he had his own. I was always small so my size 6 Patrick pigskin moulded boots which had been stolen from Jan Molby's locker at Melwood, would be a perfect fit for young Tony Grant.

A week later the boots were returned and it was good news as Tony had been taken on by his beloved Everton Football Club on schoolboy terms. With the knowledge that my boots possibly helped Tony out, the next time I wore them, it filled me with a certain pride and achievement, I don't really know why but that's how I felt back then.

Although community spirit was always on show, that didn't mean that you couldn't end up on the wrong side of some of the shit that was going on. The flat was burgled twice and ransacked as a result of me and my sister being too trusting and letting certain fair-weather friends know too much. It took about a year to find out who'd done it and it hurt more than a good beating when it was confirmed. You both know who you are. I'll leave it at that.

With me knowing every kid on the estate, it didn't take long to find out things. Take the time when my Auntie Brenda, who had a great job at Coca Cola - had her beloved Ford Orion Ghia broken into outside my Nan's house in Studland Road, Sparrow Hall. As soon as she realised what had happened, she contacted me and said she wasn't bothered who broken into her car, but she needed her purse which was in her glove box with some other personal items, returned. She pleaded with me to try and get these items back, so I went about the estate putting the word around.

I told everyone that they had until 8 o'clock that evening to leave the purse and other documents under a certain bush in a certain garden and no questions would follow. I gave them my word. I carried on with my day regardless and just after 8, went to the location to discover all the documents and a tan, leather purse that was bulging, but without any cash inside. There were credit cards and other work-related cards in the see-through compartment intended for photographs of loved ones and the like.

With all the items tucked under my arm and my tracksuit top zipped right up, I ran to my auntie's house, knocked on the door and caught my breath while waiting for it to be answered. The net curtains went back to reveal my ferocious Auntie Brenda.

She opened the door with such venom that the door knocker began to swing to and fro, making a rapid clatter. Before she could put her head round the door I had the documents and purse held out waiting for her.

"Who took them?" She demanded with this rabid-dog look. She was shaking as I handed them to her.

"I don't know Auntie Brenda, I just asked about today and they've turned up."

"No! You know who took them, if you say you don't, then it must have been you!" Her mouth was open so wide that I could see the plaque on her bottom teeth.

I was expecting a pat on the back but now I was being accused by way of a doorstep kangaroo court. She carried on with her rant and threatened to get my legs broken by other local gangsters who she claimed to know. She went on and on until I snapped back and gave her a mouthful of anger and amazed rage.

"Shut your mouth you silly, left-on-the-shelf, trouser-wearing dyke!" Oh yeah, I said what most of my family thought but would never speak about. Her jaw dropped below her belted-up high waistline as I spun on my heel and gave the final insult.

"ARGHHH FUCK OFF YA DIVVIE!"

I could hear her still shouting as I walked calmly down the road, knowing that I'd tried to help a family member and somehow become the victim. I was gutted and went right to my mum to tell her that her crackpot sister had an assumption malfunction and got it all wrong. Mum knew I was telling the truth; I've never spoken to Auntie Brenda from that day and to be honest I couldn't care less about her.

Every family has one or two members who are wired slightly differently than the rest. Being a huge Catholic family, ours was a case of having a few more than your average. Mum was from a family of 13 kids, we had nine in our family and countless cousins and second cousins. Cranks would be everywhere but the majority were decent people, you know, the type you have a buzz with at family parties.

Another car-theft incident had a more direct effect on our lives that Christmas. My sister, Pat, had a silver Ford Fiesta and would use it to go to one of her four jobs; she was a proper hard worker and hats off to her for that.

One of her better-paying jobs was in the Adelphi Hotel in Liverpool town centre. I think it was the tips that made it a good earner and Pat was an attractive woman who was good at her job. As it was around Christmas, her hours became longer so she asked me to be a sort of stay-at-home sitter for Antony. This was no problem as I was domestically well trained; knew how to use the cooker and clean up - not to Pat's high standards, but I could pull my weight. I would pick Antony up from school and feed him, play footy with him and get his uniform ready for the next day. So when he broke up from school, I became a full-time dad for him. I was 16 years old.

On Christmas Eve, Pat had to work. She left her car outside the flat in Sparrow Hall so she could have a few Christmas drinks with her mates at the hotel. Earlier on, we'd decided to hide Antony's wrapped presents in the boot of the Fiesta so he wouldn't find them on the annual Christmas Eve mooch; we've all done that. Everything was set, Pat would be home at 1.30ish and she'd bring the prezzies in with her to place beneath the white Christmas tree.

It all started to go wrong about 6 o'clock when I heard noises outside. I looked out to find the car boot open and two lads legging it in different directions with Antony's toys. Fuck me, I was out the door like Ed Moses, hurdling bollards bare-footed like a crazed lunatic. I caught up with one of the sewer rats and brought him to the ground like a lion would bring down its prey. The bag split open and the prezzies bounced off the nearby kerb as I kept hold of this lad's waist. I grabbed his neck and pushed him up nearly taking him off his feet. He kept on saying 'sorry' and asking me not to hit him. I knew this fucker from the estate and knew where he lived.

"Now you're gonna tell me who's got the rest of them otherwise I'm gonna smash your teeth in ya little prick, then I'll drag you to your own house". I was seething.

"It's Phil, you know him, Phil from the Strand." The beaut had blood coming from his lip.

I marched him back to the car and told him he had 30 minutes to go and get them back otherwise me and my brothers were going to cancel Christmas for him this year and maybe every year. I instructed him to bring Phil back too because if he didn't, I'd be at his mum's in one hour. That was promise and it'd be ten times worse for him if he didn't.
As I took the ripped bag back into the flat, I noticed Antony hadn't moved from watching a video in his bedroom; good, he was none the wiser but still had half of his prezzies missing. I reckoned the

kid would bring back the rest of them as he knew what the consequences would be.

On cue he turned up, but without Phil who was terrified and had pleaded with his pal to take them back alone. I snatched the rest of them from him without checking them; I wasn't sure what was supposed to be there anyhow, then as he turned around, I toe-ended him right up his arse with all my might.

"Tell Phil I'll be at his mum's in an hour, you little fuckin shit!" I said while spit was coming out of my mouth with anger. I phoned my brother Stephen and told him what had happened and to deal with it ASAP.

"No worries Kidda, am on it."

It was dealt with and I hoped all the prezzies were intact. I had a quick look through and all looked good, so making sure Antony had a bath and was in bed for 11ish was next on the cards. This all went without a hiccup so I waited for Pat to come home so I could tell her about the break in.

There were no police involved as we dealt with things ourselves, so Pat would be none the wiser. Two o'clock came and Pat hadn't appeared. Three then four passed, then the house phone rang. It was someone from the Royal Hospital in Liverpool telling me that an ulcer had burst in Pat's stomach due to the intake of alcohol and she'd be there for a few days or so. What the fuck else can go wrong might you wonder? Well, I'll tell you.

In my wisdom, I decided to get the Christmas dinner ready. I put the turkey in the oven and proceeded to peel spuds, carrots and sprouts. I thought the turkey should stay in the oven for about four hours because that's what it said on the packaging. In the morning when Antony woke me up about 8ish, I could smell the foulest stench coming from the kitchen, lo and behold it was the turkey. I'd forgotten to remove the giblets in their plastic, sealed bag. It fucking stank.

We both went to the fridge and noticed a Fray Bentos steak pie. By this time, Antony was buzzing with his prezzies and after we'd phoned the hospital to get an update on Pat, it was time to visit my Mum. We walked over to her house to tell her about Pat in hospital and our exciting adventures. I was happy when that day ended. Pat returned home a few days later but I'll never forget those 24 hours.

Heroin hit the streets and like water comes down a wall - it eventually makes its way to the bottom and forms puddles. I told myself to stay away from it in any way, shape or form, there was no mistake in its first nickname on the streets of North Liverpool, 'Nasty'. Nasty would have many pseudonyms along the way but ask any Scouse street kid and they'll know what you mean.
I'd started to have the occasional go of a hot knife or bong in one of the lad's houses when his mum was working late. With this came a few new mates - or so-called mates.

My new pals would come round to the flat in Sparrow Hall and mooch around the estate when we had nothing to do. This became a routine for one of them and he would knock early in the morning. He was supposed to be at college but was blagging it and sitting off with me all day. One morning he knocked as I was in the bath at about 10ish. I opened the door dripping wet, wrapped in my huge, red-and-yellow Liverpool FC towel. I let him in and jumped back in the soothing warm bath.

"Do you wanna cup of tea?" He asked as he made his way into the living room.

"Yeah, go on then, I'll be done in ten." I replied, soaping my hair up with Vosene.

"I'll go the shop first, do you want anything?" I heard him say, it was, muffled but it was clear enough to understand.

"The Daily Mirror and a custard slice from Sayers... have you got enough money?" I was buzzing with the knowledge of my favourite cake and daily read en route.

"Yeah, no probs, I'll be five minutes so I'll leave the door on the latch if that's ok?" He bounced past the bathroom, down the hallway and out of the door.

I carried on with the usual bathing ritual of putting my ears under the water and listening to the world in a weird underwater tone. I heard the noise of the latch click while I was submerged and burst up out of the fluffy bubbles and shouted.

"Is that you, lad?" His head popped round the door half way down with a big grin on his face and a Sayers bag in his hand.

"Here lad, there's ya cake and ya paper's on the floor." He slid the bag and the Daily Mirror towards me.

I dried my hands, sat upright and looked at the sports section on the back page as it was face down on the floor. He asked if I wanted a cuppa which I did and pulled the Sayers bag closer to me. The tea was placed on the side of the bath as he put the lid down on the toilet and started to talk to me about going to the youth club for a game of footy and pool.

The cake and cuppa were a Godsend and the Daily Mirror just helped with the relaxing mood. I turned the hot tap back on to top up the heat levels in my bath and spent about five minutes chatting while I was still in the bubbles and even-hotter bath, then he upped and left saying he would see me in the' Youthie' later on.

For some reason I felt weird so I looked at my hands and noticed they had wrinkled a lot more than usual, the water was only warm but something was amiss and couldn't put my finger on it. I topped my bath up again and lay flat for what seemed like ages. 'Oh my God, I'm off my barnet!' I thought, looking at the huge ridges in my wrinkled fingers.

I stepped out of the bath and popped my head round the door to look at the clock in the hallway. It was saying it was 1.30 in the afternoon, I'd been in the bath for over three hours and was off my nut in a bad way.

I tried to work it out and it hit me; my pal, the custard slice and the cuppa, what the fuck had he done? I was fuming but that much off my head, I was having crazy rushes whilst trying to control my breathing. I needed to find him and find out what he'd done to me. I got myself dressed sharpish and left the flat in about 30 minutes. I couldn't even iron a pair of kecks properly, I was in a right tangle and needed answers.

My first port of call was a place called *'The View'* on Townsend Avenue where a group would hang about who knew the lad who'd got me in this state. There were three lads I knew by the street lamp on the corner when I got there. As I got closer they seemed to move sideways together; one way, then the other. They swayed and rocked together as I stood right in front of them.

I asked them if they'd seen him and they just continued to sway this way and that. It was freaking me out.

"Stop swaying," I said with a frown and what must have looked like the biggest eyes in the world.

"What are you on about? We're not swaying, you are." They were looking at each other and grinning. It was properly freaking me out,

I just stared at them and started to walk up Townsend Avenue shaking my head thinking how fucked up it was. They were deffo swaying, I was telling myself over and over again.

I got to the youth club in one piece but feeling fragile and walked into the main room where the pool and snooker tables were situated and surveyed the room. Everyone was swaying in tandem; my mind was flipping, my head nearly fell off.

I carried on looking around for my pal and noticed him laughing in the far corner of the snooker room, he was swaying too. As I looked around, everyone was swaying from side to side. I was freaked out and shouted

"What the fuck are you all swaying for? Ya fucking divvies!" There was a burst of laughter and howls of,

"We're not rocking, you are!"

Oh my God, my head nearly burst open. I was livid so I just fucked them off and walked back to the flat to try and sort my head out.

About 9 o'clock that night another friend who'd heard about my ordeal knocked at the flat. I was still off my head and struggling to come to terms with the swaying routine. He told me that there were three purple mics LSD trips in my custard slice and when my pal left, he'd told anyone and everyone en route to the Youthie and asked them to sway. When he told me it was a reality check. I really thought I'd lost the plot, but actually knowing, eased my paranoia.

The next four hours shaped my mind forever. At one point I actually thought I'd traced my blood line back to Jesus Christ and was directly related to him. That's how much my mind was working overtime and I really believed it too. I don't know whether my mind was shaped for better or for worse, but it left an imprint deep in my psyche like a meteorite leaves a crater.

Obviously, the so-called friend thought it was hilarious and buzzed off my LSD-laced custard slice, but not long after that he had his own run in with a monster. The beast locally known as Nasty got a hold of him. He robbed his own mother's house, his brother's cash stash and became the local hunchback on street corners looking to score. My trip wore off the next morning, but his trip ended in robbing and mugging bus drivers for loose change.

Rome and Heysel

The 1984 European Cup final was to be played in the Olympic Stadium in Rome. My beloved Liverpool had reached the ultimate club football match in the world again. This would be their fourth final since 1977. What made it more daunting was the fact that their opponents would be Roma; the Italian champions of the previous season. This was their city and the venue was Roma's home stadium.

Rome was last invaded by the red-and-white clad Scousers in 1977 when Borussia Monchengladbach were defeated 3-1 in the same stadium Kevin Keegan played his final match for the mighty Reds. This, however, was to be a different occasion altogether; a night of intimidation on and off the pitch.

As my Dad was unwell at the time and losing weight faster than Greeks spend borrowed Euros, I wasn't allowed to go to Rome. There was nobody to take me, but the real truth is that every day was precious. Dad's time on this spinning ball of gas, water and rock was ticking away. We sat in the living room and made a cuppa, waiting for the kick off. We'd recently had the living room and parlour knocked into one and the whole room had been artexed in a thick bark texture - except for one wall which had velveteen black and white paper, with a huge Sarah Moon print hanging in the centre.

The plush, purple carpet (on which I'd had a fight with my sister, Lynn, because I thought it was black and she thought it hilarious to buzz off me with her visiting friends, making me lose my rag on numerous occasions) ran through both rooms which was now one big space.

We had an archway where the partition wall had once been; I thought it was the dog's bollocks and was now comfortable having my friends in the house. The only reason the work had been done was because Dad had taken an early pay-off from the docks which amounted to £24 000. It felt like millions to me back then and our house was bought and decorated in the style of 1984 Liverpool; 'Scouseness personified'.

Six months after Dad took his money, he was diagnosed with terminal lung cancer.

We watched the whole match in our Scouse house, mostly on our feet, screaming at the telly. It ended 1-1 at full-time and went to extra time; another 30 minutes spent screaming and shouting until hoarse, then the final whistle blew and it was to be decided on penalties. The rest is Scouse folklore: Bruce Grobbelaar's wobbling antics on the goal line to put the Roma players off as they were about to take their shots will be an everlasting memory ingrained into mine and countless other football fans' souls. The plan was working until I realised our last penalty taker was Alan 'Barney Rubble' Kennedy, our left back who scored the winner in Paris in 1981. He was one of the most unorthodox players and looked shattered as he walked up to take his shot.

For some strange reason, both Dad and I felt uncomfortable about him taking what could be the winning penalty. I closed my eyes and listened until I heard the commentator mention his run up, I opened them wide while keeping my hands pressed firmly onto my head harder and harder with every breath.

He scored! "Yeahhhhhhhhhhhhhhhhh!" I yelped at the top of my youthful-but-breaking voice.

I jumped around the living room with Dad until I noticed him getting out of breath and he started to cough. For that brief moment I'd forgotten Dad was ill. He sat down quickly in the safety of his chair and I carried on with my celebrations, taking them on to the street with all the other dancing Liverpool fans who were cheering and running around lampposts, delirious. Somebody had their car radio on full blast and the commentator was hoarse from shouting over air horns which had been hooting non-stop by the Roma fans for the entire match and drowning him out. The atmosphere in the street was electric.

The DJ played a song by Deniece Williams that was in the charts at the time; *'Let's Hear it For the Boy'* - and everybody in the street was doing the conga, vigorously joining in the chorus. The numbers swelled by the second as everyone joined in from the adjoining streets.

That was the last thing I ever did with my dad; the next week he took bad and was bed-ridden in the makeshift hospice in the back of our new living room. I was moved out of the house and in to my sister's across the road in Sparrow Hall, but would come back and stay whenever I wanted to. It gave me a chance to avoid the ever-decreasing situation and the state Dad was in. Looking back, it was definitely for the best.

He passed away on 25th June 1984, exactly one month after we'd jumped up and down in the living room. I was sent to Ibiza so I missed the worst of his deterioration and his final days. I do remember the Roma memories fondly and kissing him on his head the morning I left for Ibiza. They're everlasting pictures I've taken and put in a place in my mind. I will treasure them always.

Dad's Stash

The next year was tough and I decided I would travel to most of Liverpool's away games in between playing myself, of course; the odd mooch around the estate was also a priority to make myself a few quid. Mum took Dad's death really badly and wanted to join him at times. I found that tough and witnessed a lot of grief. I wouldn't wish it on anybody.

With this huge loss in my life, I found some space available to do more shite and more mooching. Dad always said, 'Don't do this and don't do that', so what did I go and do? Everything he told me not to, obviously. I was a young, smart arse - or so I thought - who'd been given a joker's card to play whenever I wanted to. It was getting played as and when I saw fit.

Every time I'd see one of my Dad's pals on the estate, they'd tell me stories about him which started to paint a picture of a person I knew so little about. Strange really when he was my father. With all this new information in tow and the go-ahead from mum I was allowed to rummage through Dad's aviary, which he had built with his own hands over the past 20 years. This was no ordinary bird house either; if Carling did aviaries then this is what it would look like. It was truly amazing.

It was immaculate and guarded with better security than our house. I'm not kidding. TV, fridge, collectables, a workshop, library, massive oil heaters, bars on the windows and sensor pads. Whatever was in there he wanted to stay there. Mum was adamant that money was stashed in there along with a black book with names of people who owed him money for one reason or another. Upon numerous insidious questions to mum, she let slip that Dad was some sort of money lender.

Armed with this knowledge and with a tear in my eye, I got the key from Mum and opened the cream-coloured, thick, wooden door with 83A in bold black lettering on the top: our house was 83, hence the numbering system.

Mum had been generally looking after, feeding and watering the birds since he'd died so it was a bit dusty, but at least the budgies, canaries and zebra finches were all fine. I sat and cried alone for about 20 minutes before I eventually turned on the white Bush portable TV and fiddled with the dial to get a clear picture. For me, one tear cried alone is worth more than a million wept in front of someone, I truly believe this to this day. I started trying the selection of keys to find the one which opened the numerous locked cupboards; there were several. Memories flooded back with every door I opened and crevice I peered into which in turn brought on bouts of blubbering tears from a grieving son.

Each cupboard was searched without making any mess; for some strange reason I still felt the presence of my father so I showed respect. It was immaculate and the tool cupboard had a shadow board with only one tool missing; a wooden mallet. I've got to admit it did baffle me to the whereabouts of this mallet, but only briefly.

I was searching for about two hours when I returned to the cupboard which had the best lock. I opened and closed it about five times until the final time I slammed it shut and to my utter disbelief a false bottom fell from underneath revealing a secret tray about two feet long, a foot wide and two and a half inches deep.

I couldn't believe it, my jaw dropped in amazement. There were two hard-backed books, one accounts book, two plastic money bags filled to the brim with notes and a biscuit tin filled with 50p and 20p pieces. It wasn't the money that struck me, it was the books: *The Count of Monte Christo by Alexander Dumas* and *Chariots of the Gods by Erich von Däniken*. The Count of Monte Christo, I'd heard of, but the other one had me scratching my head in bemusement.

I picked up *Chariots of the Gods* and looked at the front cover, then turned it over to read the back wondering what it was all about. I ran to the house and shouted mum at the top of my voice.

"Mum, mum…I've found it….dad's bits and money too."

"What did you just say?" She seemed to float downstairs as I couldn't take my eyes off her eyes. I explained the discovery of the false bottom, books, money and grabbed her hand to lead her into the garden towards the aviary. She took one look at the stash, looked at me and still smiling said,

"The sneaky fucker! I knew he'd have some sort of stash."

We shared a moment in the aviary that day knowing that we'd unearthed some of Dad's secrets. Under the accounts book was a brown envelope with his seaman's pass from 1949 when he worked on the banana boats out of Liverpool Docks to Rio, Belize and other exotic destinations. I was hooked on the footsteps my father had taken and what happened to him when he was my age. I found myself somehow in his shoes, even if it was only second-hand.

Bringing Dad back to life was a wonderful experience; it was only for a brief moment, but nevertheless, magical and everlasting.

With the two hard-back books in my hand, I retreated to my bedroom and started to read. *Chariots of the Gods* was obviously first as it puzzled me big time. I never moved out of that bedroom for two days except for toilet breaks and collecting food from the kitchen, which I would eat in my room while scrolling intensely through the book. I only ever read school-based books so this was a new experience for me.

As the words poured past my eyes and fingers, I tried my best to absorb the theme of this Holy Grail in my young, grieving heart. Things started to register on the second day as I was reading and asking myself questions after turning each page. The penny finally dropped as to why Dad had hidden these books. *Chariots of the Gods* was an opinion-based book with some interesting facts to back it up. It suggested that we're space gypsies and somehow the whole history of mankind will need to look to space for the answers. Maybe we originally came from space or maybe we evolved from single cells in the bottom of hot-water pools, who knows?

What I do know is that in the early 80s, if you thought aliens or something else existed out there, you were in a minority and would be looked upon as a bit of a weirdo. This is why he'd stashed it away. Wow, Dad had a secret which I'd unearthed and now treasured. It was mine to place in my psyche forever. This triggered my imagination, left me with questions and opened up possibilities that I'd never considered before.

Later on, mum would tell stories about all the girls being after dad, but it took a woman to grab him. Seeing Mum without Dad was now a new and weird perceptual viewpoint; it was so very different and Mum was heartbroken and devastated. I knew I'd have to keep an eye on her behaviour, even if I was only 15; I had responsibilities that never came to mind before.

The next year was strange without Dad around. I carried on playing football as much as I could and travelled to watch Liverpool FC playing whenever I had time. Mum allowed me a few quid to get some new clothes, trainers and footy boots. Robert was part of a running club in Kirkby and would get *Running World* magazine which advertised trainers from other countries. In the back of the magazine was a mail order section and the selection was amazing. I ended up getting Mum to fork out for a pair of new Adidas ZX500 in grey with yellow stripes. The total cost including P&P was £85, this was expensive back in the day and was not far off a weekly wage.

In Liverpool town centre, just off Bold Street was a small sports' shop called Wade Smith (Neil's Corner). All the grafters would sell their acquired trainers from across Europe to Wade Smiths when they got back home. There was always a few pairs of exotic-looking footwear in the window or on the shelf behind the till to tempt the punters in off the street.

When I bounced in with my gleaming, new size 5 ZX500 his face lit up like a kid with a new bike and immediately asked to buy them from me. I told him he had no chance. I'd bounced in a few times with new trabs before, which my brothers would buy every now and again, as I was the youngest. Diadora Ed Moses; white with a red logo had turned Wade Smith's head earlier in the year, as did my Asics Tiger; white with a red and blue logo. I was a bit of a trainers' nut and looked after them all to the point of being weirdly obsessive.

My choice of football boot at the time was the only unusual coloured pair since Alan Ball had his white Hummels in the 70s. I bought a pair of navy blue Adidas Profi which were wonderful. The huge leather tongue with the Adidas logo bent over the laces to protect them and advertise the brand at the same time. I thought I'd smashed it with the variety of footwear I had at my disposal. That's how it was in Norris Green back then, not just for me but for most lads of my age and older.

With my new trainers and my blue combat kecks along with my blue, red-and-white, horizontal-striped Lacoste T-shirt, I was equipped with my travelling football rig out. The Liverpool supporters would amaze their rivals with this newly-acquired dress sense which turned many opposing fans' heads along the way. The Peter Storm cagoule from Wakefield Camping shop on Church Street would round off my look, making me stand out from the other fans around the country and create a uniform for the travelling Red Army.

There's a myth about Scousers wearing tracksuits and trainers at all times; the one which Harry Enfield stereotyped in his TV show. The reason for this rig-out enigma was due to inter-estate mass fights back in the late 70s and early 80s and the running battles that would erupt on the streets of North Liverpool. The police would obviously turn up at some point, so a story was needed to use as an excuse.

All the participants in these fracas would be wearing tracksuits and trainers so that when trying to avoid capture they had a blag, which was, 'I'm just going for a jog, Officer.' If you did get collared and were wearing jeans and a coat and you used the 'jogging' story, you'd get buzzed off, then thrown head first into the back of a Bizzie van.

The tracksuit-clad Scousers had really good street acumen at the time, so don't knock it because it got many a rogue off criminal charges, not to mention the possibility of a beating from the coppers. This tracksuit culture was born from the football hooligans and their exploits around the globe, so we have to bear that in mind for the purpose of this book and for future generations.

The travelling Liverpool fans had a proper buzz and would be rewarded with a couple of finals along the way; it seemed to be rude if we didn't reach the odd major final or two. We had another great season and ended up reaching the European Cup final in Brussels, where we would play the Italian Champions again – this time Juventus, but not on their own turf.

Everton had improved and had a great team which had reached the European Cup Winners' Cup final, to be played in Rotterdam the week before our final in May.

They played Rapid Vienna with the European legend, Hans Krankl, in their line up and in the end defeated the Austrians 3-1 - to the delight of the Blues who'd travelled to Holland. Apparently, the weed, alcohol and prostitution trade had a massive increase the few days before and after the victory, but I don't believe that for one minute, do you?

Rotterdam, Amsterdam and the surrounding areas had been traumatised, terrorised and left gasping for normality after the Scouse masses devoured all in its wake and UEFA made a huge point of giving stern warnings and threats of impending bans if it happened again.

After Rotterdam, loads of Evertonians met up with the Liverpool supporters in Eindhoven where Dire Straits had arranged a leg of their *'Money For Nothing'* tour and the release of the new, music sensation, CDs, by their sponsors, Phillips. Liverpool is a huge music and football city so any time the two can be combined, it's 100% happening and travelling fans would plan that into their European adventures.

Antony had started to go to the home matches with me so his first European Cup final was on the cards. His mum, Pat, decided to come to Brussels with us, too. On occasion she would come to the home games so it made sense to have her as our minder and to look after the two, staunch, red noses in her family, plus she liked the male attention that went hand in hand with it; so it was a win-win situation for all of us.

WH Smiths in Liverpool town centre had offers in the Liverpool Echo to travel by coach in the early hours of match day to Brussels, arriving back mid-afternoon the day after the match, which would be played on a Wednesday night. This was the only viable option at the time, so we booked and paid in cash to avoid any disappointment.

Antony and I both had season tickets, so we knew tickets for the final were guaranteed. When the tickets went on sale, Pat went with me bringing our documentation of travel from WH Smith and passports to show to the ticket-office staff. While we waited patiently in the queue, Pat and I talked about trying to blag another as she was our chaperone and didn't have a season ticket.

As we approached the window, leaning over the back of the ticket woman's chair was Peggy from the main office who I knew from back in the time when I was reserve-team ball-boy. She caught my eye and smiled, then walked over and started chatting. I introduced my sister and stood back to let the women talk. In the same way that you mustn't separate a dog from its bone, you must never get in the way of two women deep in conversation. I did earwig and heard every word of Peggy ordering the staff to give Pat an extra ticket for the final, there was now no need for me to revert to dipping again; thank God for small mercies.

You'll never know how I felt walking away from Anfield Road with three tickets for the 1985 European Cup final firmly zipped in my inside pocket, instead of two. I was so happy, I forgot to say thank you so I ran back and pushed to the front of the queue, squeezed into the ticket booth and shouted over to Peggy. She was just about to light a cigarette when she heard my shouts. She took a few steps closer so she could hear me more clearly, nodded and smiled while reaching for her cigarette.

"Thanks Peggy!"

"No problem, Cutie. Any time you need tickets, just come to the main office. Isn't your sister lovely?" Peggy said, as she dragged on the lit cigarette.

I smiled, nodded my head in agreement, backed out of the growing line, and ran like the wind to catch up with Pat who was already back at her car.

The coach was leaving at 1am on the Wednesday morning; all travelling fans were to be there at midnight to check in. We arrived at 11.30pm and there were loads of people who'd brought ale for the journey and were already pissed and singing at full throttle.

A few days earlier, Antony and I had customised a Liverpool flag to put our own small, but significant, mark on the occasion. We'd made our way to the back of the coach to put our flag in the back window and then waited anxiously for rest of the passengers to arrive.

One o'clock came and the coach was full. The doors closed and we were off – *'Brussels here we come'*. The singing started and we all joined in at the top of our lungs, adding to the upwardly-mobile atmosphere.

Pat was a dab-hand at cooking so our food supplies kept half the coach in munchies for the outward-bound journey: London, Dover, Calais and then on towards Belgium. By 10 O' clock, Antony was asking how long until we arrived, in fact, I had to tell him if he asked me one more time, I'd flick his ears severely. I was quite the champion ear flicker so he knew not to ask again.

We'd arrived in Brussels at about 1.30pm and had been directed by the police escort to a carpark by the Expo building. There were alien-looking *Space 1999* pods that stuck out like sore thumbs in the Belgian skyline against the backdrop of pre-war-stained architecture.

We emptied out of the stale and smoked-filled coach and stretched our legs and it wasn't long before we were ordered back on to collect our belongings. Before I knew it, we were somehow being herded into a nearby huge square by armed Police. It had been equipped with a massive stage and live music to entertain the travelling Scouse army, but more importantly to keep us in one place and under observation.

Before too long, we bumped into the Evertonian crusaders who'd made their way from Rotterdam a week earlier. It was funny seeing the occasional blue scarf amongst the sea of red. It wasn't long before we bumped into lads from our estate and others who knew me from my dipping adventure in 1981.

Pat, Antony and I were treated like royalty in that massive square. We didn't have to put our hands in our pockets once, the lads must have had a good week because the beer, food and mementos flowed in abundance. When I say the lads had a good time, I mean they would have robbed and purloined goods to fund the adventure ahead. They always had a few stories attached to their journey but this would be spoken about in certain circles; for now we just enjoyed the spoils of their bounty and asked no questions. The booze flowed while they handed Antony and I strange-looking bank notes.

The square filled rapidly with high-spirited, singing Scousers and local onlookers seemed amazed by the invasion. There weren't many Juventus fans around so I thought it was going to be the same as Wembley 1978 and Paris 1981 when the whole of Liverpool seemed to relocate.

Antony was eager to get to the ground and claim his position to watch the game. You can't blame a 7-year-old for that, so we made our way to the Heysel Stadium. Once we'd left the red-and-white square, there didn't seem to be too many Liverpool fans, but there sure was fucking loads of Juventus fans clad in black and white. In fact, the closer we got to the stadium, it was 'spot the Liverpool fan'. It was black and white as far as the eye could see.

The atmosphere was electric and intimidating at the same time. Spivs and ticket touts were all over the place with hardly any police in sight. British fans had a reputation for hooliganism and given the present company - Italians who also thought of themselves as tasty; this was a firework, waiting to be lit.

Pat grabbed us both by the hand and rushed us to the turnstiles to keep us out of harm's way, as the mood was changing rapidly. Once through, we were up the side stairs and on to the weed-laden terraces to get a view of the pitch. It was about an hour before the kick off and the sheer number of Juventus fans already in the stadium indicated that we were seriously outnumbered and it changed my demeanour instantly.

I'd never experienced this on foreign soil, so the intimidation levels went through the roof. We headed off to find a suitable position on the dilapidated terraces; high up, directly above the goal to the left of the players' tunnel was our fenced pen for the foreseeable duration.

The terrace behind the goal was divided into three, equal-sized areas. Liverpool had the two right-hand sections and Juventus the other one nearest the main stand, as well as all three sections behind the other goal.

As we settled into our positions we had to dodge the occasional missile which headed our way; bits of terrace, beer bottles and cans landed nearby on several occasions. Within the next 20 minutes, all hell broke loose.

The state of the terrace played a huge part in what happened next. Huge pieces of concrete had been smashed off and both sets of fans retaliated, bombarding each other with the rubble. Broken bits of terrace bounced off skin, bones and anything you could protect yourself with.

A gaping hole between the two sets of fans appeared which indicated the length and width of the throwing zone. By this time, Antony had started to cry and wanted out. There were only thin wire fences separating the rival supporters and by the time we made our way to the back, the fence had been torn down and a violent, running battle had erupted.

As both sets of fans ran from the trouble, the Liverpool fans moved into the segment where their own were, while the Italians only had the exit to run to in the far corner, where a huge wall separated the terrace from the main stand.

We ran for our lives as the Italians at the other end of the pitch broke down the feeble fencing, got on to the track around the perimeter of the pitch and began to surge forwards, armed with sticks, bricks and what looked like a pistol in one of the oncoming fan's hand.

I was scared shitless and we all feared for our lives. Surrounded by trouble, panic set in and as Pat had two young kids with her, she appeared to be given right of way and preference in making good our escape. It was more or less every person for themselves and utterly terrifying with every second that passed.

As I looked back, I could see a huge group of police and emergency services gathering by the gap between the stand and the Juventus fans. It looked serious, but so was my mood and our only thoughts were about escaping from this hell. It lasted for about 20 minutes but somehow seemed like forever.

We ran from one exit to another until eventually we ended up at a wall with a Perspex partition about 15 to 20 feet high. There was no way over this, so we decided to kick the bottom of the wall with our heels as hard as we possibly could. With the shabby condition of the stadium, to our great surprise and relief, a hole appeared quickly. The spectators on the other side had helped by banging a metal, mesh bin in the same place as we were kicking. We squeezed through the makeshift hole to our utter relief.

The Liverpool fans who dragged us up off the floor had bought the expensive, seated tickets and that was why they were on the other side of the Perspex. Our saviours calmed Antony down offering us fizzy drinks and sweets from a huge sports bag that was squeezed under their seats.

I couldn't take my eyes off the pitch as huge police horses tried to force back the angry Italian fans. By this time, the ground had almost reached capacity; we were totally outnumbered, I felt seriously uneasy and my heartbeat became the most important thing to me at that time. The commotion still ensued in the corner with the ambulances and now helicopters began to land behind the main stand. 'What the fuck's happening?' I thought as the atmosphere changed and the roar of the Juventus fans became louder and louder.

The tannoy was blaring out instructions for people to calm down and not to leave the stadium, but I just wanted to go. Even if we wanted to leave, the police wouldn't allow anybody out now. I looked at Pat and Antony and noticed that they both looked as worried as I felt. The next thing, I heard was the Liverpool manager, Joe Fagan, trying to make an announcement asking for calm and order.

About 15 minutes later, the two team captains, Phil Neal and Michel Platini came on to the pitch in their track suits holding microphones. 'Oh shit!' I thought, as the helicopters poured in behind him like a scene from Platoon. This was bad.

Some semblance of order ensued after the captains' message and finally the game went ahead as if nothing had happened. The atmosphere was still palpable, plus the ever-increasing Italian fans' mood was worrying me more by the minute.

Juventus won with a really dodgy penalty, but if they hadn't, I'm sure many Liverpool fans wouldn't have made it home alive that night.

As we made our way to the coach park through the thousands of Belgian police, we started to hear rumours that 40 people had died. My heart sank, but it wasn't until we sat down on the coach that the driver told us it was Juventus fans who'd died and the blame was firmly on the shoulders of us Liverpool fans. Every person on that coach sat in silence as we made our way back home in disgrace.

That journey dragged until everyone's stories started to come out. After a few hours of discussion and debate, everyone was of the same opinion – 'Who the fuck decided to play that match at that stadium? It was falling to pieces and the segregation was a joke'.

The following days brought the English football clubs a blanket ban of a minimum of five years from European football from UEFA's head honchos.

The debate raged and blame was apportioned as well as prison sentences for those who were named and shamed for being involved in the fracas. All in all, the kangaroo UEFA court worked for the authorities at the time and definitely lost English clubs the firm grip that they'd had on European football since 1977. A new era now dawned which was about to change Liverpool Football Club forever. This was the day that I declared, 'I saw Caesar die'.

The sight of Joe Fagan crying and being consoled by Roy Evans on that tarmac at Liverpool Airport after arriving from Brussels will always stay with me, just like the sight of the funerals of the Italian fans who died on that tragic night. May they rest in peace.

That was a rough 11 months for a 15-year-old kid to endure. Weirdly it was Kenny Dalglish who made me realise how to come to terms with life and death as a really young kid, and now he was appointed player-manager of Liverpool Football Club as Joe Fagan had had enough and retired after returning home from Brussels.

That summer didn't really strike any major chords in my fun levels, but I do remember getting down on my knees and praying a lot, not to God but to my own personal God, my Dad. I often asked him for help and guidance, and boy, did I need it that year.

King Kenny

The 1985/86 season was all-conquering for Liverpool's new player-manager and my new away-day friends in our metallic gold RS Ford Mexico. The car was a belter, it had style, speed and five, carefree lads, blasting up and down the M62 on a regular basis dressed in our Scally clobber. Buster, Brian Mc, Mini, Orlley and myself had now forged a group to travel the country watching the Reds.

Every time we'd meet to plan our next trip, a quick glance to clock if the lads had any new items of clothes would always take place. You couldn't make it obvious as we had a sort of reputation to keep it cool and au natural.

The previous season was always a topical subject during our travels and at our new local watering hole; *The Green Peppers* in Broadway, Norris Green. This was where we would meet as it was around the corner from the Youth Centre where we'd spent the last few years. It was also middle ground as we lived in different corners of Norris Green.

On occasion, we 'friendly kidnapped' unsuspecting drunks from the Peppers and took them with us to away matches in the boot of our car. As you can probably guess, this went down like a lead balloon with these unsuspecting, unconscious drunkards when they awoke.

With this new watering hole came a new direction in my life; weed. It was smoked openly in almost every pub in Liverpool in the mid-80s. I wasn't a smoker, in fact, I hated the smell of tobacco, but for some reason, I did like the smell of burning weed. I often wondered what all the fuss was about and had asked the regular pot smokers about the effects of this solid, dark matter. Mostly they said it was just like getting pissed but without the falling over and it was cheaper. The other most common reply was that they needed it to chill out and stop them from killing their Missus – but that was always said tongue in cheek.

It painted a picture that ended up looking like a pound sign to me as every fucker seemed to be on it, not just in my own age bracket; it was across the board, it was endemic.

This was an eye opener; I needed extra cash. Pat had worked in the Adelphi for years and asked me if I wanted a part-time job there, cash in hand. I already had a few quid from my mooching adventures, but that was getting thin due to the regular away trips, so the chance to earn a few extra pounds for my coffers was grabbed with both hands.

There was a problem that came with the job though, weekend work. I had to make sacrifices one way or another and they weren't easy. My away trips had to be limited to no more than an hour-and-a-half's drive as I'd often have to start work at 7pm. I was wounded, but after a few weeks of steady cash rolling in combined with the job actually being a buzz, the wounds healed without scarring.

After a month of working all the hours I could get, I'd saved up a few quid as I hadn't been to one away match since I started work.

Extra cash was burning a hole in my Birmingham Midshire building society account which I'd been asked to open by Pat. She'd had ideas of me saving up, but I had other plans. Weed. Even the waitresses and hotel bar staff had a blast of a joint; it was widespread in Liverpool with no exceptions. I was going to exploit my position and plan my future moves. Money was firmly on my mind. I made enquiries to certain people I knew and bingo! I had my first ounce of Moroccan resin, or as it's known on the streets, rocky.

I was now in the drugs game and all I needed were some regular punters. This wasn't difficult as I had loads of people at work, The Peppers, The Crown and on the estate who smoked their socks off on a regular basis.

My weed-business cash started to roll in, as did items that people exchanged to get hold of a piece of this Moroccan resin. I tried not to take people's bits or possessions but sometimes I had no choice, so I ended up with things I'd have to move on; bracelets, watches and rings. This kept happening for a few months so I continued in the direction of weed, work and watching Liverpool's home games on Saturday afternoons. This now became a lifestyle choice.

The weed game opened a few doors that could change my life if I'd decided to walk through them; now open I thought it rude not to, and I did. I was impressionable and fatherless. I took that chance and met a group of serious people who took me under their wing and educated me in how they expected me to behave, stay vigilant and ultimately, avoid getting nicked.

This would become my way of life for the next 20 years and would dictate who, what, where, when and why I did everything. Mind you, it was only in the early stages of a life of crime, but the seed was planted.

It wasn't long before I was buying a '9 bar' of Rocky every two weeks, as well as working midweek now - the money was flowing, as were the gold chains and other jewellery. I'd amassed a large mound of gold and looked to get rid of it because it was no use to me, I just wanted cash.

One of the older fellas who'd taken a bit of a shine to me said he'd give me scrap value or just above once he'd weighed it. This guy seemed to pop up everywhere I was and offer me a lift. I think he just wanted to get in to one of my sisters' good books (or knickers), if you know what I mean.

Now this fella never said much but what he did say was always worth listening to; no bullshit, no frills just common-sense and he had an aura of mystery and power surrounding him. He appeared to call the shots in his clique and whoever didn't toe the line was sent packing; that's what I'd heard anyhow.

Liverpool and Everton were now the two best teams in England, if not Europe, but as neither of us could play in Europe, I suppose we'll never know; much to every die-hard Evertonian's total resentment. That's another point to go down in the folklore book of 'would have, could have and should have'. Just how good were Liverpool and Everton?

It was touch and go as to who was going to win the League in 1986; both of us were neck and neck going into the last month of the season. The FA Cup final at the end of May was between, yes, you've guessed it, the Reds and the Blues from across the park. An 'All-Merseyside' Wembley final would add to the run in as both could do the double and make history, but better still, have the city's bragging rights.

I took a few weeks off work to join my mates on the road for the last two league games that would settle the destination of the Football League trophy. The first port of call was Leicester and the final game against Chelsea away.

The Leicester match was midweek and Everton were playing at Oxford the same night. We both needed to win, but Everton stumbled and we won 2-1 with Ronnie Whelan on the score sheet. We went into the last game needing a win to clinch the League and Everton, who were playing Southampton at home, were counting on Chelsea getting something from the game. Game on and I was going by way of a road-trip in the Ford RS Mexico with the lads.

Saturday came quickly and so did the lads to my front door once I'd phoned them early that morning telling them I'd made them sausage on toast. Nothing like sausages on brown toast with brown sauce and a steaming mug of tea to get your arse into gear.

We seemed to float down to London in the cramped car listening to ELO, Supertramp, Genesis and Jon & Vangelis and before we knew it, we'd parked up and made our way to the meeting point for the scally travelling fans; a pub about half a mile from the stadium.

Now the rule of thumb for the lads was not to wear your colours for two reasons; one it was a tell-tale sign you were an away fan and it could result in getting your head kicked in by waiting bandits, two is that it was classed as uncool and the lads would think you were a bit of a knob.

With that in mind that morning, I'd put my short-sleeved, Crown-Paints sponsored top on under my sweatshirt as a good luck charm (obviously saying nothing to the lads or they'd have ribboned me for the entire journey).

The boozer was rammed with all the usual travelling scallies, grafters and fanatical pissed-to-the-core Reds singing non-stop like it was a sponsored sing-a-thon. Banners were draped from every available wall or hook and gave the impression that we were drinking in Liverpool, not London. The only Cockney accent was that of the overweight barman who was sweating like a yeti in a hot tub, trying hard to look like he was in charge. Let me tell you though, he definitely wasn't on this day.

The smell of weed was rife and an ever-increasing number of Reds squeezing through the double doors gave the Cockney Yeti more problems than he'd bargained for when he'd woken up that Saturday morning - the poor bastard.

It was roughly 2.15pm and the troops in the boozer started to round everyone up, as 'safety in numbers' was the name of the game for the half-mile walk to Stamford Bridge. The talk of the impending hostile greeting from the Chelsea fans was on everybody's lips as we drank up and corralled outside; still singing at the top of our voices like warriors going into battle.

The walk was colourful, especially as we only needed to win and the title was in the bag, again. This knowledge kept every Liverpool fan buzzing on the walk but I was vigilant. The tall, blue gates outside the away end separating the Chelsea Head Hunters from us looked like a scene from Midnight Express as I glared at the faces between the railings. Hundreds of hard, worn and scarred faces pressed tight against the bars, their knuckles white from clenching in rage with gritted teeth showing, all because we'd arrived in numbers to celebrate our potential triumph and were out-of-towners.

Some of the Liverpool fans looked like the British soldiers in *Zulu Dawn*, dressed in red and white, while the rest of us tried to blend it with our casual look but we stuck out like sore, red thumbs. But we didn't care about any of that as we knew the title was on the line and we had a formula that had seen us win many a tight fixture; togetherness.

I made sure I got into the ground as soon as possible, especially as the Heysel tragedy was still fresh in my mind. I got in with minimal fuss and was safe with my pals.

Once the game started it dragged and seemed to last forever, in fact, it was like we'd discovered a parallel universe and the perception of time was one hour to one of our earth minutes. It took a technical take down on his chest and angled volley into the back of the net to break the deadlock from of course, my King Kenny.

We leapt all over each other as if gravity was non-existent. It was a mass of joyous bodies writhing in absolute ecstasy, having an out-of-body experience.

Once I caught my breath and gazed around at the sea of red and white, it didn't take long for me to reveal my colours, my sweatshirt was quickly tied around my waist to the sheer delight of my pals who'd only ever seen me wearing my colours playing 5-a-side. We all jumped up and down with hands clenched and raised above our heads in tandem, singing,

'We're gonna win the League, we're gonna win the League and now you're gonna believe us, and now you're gonna believe us ...' this seemed to be non-stop.

There was about 6000 Scousers who travelled to London to witness the ref blow the final whistle. The tannoy rang out with *'We are the Champions'* to every one of the Red fans' sheer delight. *'You'll Never Walk Alone'* was next and sung with heart and passion; it was as if we'd brought back the spirit of Bill Shankly through the power of song. The famous *Shankly, Shankly, Shankly, Shankly* chant was sung and my eyes started to well up, I had to hold it together to stop myself from flooding that terrace with tears of remembrance and joy ... looking back now, I wish I had.

The scenes of the fans and players celebrating on the pitch that Saturday tea-time will be forever in the memories of lucky travelling fans who made the trip to Stamford Bridge that day. And do you know what? My pals and I were there, in the flesh; we felt it, touched it and the journey home gave us time to make sense of it and smell it too. Next stop was Wembley in a week's time against our Blue neighbours, Everton. Bring it on!

On the car radio we heard that Everton had beaten Southampton 5-0, but it didn't matter to us, we just carried on singing all the way home with the occasional Chris Rea song blaring out on the cassette player, *'I don't know what it is, but I love it ..'* which was an unofficial anthem for the travelling fans over the previous few seasons and made the journey home that much quicker and somehow smoother than the outward-bound one.

On the way home, I remember wondering whether life could get any better. Only time would tell as the all-Merseyside final was only seven days away.

The week flew by and it was the same as the previous week except that we'd been out the night before so a heavy-headed, early Saturday morning wasn't welcome, but what the fuck, it was the first all-Scouse FA Cup final and we were on our way.

As we exited the city, the houses were all draped in blue or red; it was like a competition with bragging rights as the prize. FA Cup fever had taken control. Grannies, butchers, shop keepers, bus drivers all showed their colours; some had splinters in their arse from fence sitting, showing red and blue so as not to lose business. Not me and my pals though – we were red through and through; we even spat red.

We checked in to our hotel, had a quick lager shandy, and set off towards Wembley. The streets were laden with blue and red walking side by side, cars with both colours and couples with different colours holding hands, all heading in the same direction. This could only come from our wonderful city, that's what I thought, as I passed through the London streets that Saturday afternoon.

The scenes outside trying to get in were frantic for some people. Grown men hanging 20-30 feet high above the ground by one hand being hauled up by their mates hanging off the stairwell gaps. People being pulled up on makeshift rope made out of banners and scarves having to swing like fuck to get a foot hold to gain some purchase so they could get inside. There were even people on the roof, yeah, the roof and they'd been drinking. People risked serious injury and death just to catch a glimpse of the action, that's how much it meant to them.

Our viewing point was behind the goal facing the famous, huge Wembley tunnel, high on the left-hand side. We'd queued and struggled to gain access but once we'd reached the turnstile, we were past the point of no return. Even if you wanted to, you couldn't have turned around as the sheer number of fans created a fast-flowing river of red and white.

The build-up was fantastic and flew by once we'd settled down and started to join in with the songs that had become anthems for us by now. The players ran out to an almighty roar and a cascade of emotion that I'd never experienced, ever. This was special. The match was underway while I was still coming to terms with my delayed hangover and wave of emotion.

Everton scored first, Gary Lineker put the ball in the net right in front of me on his second attempt. I felt deflated and realised my dreams might not come true. Everton seemed to be playing well or was it us playing badly? I just didn't know and it was hard to figure it out. I couldn't wait for the half-time whistle and flopped to the terrace floor with sheer exhaustion, dripping in sweat.

I began to sing 'Walk On' in my mind over and over again until suddenly my Dad popped into my head. It was like somehow my dead father had channeled himself into my soul in my moment of need. I started to pray quietly and asked Dad to do everything he could to help me and our team out. I seemed to do this while still singing in my mind. I picked myself up off the floor and instantly felt rejuvenated. I had hope, there was 45 minutes remaining and hope was still alive.

The second half started like the first and Everton almost scored again when Graeme Sharp had a long-range effort saved spectacularly by Bruce Grobbelaar. That was the turning point or maybe it was the fight between Beglin and Grobbelaar in our own penalty area over some mix up. After that, Liverpool found another level and Ian Rush equalised to our sheer jubilation and relief.

The Reds took the game by the scruff of the neck and Molby and Dalglish began to call the shots. Before you could sing 'Walk On' again, we were leading 3-1; another from Ian Rush and one from our Australian midfielder, Craig Johnson. Oh my God! My prayers seemed to be answered; they definitely had once the ref blew the final whistle.

With celebrations now firmly underway both on and off the pitch, it was time for a quick thank you to Dad in the way of a prayer. Not a, 'Oh God, my father, I thank thee' type of prayer, more of an imagined hug for a father from his loving son, kind of prayer.

It was always comforting knowing that I could turn to my deceased father for support; thanks Dad.

Seeing Things

In the summer of 1986, there seemed to be an explosion of speed (amphetamine) on the Liverpool estates. It found its way into the pubs, clubs and dancefloors and kept many a night clubber talking utter shite all night to the nearest available person. It didn't even matter if you knew the person, anybody would do for the purpose of a few hours of drunken, drugs-crazed ear bending.

One night, somebody gave me a bit wrapped up in a Rizla paper; he called it a speed bomb and I tried this free sample without hesitation. Hours passed and it kept me awake all night and most of the next day – I felt terrible. It was like standing next to a huge speaker all night and the vibrations somehow infected my bones with a trembling sensation for the next 24 hours. It was the first and last time I had that drug, it was a 'once bitten, twice shy' type of situation for me, although it seemed to be popular with the females I didn't know why then - but maybe I'll be able to answer that later on.

Some of the older lads who'd been hovering around gave me the occasional LSD trip to have a look at – what I mean by that is they wanted me to take it and let them know if it would catch on at street level. I didn't take them all the time and some of my pals absolutely loved them, they would plead with me for more when I had samples. They were free of charge, of course, so more often than not I would pass them on and stay with them to view first-hand the effects; it was like a lab experiment to gain feedback. I witnessed some crazy antics and watched loads of my mates go under due to the strength of some of those tiny microdots, blotting paper or strange-looking gel-like trips.

On occasions, my football away-day match pals were off their nuts before, during and after the game, which made the journey home a long one, but also hilarious at times. As you can most probably gather, due to the LSD experimental phase we appeared to be a part of, the 1986/87 football season came and went in a sort of blur… and sometimes in a kaleidoscope of coloured oils raining on to my eyes and the window to my weird world was awkwardly cracked on occasions.

My weed business was nicely ticking over while I still worked in the hotel as and when they required me - which was becoming more frequent now, so away matches had to be limited. The older lad who'd taken an interest in me was now a friend, he would often turn up outside work at lunch time and clocking off time. He'd always ask why I worked full time for a living and picked my naïve brain one way or another; this was to find out how I ticked as he was a total head-worker.

He slowly took me into his confidence and would let his guard down occasionally to reveal his true self. I enjoyed this psychological experience and weirdly it gave me confidence in letting my own guard down because I felt comfortable with him. This would be a huge lesson to me when I finally decided it was time to grow up later on in life, but for now it was all good as I was making influential friends and cash on a regular basis.

I was still floating between Waresley Crescent and Faversham Road, Norris Green, and I had my own room at both. I had the knack of turning up at meal times, it was freaky how often I'd land at either door as food was being put on the table; in fact, I'd become a black belt in this food art form as I'd do it at my friends' houses, too. There was always a meal for me knocking about, I made sure of that, and it still happens to this day.

My sisters would also come and get me at the weekend and take me to their houses for slap-up munches and Sunday roasts; Kathy, Kim, Pat, Sue and Shirley would be regular visitors and either take me to their home or bring piping-hot meals to wherever I'd be. You could say I was the spoilt baby brother, whatever it was, I made the most of it. Doorstep deliveries of food were never turned away.

Every day that passed I seemed to dive deeper into doing exactly what my father and now my sisters told me not to. I was going down the route of 'money first, second and third', thinking I'd deal with the consequences when necessary. I was mulling around the estate and meeting loads of new faces, especially girls as the word had got out that I was upwardly mobile. There were a few girls who I fancied and now and again the odd girl would 'apparently' fancy me, or so I'd been told by some of my mate's girlfriends who'd always try to hook me up by proxy.

I'd had a girlfriend right through school, Tina Townsend. To be fair though, I didn't really know what I was doing as she was my first girlfriend and I'll have to apologise when I next see her for being a bit of a plank. We just seemed to drift apart when we left school; she was a nice person and I enjoyed many a Friday evening in her house eating Rich Tea biscuits having a cuppa and a chat about footy to her half-drunk older brother, much to Tina's disbelief at times. The rolling of the female eyes can be spotted from several light years away.

My first proper girlfriend was Josephine Farley from Broadway. She lived just behind the youth centre in Norris Green where I spent most of my spare time. I first met her in the summer of '87 when I was a regular visitor to the Summer Youth Camp, as I'd packed in my job at the Adelphi due to an incident that involved the police; I'll have to leave that there for fear of more bollocks from the law. I now had more spare time to participate in peer-pressure get-togethers and council-estate shenanigans, as that's what teenagers did then.

There were badminton tournaments in the youth club on a daily basis. As I was as fit as a greyhound on race day and loved badminton, I would take the court in a positive fashion. Josephine and her mate, Lyn, who were a few years younger than me would watch me hurtling all over the court from the side-lines, so it wasn't long before I was spending a bit of time getting to know her. She was very pretty and well developed, if you catch my drift.

I was never really serious about girls because money was always first on my mind so it wasn't fair on her. I really wish I'd had the sense at the time to express that but I just didn't. I was young in the head, naïve and too wrapped up in myself to be bothered about anybody else. Plus, I was really quiet at the time and never said boo to a goose.

Much of my time was taken up trying to create a sense of worth within my peer group, you know, trying to fit in. I was 17, fatherless and hungry for a type of success that doesn't even exist, but I didn't know that then. I just wanted to be one of the lads and that was that. I was becoming a direct reflection of what the people I hung about with wanted me to be.

As Everton had won the League the previous season, it was 'game on' with the banter flying round between the Reds and the Bluenoses on a regular basis. Sometimes it would result in football matches being played between rival supporters, which were funny on occasions. There was one particular Evertonian from our estate called Pete who was supposed to be one of the proper lads and often played in those matches; he was 10 years older than me and had a particular swagger.

Word got about that a match was being arranged one summer's afternoon on the LBA pitches on Long Lane and Pete turned up with a really tight, neat, curly perm that had been coloured darker than his original barnet. It was so obvious, that you could hear the sniggers behind his back, coming from every angle and everyone seemed to join forces to rip him another arsehole.

After about 10 minutes, the heavens opened with a typical summer downpour which flattened Pete's newly-acquired belter of a perm into a Tony Blackburn-esque melted vinyl record. Not only did his curls disintegrate, but the moisture made his new colour run into the shoulders of his new Everton kit. It was funny to the other lads, but Pete got the right hump and made a sharp exit in his flash car to the roars of laughter. 'There's only one Tony Blackburn, one Tony Blackburn', rang out from the side-lines while the rain battered the ground.

I'd started going out to town more with the older lads at the weekends. Daley's Dandelion on Dale Street and the Harrington Bar around the corner from the old Cavern Club on Mathew Street in Liverpool town centre were now on my radar at weekends. The routine would be: The Crown, The Green Peppers, County Road for a pub crawl and then off to town for the evening. I'd discovered another side to growing up now and I was enjoying it while making a few extra quid on my travels.

My weekends out on the town would now include having weed and trips with me to sell, you never knew who might want them or who you'd bump in to. I wouldn't go out looking for punters as it was all on the QT, but on the off chance, I was equipped with a few extras.

The weeks and months passed with me going to nearly every Liverpool match, home and away, while I was building my cash stash and network of people every time I ventured to pastures new. It was all very estate minded as I didn't want to let people know anything they didn't need to. While I was out on the booze I would always seem to bump in to Josephine and Lyn, which resulted in me going home off my barnet or half-cut with Josephine. It wasn't planned, it just happened.

The older lads passed me trips they called 'window panes' over the Christmas and New Year period to see what the score was with them. It was shortly going to be 1988 and I had a new product to test on my unsuspecting pals on the next football away-day jaunt. For one reason or another, we never went to the away fixtures over Christmas period, so me and a pal decided to neck one of these new trips and go for a drink in The Crown, our local boozer.

It took about two hours for the full effects of this clear, square gel of LSD with a red band running through the middle of it, making it look like an actual window pane, to get a grip of me. It was as if somebody had poured coloured oil on my eyeballs and jammed them open in a rainstorm. The colours would melt into each other like a Salvador Dali painting making its way off the canvas of my mind and on to my eyeball. I was in wonderland for as long as this piece of gel would allow me to be. Yeah, this was ok and lifted my senses to weird new levels.

It wasn't long before we peeled ourselves off the blag-leather seating in The Crown, moon-walked into a taxi and headed for town. As we looked out of the window, passing car lights would hang in the air like a sparkler on bonfire night and leave traces, as did the traffic lights as we made our way through the streets of Liverpool. This was like our own movie and the special effects team had won an Oscar for the fabulous lighting. Even our hearing seemed enhanced, making every bump we drove over sound like a crater, giving the impression that the taxi was going to fall apart at any moment. My senses had been spiked, pushed and transported to another dimensional avenue which led to Narnia.

There were times that ultra-paranoia raised its ugly head, then self-analysis would slap you in the face to tell you that everyone was looking at you when you were tripping out of your mind. You had no choice other than to snap out of it, otherwise you would melt into the background and never mentally be the same again – well, that was the thought process the inner cogs in my head evaluated and processed this experience into some resemblance of reality. I would trance in and out of dual emotions on the 15 minute journey into town.

We couldn't get into our usual haunts, so we tried a Beatnik type of club called *The State* on Dale Street, about 50 yards from Daley's. This was an old ballroom with marble floors and polished brass handrails, reminiscent of the opulent Art Deco era.

We made our way down the spectacular, sparkling hallway to sit in the glorious studded-leather seated area, which allowed us the best viewing point in the club. The LSD trips hadn't worn off; on the contrary they gave me rushes and seemed to make everything look like it was dripping with wet paint. As we sat discussing how we felt, I noticed out of the corner of my eye what looked like a dwarf. I stared until he got closer and looked at my mate in LSD-induced amazement. 'No way!' I said while my senses took another blast of reality.

A quick glance back in the same direction and there were now three male dwarfs heading our way. 'Nar this isn't happening', I thought. Was my imagination playing tricks on me? Another quick glance and I counted five dwarfs coming towards me. We looked at each other with huge eyes and jaws gaping and by the time the dwarfs were about a foot away there were seven of them.

"What the fuck is happening?" I asked, looking the dwarfs up and down like they were from another planet.

"No way! There's Snow White with them!" my pal was laughing so much, he couldn't keep still.

I looked up and saw a beautiful woman with jet-black hair with seven dwarfs standing right in front of me, like they'd been painted. Was this really happening? By now they were all looking at me; my mate was hysterical and I was shell-shocked. I froze for a few seconds while my senses readjusted.

The woman leaned towards me and whispered in a sweet, posh accent,

"What's the matter with your companion? Is he mocking my friends?"

"No, no, Luv, he's just off his head, don't worry. Do you want a drink?" I asked, trying to smooth things over.

"No, we can't drink, we're working in the morning at the Empire Theatre doing Snow White and the Seven Dwarfs". She smiled revealing a perfect set of gleaming, beautiful teeth.

'Fuck me!' I thought as she breezed back down the hallway with her dwarfs in tow. As they got out of sight, I fell on to the floor in a heap of laughter, as my pal appeared from the bar holding two more cans of Red Stripe while trying to lift me back on to my seat. It was surreal and my warped mind was trying to figure out if this was reality, a cliché drug-fueled moment, or were my processing pathways fucked?

That couldn't be topped the whole night, no way. Those window panes seemed to be never ending as the taxi ride home was just like the journey into town earlier, except now the dwarf story was firmly imprinted in our minds.

The downside of these small but massively-mind-blowing influential trips was the deep-rooted scars they grooved into your psyche forever. Chasms of doubt and floods of self-awareness would play like a film reel, while paranoia took the best seat in the house. I would often self-talk and tell myself to get a grip; this was my final evaluation and would allow me re-entry back into reality of sorts.

We stopped the cab on the East Lancs Road by the Arches which lead to Bullford Road. As it was raining, we took refuge in the archway for about an hour just staring at the streetlamp being trounced by dancing rain in high definition; giving the effect of it dripping like a packet of never-ending rainbow drops.

That night was colourful and weird; from the taxi ride to the dwarfs to the archway, it drifted in and out of reality like a demented metronome. Let me assure you, there was no real rhythm to the whole evening.

The next day, I was up and out of the house to find my lad who'd given me these window panes. These trips worked and would fly out on the streets as they didn't seem to be really heavy; you could have a good night out and not be totally fucked the next day.

When I eventually found him and broke the news, he told me to sit tight and he'd be with me as soon as he could get his hands on them. I went to my mates with this news and told them we'd fallen on a little gold mine and window panes would be available to the masses on our estate soon.

Before too long, it was that time of the year when the football season was reaching its climax. Liverpool had sewn up the League with some of the best football I've ever witnessed by a club side to date. To be honest, by the second away game of the season, we knew it was inevitable; that was against John Sillet's Coventry City at Highfield Road when we conquered them 4-1. It was one-way traffic and showed the gap in class between us and the rest of the league at that particular time. I'll never forget the balding John Sillet on the pitch at the end of the game heading for the thousands of travelling fans and bowing towards us as a mark of respect. To be fair, we never shut up for the whole 90 minutes, constantly singing our now-legendary anthems.

The return journey with the lads was wonderful and when we got closer to home, the window panes appeared out of my plastic money bag down my sock much to everybody's delight. Let the colours stream down our eyeballs!

In the summer of '88, my sister, Pat, tried to help me out be getting me an interview with an engineering firm which made high-pressure valves in Burscough near Ormskirk, Lancashire. As I'd fucked the job up at the Adelphi, Pat took it upon herself to guide me towards manual work. I had different ideas though. As I was living with Pat, I thought it only fair to go for the interview and see what happened.

To cut a long story short, it wasn't long before I was up at 6.30am and earning over £225 a week as I worked weekends too. As well as this, I still kept my little drug business ticking over so I was earning proper money – about £500 a week and decided to buy a car for work and another car to graft in. I was getting richer and staying under the radar of the police.

It was around this time that our estate was shaken by a murder; one of the lads was shot, yards from his front door. This opened a huge can of worms for the police and gave them a blank canvas to paint the picture they saw from the aftermath.

It changed all the older lads' directions and forced people into corners they didn't want to be in. It wasn't long before doors were getting booted in and arrests being made regarding a robbery on a Preston Bank, where the manager's family were held until he did as he was told. This was major news, not just locally, but nationwide, and it changed the workings of our small area of north Liverpool forever. I knew all the lads on a first-name basis and would see them regularly, but not anymore.

That wasn't the end of it, the open can revealed another mob. In fact, when I say that, it wasn't worms, it was rat shit. He blabbed everyone's business under pressure. Some of my away-day pals were involved and ended up getting heavy sentences, turning their worlds upside down.

This was close to me and I felt it. These lads had been like family for years and were always in our house when I was growing up. It was an eye opener and I had to keep the weed and trips low for a couple of months. The only Godsend was my job, I wasn't going out much either so my funds kept growing. I still loved money and thought money loved me.

A short time later, I got a call at work giving me news I was going to be a father. I shit myself. I was way too young to be a father, I had things to do and this wasn't in my plan, but Josephine said she'd told everyone including both our families and that was that. Selfish me wasn't ready to settle down, no way, but I came to terms with it and got on with doing what I'd always done; working to try and get on. I was a selfish twat then, tunnel vision with no real long-term plan other than to be one of the lads.

I had to try and grow up quickly, I had plenty of responsibility landing on my young shoulders. What should I do? I decided to go out on the town at every available opportunity.

It was April 1989 and Liverpool were due to play Nottingham Forest at Hillsborough, the home ground of Sheffield Wednesday in the FA Cup semi-final. I was about to make a discovery that not only changed my life, but changed the face of modern, popular culture forever.

The State

At the turn of 1988/89, I was always in The State, listening to great Indie music and attending Daisy Night. This happened on Thursday evenings when you paid a penny to get in and James Barton, the founder of Cream, would play unusual tunes; Big Audio Dynamite, Lloyd Cole and the Commotions, Waterboys, The Clash, The Cure and many more obscure artists who made underground records.

There were projectors with kaleidoscopes all around, transforming the Art Deco interior into something out of the Hippie era. It worked. I loved this night and wouldn't miss it for the world. With weed and trips down my sock, I'd bounce around to the left-hand side where the North End Liverpool lads and girls would stand. The right side was for the South Enders, who knows how and why it was like that, but it was.

It all changed one night when a group of lads and girls, mainly from Huyton, bounced in wearing waistcoats and huge Elton John sunglasses; carrying inflatable bananas, crocodiles, hammers and palm trees. Not only did they look way out and fantastic, but they sounded like they'd just won a famous battle and were returning home in fine fettle. They were loud in every possible way and it wasn't until the following Thursday that the news had somehow reached me about a new drug called Ecstasy in the form of red and black capsules, called Dennis the Menace.

It took another two weeks until I got my hands on some and me and a few of the lads in The Crown had half a white tablet at about 9 o'clock on a Thursday night. Nothing happened for about an hour, then after a quick spliff in the toilets, it kicked in big time.

Head rushes like never before made me feel absolutely wonderful, in fact it was better than that, I became loving, agile and out of nowhere, I decided I wanted to dance. Now, apparently tough guys don't dance but that night, the wave of ecstasy and emotion gave me something I'd been searching for, for years and I found it. Unrivalled, unrestricted, unparalleled freedom of mind.

What happened to me that night happened to millions of teenagers of the same ilk over the coming years but I can honestly say I was at the birth, not the conception, of modern dance culture that went hand-in-hand with ecstasy. The dance culture was unleashed on society but it took a few months for it to become widespread; for now it was underground, but not for long.

While this crazed, off-its-head culture was finding its feet, another cultural movement was looming for the whole of Merseyside. The FA Cup semi-finals were upon us and both Everton and Liverpool had reached them. Everton were playing Norwich at Villa Park and Liverpool playing Nottingham Forest at Hillsborough. This could result in another all-Merseyside final if we both beat our opponents.

My away-day pals had discovered Es by this time and decided to go out the night before the match, so I made other arrangements to travel across the Pennines. Stephen was going in his red Ford Orion 1.6i Ghia and said there was room for me as he was going with his pal, Eric Dunn, and our nephew, Antony.

The away-day morning routine was the same as usual, only it was my mum who made the sausage on toast and piping-hot mugs of tea to fill our bellies. She also made some cheese and onion, corned beef and pickle and ham salad crusty cobs for the journey. She wrapped them in tin foil, placed them in a Sayer's bag with two huge packets of crisps and off we went, licking our fingers clean of the brown sauce that had seeped out of the sausage butties.

With Stephen in the driving seat and me sitting beside him, Eric Dunn and Antony got themselves comfy in the back. I turned on the Phillips radio-cassette and tried to catch the news as it was just before 10am when the doors were all slammed shut. We waved to Mum and pulled out of Faversham Road, turned left then right onto the East Lancs, and we were on our way.

Stephen and I discussed the length of the trip and tried to estimate our arrival time; the conclusion was about 1pm taking into consideration stops and possible delays. We were all set and it wasn't long before we hit the motorway and then Snake Pass.

Stephen had taken this route the year before and said it was the best way. Nobody argued as we tucked in to Mum's home-made (and now flattened) crusty cobs while winding through the scenic Yorkshire countryside. As the regional radio signal faded, we flicked through to stations to find another one. Finally we tuned in to BBC Radio Sheffield just in time to hear... *'It's midday and the date is April 15th. This is the Radio Sheffield newsroom.'* The signal was strong so I knew we'd broken the back of the journey and were closer to our destination than anticipated.

Another 15 minutes passed and we hit a traffic jam that lasted for 20 minutes. The reason for the delay was that the South Yorkshire Police were stopping and searching cars heading to the match for alcohol.

We were pulled to one side and taken out of our car while two coppers searched inside and opened the boot; they even looked in the spare-tyre well for booze. There wasn't one drop in our car, the coppers looked at each other, shrugged their shoulders and told us we could go.

Antony was getting excited by now and was glued to the window waiting for a glimpse of anything to do with the semi-final. It wasn't long before we came over a hill and spotted the Owls' crest above one of the stands. We parked up in a terraced street and walked towards the stadium following the red-and-white masses.

We made our way to a pub not a stone's throw away from the Leppings Lane End. Antony and I stayed outside while Stephen and Eric squeezed through the crowd and five minutes later appeared with three pints of lager and a bottle of White's lemonade for the lad.

We sat on a low wall watching the crowds move about like worker ants. We stayed for about 30 minutes on that wall as we kept bumping into people who knew one of us. It was about 2.15pm when Antony was becoming agitated and wanted to get inside the ground to get a good spec. It was only four years earlier he'd experienced the trauma of Heysel, so we grabbed our coats and headed towards the huge crowd outside the turnstile.

The 15 minutes it took us to get into the ground was horrendous. Police horses swayed to and fro not knowing what to do as thousands of fans were crushed, shouting advice, abuse and pleas to the coppers on top of their horses. Antony was protected by us as we made a human-cocoon-type of shield and ushered him safely with our arses sticking out and grabbing each other's shoulders to reinforce our buffer.

We fought our way through the metal-barred turnstiles and were surprised to find it was relatively-sparsely occupied; it made you wonder why all the fans outside were panicking when it seemed so calm once you got into the ground. We bought a few match programmes and made our way towards the Leppings Lane End.

Antony and I went to enter the middle section, behind the goal. As we looked down the tunnel it seemed full yet it was only 2.30pm, still a full half-hour to kick off. We started to make our way down when we spotted another friend, Pat Neddy, who shouted,

"Don't go in there, it's rammed and I was in there last season and I couldn't move. Let's go in the next one." And with that, we all moved to the next entrance and calmly walked down the brick tunnel to come out to a wall of noise and our pen wasn't even half full.

Our vantage point was about two feet from the blue, dividing metal railings half-way up the terraced steps. To our right, the middle pen was jam packed as it moved with heads and shoulders like a swaying ocean. We joined in with the songs to keep fully in the spirit of a semi-final as we waited for the players to come out on to the pitch.

The noise levels rose as they came out of the tunnel to our right, as small pieces of paper came down from the stand behind us like tickertape. The game was nearly upon us as the players went through their last-minute preparations on the perfect, velvet-like pitch and the noise behind us seemed to increase again. Some of the fans directly behind Bruce Grobbelaar's goal had climbed on top of the spiked, blue railings and seemed to be looking back into the middle of the packed terrace in fear.

The match kicked off and for the first half, Liverpool were defending the goal at the Leppings Lane End. Liverpool broke early and nearly scored and the surge from the middle pen seemed to force fans on to the railings. Stephen pulled my arm and pointed to the entrance at the back of the middle pen where fans were trying to get into the seated area about 12 feet above them. They were clinging on to the outstretched hands of fans above them in an attempt to flee.

In the next few minutes, all hell broke loose with the police thinking something nefarious was going on that so obviously wasn't. More and more people piled over the fences and onto the pitch, pleading with the police to open the gates at the front of the terrace, but their pleas fell on deaf ears as the police thought there was going to be a pitch invasion. It took a few more vital minutes before the penny dropped and the bottom pen gates were opened to allow the fans to escape the crush.

On the terraces, crush barriers were strategically placed on every couple of steps. Ironically, they were there to protect, but fans were stuck behind them and couldn't move. We could hear the shouts, groans and screams of our people being crushed.

After speaking to the police, the referee took the players off the pitch and with this dramatic action came dramatic thoughts. We all looked at each other in disbelief as we listened to the pleas and cries of help from the pen no more than two-feet away.

We all helped people climb over the railings and made sure they were safe. I'd forgotten about Antony for a split second and by the time he'd come into my thoughts and looked around for him, he had vanished.

"Oh shit! Where's Ant?" I was sweating and panting with the effort.

"He was here a second ago," said Stephen, as we all climbed on the barriers to gain a better view of the terrace.

We were frantic and started to panic as we couldn't see him and by now there was an ambulance in front of us, attending to what looked like injured fans. I bounced down four or five steps at a time looking for my nephew with my eyes peeled like never before. As I got to the bottom, I noticed his red Adidas kit with a number 9 on the back. He was clinging to the railings. I grabbed his shoulder and spun him round.

"There are dead people there, Paul". He said in an innocent-but-knowing way.

"Are you sure?" I pulled him off the railing so I could see for myself. Fuck me! There was about 10 bodies lying motionless and another dozen receiving CPR or being lifted onto makeshift stretchers. I looked on in total disbelief when I noticed a lad from our estate, Gogs, who was kicking fuck out of an advertising hoarding to make a stretcher for the injured.

I shouted him three times, on the third shout, he turned and gave me a look as if to say, 'This is a matter of life and death, no time for talking.' I watched him run the full length of the pitch with three other men and a body, then return with his empty stretcher.

By now, the police had made a human cordon on the halfway line as they still must have thought it was the Liverpool fans causing some kind of trouble.

Antony and I ran back up the terrace to be greeted by Stephen, Eric and Pat Neddy, who by now had decided it was time to go. There was nothing we could do except try and find out what the fuck had happened and get Antony out of there, pronto.

On the way out of the ground, there were rumours flying around that 20 people had died, then it was 40, then 100; with 200 injured. We all ran from Leppings Lane towards our car stopping occasionally to try and use a public phone to call home and let mum know we were OK.

All the phone boxes had crazy queues and even after we waited for 10 minutes at one, when we eventually got through, it was engaged. Every household in Sheffield that day seemed to have their front door open and offered help and assistance if needed.

We reached our car and there was a woman standing at her front door who shouted that if we wanted to use her phone, we could. At that point, although we'd witnessed it firsthand, she seemed to know more about what had happened than us. She confirmed that people had died but wasn't sure about the numbers.
We all entered her house to crowd around her telly to try and fathom out what had gone on while Stephen tried to call home, to no avail. We thanked the kind and compassionate lady and set off

back home the way we'd come but without stopping as it was all about time now.

We turned into Faversham Road just after 6pm and noticed loads of people talking outside their houses. Standing at our front gate, I saw Mum looking anxious as we pulled up outside our house. She already had the latch cocked and was out of the gate like a shot. She glared into the car with tears running down her cheeks. When she saw her two sons and beloved grandson, the floodgates opened. She started to blab something about us not phoning and how she'd been frantically trying to call the emergency numbers given out every five minutes on the telly and local radio.

She grabbed hold of all of us, even Eric, and squeezed us like never before. To be honest, I was welling up at this point, as I noticed tears rolling down Mum's and Antony's cheeks.

They stared at the telly, Stephen rang round his mates to find out of they'd arrived home safely. I borrowed his car and on auto-pilot, drove to The Crown and The Peppers to find my away-day pals. They weren't there so I drove to their houses to be greeted by my three mates all thinking the same as me.

"We were just going to yours then. Fucking hell, your phone's been engaged for ages, is everybody OK?" Showing concern was never one of our strong points so to hear that from them was wonderful. I was just so relieved they were all OK.

News at 10 on Saturday night was all about what had happened at Hillsborough that afternoon and left me speechless and emotional. The day before, I'd made arrangements to have a Saturday night of ecstasy on the town, but with the dramas of the day still unfolding it was no time for pleasure; it was time for reflection and mourning.

That night, I cried alone on my bed watching the extended news of the day's disaster. I was there, but now, I was sitting on my bed and I was alive. Those tears I cried alone were real and as I wiped my cheeks with my Liverpool scarf that was spread across my bed, I realised how lucky I was to be able to show emotion that night. It could have been oh, so different if we hadn't taken Pat Neddy's advice about the fate-filled middle tunnel at Leppings Lane.

The aftermath of the Hillsborough Disaster was brutal and heart wrenching for everybody connected to Liverpool Football Club and in particular, the families of those who lost their lives on that fateful Saturday afternoon.

I'm not even going to mention the name of the reporter or the paper that allowed the biggest misrepresentation of the events at Hillsborough being printed and sold on a daily basis as they don't deserve the effort. Everyone who attended the Leppings Lane terrace know the facts. Those who lost their lives are always in my thoughts and reliving those events fills my heart, head and eyes with pure emotion.

They'll never walk alone.

Ecstasy Explosion

With Hillsborough still ringing in my ears, the summer of '89 arrived along with talk of the dance-culture revolution that was sweeping the nation.

My head was up my arse as I'd split with the expectant-mother of my child, found another girlfriend and while out one night, off my barnet on ecstasy, I was told the news of the birth of my son, Dayne.

I was incapable of any long-term commitment and didn't have the mindset to settle down and play house. I was caught up in making a name for myself while bopping from club to club and pub to pub selling E. It was the new drug and I was a seller of this product which brought down social-background brick walls and turned them into rubble overnight.

In 1989, The State was the place to be in Liverpool; nowhere else even came close to its reputation for being the best nightclub for an unrestricted, sweaty and mind-bending night out. It was the bollocks.

I'd arrive about 10 o' clock just as it was about to open via a trip to The Lisbon, a seedy, local gay bar where I'd purchase 20 bottles of rush. This head-exploding liquid cost £2.50 per bottle which I could quickly turn into a decent profit. The main reason I bought it was to keep the punters coming back for more ecstasy tablets, trips and weed - and if they wanted it, I'd have the rush to sell too. I was a one-stop night clubbers' dream who'd provide what they wanted; drugs.

I'm not saying I was cheap, far from it, top whack for all my goodies, but I was building a reputation as well as a business. So for £50 quid spent on rush I'd get £100 quid back which covered my travel for the night, you know like taxis, going to drop my money off and to grease the palms of bouncers and bar staff. I'd usually earn about £500 a night but I had to make sure things ran smoothly, so looking after people who looked after me also had to be considered.

My new girlfriend, Andrea, was like the acid queen and danced on every table, bar and window sill she could find. She was off her barnet on my supply and it wasn't long before she was going everywhere with me. I took her to meet my mum but that didn't go down as well as I'd hoped and it wasn't long before mum was telling me to get shut of her. 'Mother knows best', that's what she'd say to me every time Andrea left the room. I didn't listen to mum's advice then as I was having too much of a good time and making so much money I didn't give a fuck. Mum was trying to get me back with Josephine at every opportunity, so Andrea popping up on the scene was like a red rag to a bull.

A week after mum meeting Andrea, all hell broke loose which led to me being kicked out. I arrived home one tea time to hear mum screaming for me to come upstairs. She was standing over the toilet with my bag of stashed Es in one hand and her other hand on the toilet chain ready to flush. She began to threaten me,

"How dare you bring these to my house, what are you playing at?"

Oh shit, mum was about to flush a grand's worth of drugs down the toilet, what should I do? I had to think in a split second.

"Mum, if you flush them, they're worth a grand and if the fella doesn't get paid then I have to pay somehow, do ya catch my drift?" I spoke in a calm way while trying to make her understand my dilemma.

"Fuck ya mate, fuck you too, these are getting flushed. Why the fuck are you selling drugs?" She screamed at me inching ever-so closer to the toilet with the bag of drugs.

"Mum! Please don't do that, I'll get fucked." I pleaded with my mum over and over again.

"Never mind get fucked, you can go and get fucked and get the fuck out this house!" She was seething and her veins started to pop out the side of her neck which I'd never seen before.

"Mum, I'm not going anywhere without the tablets in that bag." I said firmly. With that mum began to open the bag and throw them down the stairs a handful at a time. As the tablets bounced, rolled and scattered all over the stairs mum began to shout,

"Get ya fuckin stuff packed, pick up ya scabby drugs and get the fuck out, nowwww!"

With mum's words ringing in my ears, I was on my hands and knees collecting every single tablet and quickly putting them into my side pocket of my combat trousers. Once I'd gathered them up, I went back upstairs got as many clothes as I could fit into one bag and headed off to find a place to stay.

The first phone call I made was to Andrea to tell her I'd been kicked out and she told me to go to Jackie Scott's house, who was a friend of ours. She was 10 years older but always made us feel more than welcome when we visited her house. With my tail now firmly between my legs, a pocket full of ecstasy and a bulging bag of clothes, I headed off to County Road, Walton, in my red metro van. I did stop en route at a pal's house and dropped off my drugs and money (obviously for a small fee) but at least they were safe.

Jackie welcomed me with open arms and said Andrea and I could live on her top floor, which was in essence her loft. It was a great modern conversion and on the spot I accepted the terms and conditions without getting into a conversation.
Jackie didn't know much about me but it wasn't long before she treated me like her own family.

I found myself helping her out and working in her flower shop a few days a week. Yeah, Jackie was a florist on County Road; I made the occasional deliveries and would get up in the early hours of the morning to go to the local flower market with her. As I had my own little van, it was handy because her Nissan Sooty was off the road so on occasions we'd swap vans. In fact we'd just take whichever van was nearest to the front door on any given morning. This didn't come drama-free though. I got up one morning about 9 o clock and looked out the window and noticed Jackie had taken my red van and hers was parked half on the pavement on the opposite side of the road.

The previous night I made arrangements to pick my pal up who had stashed my drugs as I had to see the older lads to do a stock take. I was dressed and out the door for 9.30 and at my mate's house 15 minutes later. I grabbed the drugs and shoved half down my undies and half down my socks. We both headed off down the East Lancs Road to Norris Green without a care in the world. Just as we got passed the iron bridge at the entrance to Walton Hall Park, I noticed a flashing blue light up my arse. There was no time to panic, just take the spin and get out of the situation intact.

I pulled over at the side of the road and jumped out rapidly to speak to the copper who was now walking towards me putting his hat on.

"Is this your car?" He asked as he picked his pen from his shirt pocket.

"No, it's a friend's," I said.

"Have you got any details on you then?"

I started to search in my pockets and after looking in every pocket of my combats I had fuck all, which I knew from the start.

"No I ain't, Officer." Now, when you start to call the copper, 'officer' then you know you're on the blag.

He leaned into the van looked into the back and asked my mate who I was. When he finished looking, he asked my mate to open the glove box and see if there was any documentation inside. He leaned over, opened the glove box and about 20 vibrators started to fall on the floor. My mate's reaction was priceless as he screamed, leaped out of his seat and jumped about like he'd just found a massive, hairy spider.

"What the fuck?!" He roared while looking at the copper who by now was laughing his cock off. There were all types of vibrators, finger and thumb ones, double ended and a big, black, huge mamba which would knock you out if it hit you, all bouncing round the footwell of the van.

"Whose car did you say this was?" Asked the copper, still laughing. He put his pen back in his pocket and took a step back from the van.

"It's a friend of mine, Officer." I replied with a look of embarrassment on my face as I smiled at him, forgetting I had the drugs on me.

"Well, tell your friend, it is a she isn't it? ... that she has: two finger and thumbs, three black mambas and a butt plug that all need a safer place than a Nissan's glove box. Go on son, you can go now but make sure you carry your driving licence with you in future."

The copper turned and with a smile on his face looked back, shook his head and said,

"No-one is going to believe me when I tell this story."

I couldn't believe that I had just got a walk-over as I shoved the vibrators back in the glove box thinking they'd just saved me from getting nicked. That wasn't my first lucky escape and it definitely wouldn't be the last.

By the time I'd done my running about and returned to Jackie's to tell her about the glove box incident, she was waiting for me with a look on her face that suggested, *'have you looked in the glove box?'*

When I explained I'd been pulled by the police she began to wince and drop her head in shame. I couldn't stop laughing as I really didn't know where to put my face, because I think I felt more embarrassed than her. I went bright red and we both looked at each other and burst out laughing while we handed our keys to each other. No way was I ever taking Jackie's car out again without checking the glove box, not a chance.

Strictly Business

Es were taking over as the preferred drug for people going out and the demand was increasing daily, so it was time to invest in a mobile phone. The Motorola 8500x was the choice I made and after forking out a grand, I felt like I was going into battle with this new bit of kit. I had to hide it under my coat as it was massive and it came with a leather, shoulder harness. Fuck me, it was hard to hide, you know. There was no other phone available at the time so I had to go about my business feeling like Action Man.

It did make life much easier as I was working on Thursday, Friday, Saturday and Sunday nights now. It was getting to the point where I couldn't even take a pill myself as it was becoming strictly business. My weekends consisted of selling my drugs in the pubs and clubs and then leaving sober so I could count, then iron the night's takings.

I loved being tucked up in bed by 1am with a couple of grand all ironed and pristine under my pillow. My older mate who was by now keeping a firm eye on me always turned up at my door at 9 o' clock on Sunday morning wanting to see his return. When I'd pull these pristine stacks of cash from under my pillow and throw them in his direction, he couldn't hide his delight. Money made this man tick and this gave him confidence in me.

The point of no return for me now was in the distant past as E had got a grip of Liverpool like a greedy bastard devours a Big Mac the morning after fat camp. It oozed out of every working-class estate and made its way to what seemed like a pre-arranged muster station on Dale Street, Liverpool.

The State was now the focal point of mine and everyone else's life at this time. It was rammed every night by midnight with wide-eyed, sweating, jaw-wobbling, drug-fuelled ravers from all over Liverpool. Different groups of people from north and south Liverpool stood together chatting, embracing and dancing, as now they had something in common; E. The love was immense and with this wave of emotion came the crashing sound of social barriers being tossed away and forging a network structure that would make Liverpool the drug capital of Europe.

Yes, it all happened in the summer of 89. The birth of the dancing-drug culture quelled the youths' desire to do nothing but dance in fields, barns, warehouses and chosen night clubs whilst off their nuts on ecstasy. Where the fuck did this come from? Who decided it was the right time for its street life to prosper? These are questions that must go unanswered for now but I'm sure someone, somewhere has a definitive answer. I was just happy to be part of it and experience first-hand the swing in popular culture that will go down in history.

With these walls tumbling and new network routes opening up, every weekend in The State came a brand new adventure for me. I'd stand in the hallway selling my drugs while other people did their thing, too. It wasn't long before I noticed that I seemed to be sorting out all the left-hand side of the club and a tall skinny kid was sorting out everyone on the right-hand side. We didn't speak to each other but we both knew what the other was up to; it wasn't rocket science.

It didn't take long for us to start chatting and swap details and telephone numbers. He told me his name was Scotty and I knew from the start that he thought, 'What the fuck is this kid doing in this game?' So after we'd had a natter about this and that I said I would be outside his house first thing Monday morning.

Now I knew he deffo thought I was talking shite and with that in mind, I made it my priority to knock at his door with a bag full of dough on Monday. He must've thought I was a fuckin weirdo when I turned up with enough money in my boot to choke a stegosaurus.

"Haha, you're fuckin' mad bringing that on this estate." He said while scanning the area to see if anyone was looking as he looked inside the navy blue and red Head sports holdall.

"Fuck me, how much is here?" he asked, zipping the bag back up and smiling.

"Twenty five grand, I told you I wasn't fucking about and that I'd be here first thing Monday." I replied swiftly as by now I started to get nervous due to his earlier comments about his estate. I was in Halewood, Torrie, as he called it, about ten minutes from Liverpool airport, and I didn't even really know this fella but for some reason I trusted him from the beginning.

"Come on," He said while pointing to the bag. "Don't leave that in the boot of the car, let's go and have a cuppa and a joint in mine."

I grabbed the bag, slammed the boot shut and followed him up the two flights of stairs into a top-floor maisonette. I stayed with him for about an hour and then his mate came around who was an absolute nutter, but in the nicest possible way.

To be honest I liked these lads a lot and decided there and then that I was going to get busy with them and that we would make a few quid together. They were quality and that's what I needed to keep ticking over, plus they lived on the other side of the city so no one would know me or my business. There was nothing happening on that particular day, so they decided to put a car in front of me and one tailing me until I gave the signal to leave once I was close to home. This gesture confirmed I'd found a good set of fellas who were on the button and knew how to graft properly.

The next few months, I forged solid relationships with these lads from Halewood. I'd be there most mornings to wake them up, to their sheer disapproval most of the time. I was always up early and out of my own two-up two-down terraced house off County Road as Andrea and I had decided to get our own house; or more to the point I had enough money to buy one for us.

Oh yeah, Andrea was pregnant too, to my mum's disgust of course, as only a few months earlier when Andrea and my mum had words, the thought of Andrea ever getting pregnant was top of the agenda. So with morning sickness making me baulk, I was up and on the road and heading to Halewood pronto each day.

Every time I'd turn up on Torrie there was something going on; one drama or another. If it wasn't a huge white van winding its way down the street with the driver none the wiser to three kids hanging onto the back with the shutter door open while they threw legs of lamb and sides of beef to their pals on every corner, then something else would open my eyes to life on this estate. It reminded me of Norris Green and Sparrow Hall in the early 80s. It was home from home and I loved being there.

I often had a few drinks in *The Halewood* boozer with my new mates and their friends in the area too. Fuck me; they could party to the bitter end. If it got a bit much for me I'd leg it, leave my car and taxi it home; better safe than sorry. I'd always leave my car outside Scotty's house and get the first person who got in touch with me the next day to take me across the city so I could retrieve my wheels.

My mate, Tom the Spark, called after one particular night out and made himself available to me. He picked me up in his white Nissan van and we set off to Halewood. We parked outside Scotty's maisonette and both made our way up the two flights of stairs, reading the graffiti that daubed the stairwell and entrance to this

Kes-like building. You could tell this was a battleground as well as peoples' homes. Social warfare at its most raw and I fuckin' loved it.

Once Scotty finally answered his bell, he looked at me while scratching his bollocks with his left hand in his gingham boxer shorts and said,

"What the fuck are you doing here at this time? I've only been in bed for a few hours, for fuck's sake!"

"You took my car keys off me last night cos I was rotten, do you remember?"

"Oh shit yeah… wait a min… they're in my coat pocket, shit, my coat's in my car outside." He threw his keys on my lap.

"Lad, I'm in need of a cuppa, then I'll go and get them." I replied, as I made my way into his kitchen and clicked the kettle down while checking the water level.

"No problem lad, I'll have one too, two sugars and loads of milk for me." He said with his hands firmly round his bollocks lying back on the couch.

"Tom, do you want one?" I was still half pissed and so was Scotty. While they were talking in the living room, my mate began to laugh then Tom bolted past me. I never heard what they were saying but Scotty started chuckling,

"Fuck me, Paul, schoolboy error bringing your mate's van full of electrical gear up here. Bandits are waiting in bushes for moments like that. What were you thinking?" he was laughing and started to get dressed quickly.

"Yeah, fuck that tea off, there'll be fuck all left in yer mates van. Let's go!"

We both legged it downstairs to find Tom staring at the open side door.

"The cunts have taken the lot, me tools, me gear and even me footy boots."

We couldn't stop laughing but Tom wasn't amused one bit. Scotty told Tom to go and wait upstairs while we found out who got the stuff. Tom was panic stricken so I reassured him that I'd replace his tools and his gear out of my own pocket. He was nearly in tears though; it was his livelihood that had been stolen.

About 40 minutes later, we arrived back to see Tom waiting by the front door and we had about 95% of his stuff in our possession. The delight on Tom's face was immeasurable and the only thing that was missing was two rolls of cable which we said we'd replace anyway.

It cost me £60 for the cable, but I would have given five times the amount to have learned that lesson and seen the look on Tom's face when he discovered the Halewood bandits had pilfered his van.

That same night I drove back over to Halewood to find Scotty as we had things to do. After spending an hour outside his maisonette buzzing with his mates about the van, I was getting a bit hungry. The chippy was only a stone's throw away so we walked over to grab some hangover-carbs.

My head was banging by this time so when the local kids were repeatedly kicking a ball at the shutters at the post office next door to the chippy, my headache got worse. THUD, THUD, RATTLE, THUD, THUD, RATTLE.

"Fuck me lads, can you turn that in?" I asked in a pained voice.

Now these kids must have been about 12 years of age and gave me a look as if to say, 'fuck off.' Scotty heard me ask them and walked over to me and said,

"Come with me lad, I'll walk you away from this racket."

He took me round the back of the shops and took me towards a black metal door that only needed a push to open it. When I looked inside there were kids no older than 12 or 13 with a lump hammer and every time the ball hit the shutters on the front, they would smash the lump hammer in time into the brick work.

I knew this was a rough-arse estate but to be fair, they knew how to graft properly from an early age. These kids wanted dough and had come up with an idea of how to get it. I know they all most probably lived not far away and they were shitting on their own doorstep, but you've got to hand it to them. It made an impression that Monet could have painted into my mind.

London and Amsterdam

The music was fast and frantic and that's how my life seemed to be as I was now venturing into uncharted territory. I'd met a few Cockney lads on holiday earlier that year when everyone seemed to be heading for Ibiza to enjoy the sun while being off it on Ecstasy.

I was in the place where almost five years earlier I'd been sent by my family to avoid seeing my father die. This time, totally different circumstances brought me back.

I went for pleasure but ended up meeting lads from London who I got on with so it wasn't long before the uninhibited nature of ecstasy kicked in and business was getting talked about. These lads were connected good and proper, I could tell by the company they kept and most of all, how much money was being flashed around while we danced our socks off every night.

We swapped numbers and I told them I'd be down to London as soon as I got back to Liverpool and arranged the funds to do proper business. I suspect their first thoughts must have been of me chatting bollocks but I knew otherwise and that's all that mattered. I had seriously high hopes of getting my Scouse arse down to London and follow my initial instinct.

These Cockney lads turned out to be the bollocks. I'm not saying everything went 100% smoothly all the time but if problems arose, they were resolved in a business-like fashion to my benefit.

One hiccup led us to the table of the top lads and that ended with a week in Amsterdam where money was no issue while business was the aim. They liked us as we did them. This all happened over a period of three months and I was so busy that the arrival of my amazing daughter, Emilly, born in Fazakerley Hospital at 3pm and weighing in at 9lb 4oz, was a welcome relief for me. My older pals showed me some compassion and allowed me to take time off to make sure everything was OK as the birth was rough.

I was at the birth and helped out as much as I could, to my sheer shock as the clinical smell of antiseptic made me giddy and just being in a hospital made me pass out now and again. I think it's called 'White-coat syndrome', and if it's not, it is now.

As I was now a dad, I went out and bought the safest possible car to carry my family around. There were a few eyebrows raised when I turned up in a year-old Audi 2.5i Sport. It wasn't flash; it was metallic, gun-metal grey with no extras on it but it had 90 000 miles on the clock. I thought that as long as the family are safe, that's all that matters. In a fashion, it was a sign of showing out and it wasn't long before my older pals had a word in my ear and talked me into buying a VW Passat estate in plain white. I always took their advice as it was invaluable in staying one step ahead of the law and not flashing your status about the council estates of Liverpool.

With money rolling in and a family home set up, it wasn't long before I had a few lads running about for me. I kept it tight and wouldn't let outsiders know anything about my business. It had to be that way; tell no-one anything - but that did come with a social cost to me. Certain people would judge me as shallow and thought I looked down my nose at others. Just because I wouldn't get into conversation with certain people when I was in my local pub, it gave them the impression that I thought I was better than them. How wrong they were. I didn't want to let anything slip that could jeopardise my situation or my liberty and everything that meant so much to me.

I had a job to do and part of that was to be secretive and single-minded. Anyway, fuck 'em, it was their problem, I had money on my mind and kept myself to myself. My close friends knew what I was really like, as did my family, and they were the only ones I allowed to get close to me.

Over the next year I buried my heart and soul into making money and trying to raise a family. The money side was fine but cracks started to appear in my relationship. The cracks became so big that no wallpaper in B&Q was wide enough to paper over them. This hit hard as I was a proper hands-on father with Emily and the thought of her out of my life knocked me for six, seven, eight, nine and 10.

It's times like these that make or break you and I'll be honest, I was wounded and the aftermath wasn't pleasant either. *'She said, they said, he said'* was getting blurted out by interfering busybodies during this stressful saga. I decided to draw a line under it and make the most of my new-found single status but not without a few sleepless weeks. What else was I gonna do? Sit and mope? I don't think so.

The lads from Halewood heard about my relationship dramas and Scotty and Fishface turned up one Tuesday morning full of beans and quality skunk.

Skunk was the new weed on the scene and if you got the right one, it destroyed you (in a good way, of course). These lads never fucked about, you know, they had the finest salad all the time. They called it salad or Greenwich to avoid anyone overhearing and deducing the real meaning - as if the smell wasn't a dead giveaway.

They'd made arrangements to go on a five-day trip to a music festival in Waterford, Ireland, without telling me. It was their way of sorting my head out and giving me a break from my dramas. They knew I would have said no if they asked me a few days before, so them turning up buzzing was the kick up the arse I needed.

A few days earlier, I'd treated myself to a new Mitsubishi Galant, 2 litre, 16-valve sports car to cheer myself up. It was discreet enough not to stand out so we decided to travel in that as I only trusted myself driving. The lads didn't object one bit, in fact they knew they could build spliffs to their hearts' content.

I was happy, they were happy, so we set off, roaring towards Holyhead with our mix tape of tunes from *The State* on full blast. The journey felt like I was inside a Space Invaders arcade game, it was a cross between Tron and The Magic Roundabout due to the constant spliffs being passed my way. I was properly stoned.

The Halewood lads had lifted me out of my bout of feeling sorry for myself and made me swear not to mention any shite about Andrea, my now-ex bird – and with me now 100% stoned to bits, I was aware of what I was saying in HD and widescreen as I put my thought process under my stoned, psychosomatic mind-set.

The Irish ferry journey and the following drive to Waterford passed without incident and even if there was something to tell you about, I was that whacked with the heavy salad the lads had me smoking, I wouldn't have been able to knock a sentence out.

It wasn't long before we ran out of weed and had to go on a recce to find a local dealer. We spent hours getting funny looks from strangers and eventually asked for help in our hour of need for weed. We needed it big time and didn't give a fuck how 'on top' it seemed to the unsuspecting Irish public.

We ended up in Cork on a housing estate like the one in *The Commitments*. Pit ponies were tied to railings outside blocks of graffiti-laden blocks of flats. I couldn't believe how many horses, home-made go-karts and shopping trollies were scattered across this what-appeared-to-be derelict council estate.

We approached a young lad who was obviously up to something, he was lurking in a doorway with is head down, kicking stones with the toe-end of his shoe.

"Hey lad, come here a minute." I said, moving my head sideways, beckoning him to come over to me.

"Wat da fuck do you want?" He replied in a broad, Irish brogue that made us all smile.

"Lad, we're after a weed … you know, a smoke …" said Scotty, putting two fingers towards his mouth as if he was smoking.

"Who the fuckin' hell are you?" He frowned, looking puzzled and shocked. He stood and stared at us for about five seconds.

"Lad, we're going to a festival in Waterford and we've run out of smoke. We're only looking to get some weed, any weed, Mate."

He walked right up to our faces, looked us up and down and said, "Giz 20 quid and wait here, I'll be back in 15 or 20 minutes. I'll get some solid, that's all I can do for you but lads, you have to give me the money first. It's up to you."

We were in no position to argue or call the shots so the cash was passed over and we watched him walk away into the distance with our dough.

"He's fuckin' not comin' back!" Fishface smirked, shrugging his shoulders.

"What the fuck can we do now except wait and see, just give it 20 minutes, eh?" I said trying to be slightly positive'. No need to be defeated yet, I thought.

The allotted 20 minutes passed and he was nowhere to be seen.

"Hahaha, we've been had, I'm not waiting any longer, lads. We've been buzzed off by an Irish tinker with a fuckin' pit pony as a pet. Come on, let's go," said Scotty, knowingly.

"Just give it five more minutes, then we can fuck off. We're here now, we might as give it another five minutes."

Time passed by and there was still no sign of the lad who'd definitely ripped us off. We jumped back in the car and as we went to tear into each other for being mugged, we heard a knock on the boot of the car and the kid was standing there with his clenched hand held out.

I wound the window down and he leaned in and passed me a block of resin. We all started to laugh and told the kid to go and get us some more. We gave him another 40 quid and off he went.

Now this weed wasn't the best but when a pot-head needs a smoke, any old shite will do, especially when you're on foreign soil.

The lad came back quicker this time as he'd sprinted under the premise that we'd give him an extra fiver to get a move on.

As we drove towards Waterford we sampled bit more of the weed and to be fair, it wasn't that bad. We were buzzing; we'd hunted down a smoke, next stop, the festival site.

We bunked into the camp site next to the race track with no problems, pitched three tents and went on the mooch trying to find a way in without paying. Of course, we weren't paying to get into the festival, not a chance, in fact it was now classed as a mission. You can't go on a crusade without returning home with treasures and local wares; that's standard for on-the-ball Scousers.

Off we marched following the crowd, as it happens, it was a piece of cake to get in. We used the blag of leaving a 10-foot gap between us and when asked for our tickets by the stewards, replied in a strong Yorkshire accent, "Me dad's got tickets, he's comin' through now," as we continued shuffling forwards and didn't look back once.

We were in without a hiccup and now it was time to mooch around and check out what was happening on the different stages and huge tents scattered around the converted racetrack. Bob Dylan, Christie Moore, Jerry Lee Lewis, The Dubliners and plenty more acts and activities to keep us occupied were dotted across the site. The four days passed in a black-liquid haze of Guinness and spliffs but on the last day, somehow we lost our weed and the atmosphere changed rapidly having mislaid the calming influence of a spliff. It wasn't long before we were heading back to Cork and the pit-pony estate to look for the kid in the doorway. We all argued like fuck on the car journey, in jest, of course but the points were taken, absorbed and spat back with venomous, comedy timing. We eventually found the kid and grabbed another £20 deal and headed to Dublin to catch the ferry back to Holyhead.

Driving down a winding, country lane on the outskirts of Cork, we all started to dish out stick and I was getting properly pissed off. Crash! Fucking hell, I'd only ploughed into the back of a white van. Everything seemed to happen in slow motion and the Halewood lads couldn't stop laughing as I'd written off the front end of my brand new Mitsubishi Galant. I was shocked and was just about to reverse and fuck off when I looked out of my side window. I'd only crashed directly outside a police station and two coppers were in the doorway, holding mugs of tea and shaking their heads. It wasn't long before they'd taken my details and given the damaged vehicles the once over, then said we could go on our way.

The lads buzzed off my fucked-up car all the way home and made sure I had the proper hump. I was so pissed off but at least they were having a laugh; albeit at my expense. To be fair, during the entire trip, I never once mentioned my messy breakup with Andrea so in that respect it was a total success. They didn't find it funny when I pulled up outside my house and fucked off with their car keys leaving them stranded for a while. It was only a small payback but nevertheless, I had to do something. I'd just been leathered all the way from Cork to Walton, Liverpool. I suppose it was funny when I hit the car on that winding, Irish country road though.

Not long after that, I moved house into a swanky, well-decorated bachelor pad in Walton Village to assist me in my new 'single' status. I also started playing footy again and joined my pals and drinking buddies playing for Bulford FC which was run from The Crown on the East Lancs Road. Before long, I was up to scratch with my fitness and became a regular starter either up front or right midfield.

The league was a rough one and our games would be played on Windy Harbour in Kirkby. I'd started to find the back of the net and was known for having a shot right from the kick off. I was a bit of a cheeky fucker on the footy pitch, you know that old adage that you put a pair of football boots on and you turn into a different animal. Well, I was one of them – at least I thought I was.

A month or so passed and I was firmly in the routine of earning a few quid, partying hard, whilst playing and watching footy. Bulford had a Cup quarter final against a team called Sacred Heart but let me tell you, there wasn't one sacred heart in that team. The week before, we played them in the league and beat them, 3-1 - I scored two belters. I was a marked man for the cup tie as I was getting kicked at every opportunity. Five minutes after I scored, I found myself hobbling off with what I thought was a serious injury, the manager said I'd run it off in a minute or two. I didn't run again, not for the next nine months, as I ended up with a spiral fracture of my tibia and fibular in three places.

Coming round after surgery on the trauma ward in Walton Hospital and looking at the two titanium rods popping out of my leg with blood dripping off them knocked me for six. As I was coming to terms with my new rods, I noticed Fishface standing at the end of my bed.

"Fuck me, Kid – that looks nasty…" he croaked, screwing up his face in what looked like disgust. It wasn't disgust though, it was sheer disbelief; it looked terrible.

I think I was off my head on whatever drugs they'd given me for the pain and it hadn't really dawned on me fully what had happened. It wasn't long before they wore off though and the pain roared up my body. I was fitted with my own personal drug drip to easy my pain when I saw fit, boy, that was a nice feeling, as were the Co-codamol tablets the nurses gave me every four hours.

My first night in Walton hospital was weird as the left-back in our team was the night porter and turned up at about 11pm with eight bottles of freezing cold Budweiser. He plonked his arse on the chair next to my bed and cracked two bottles open. I remember him passing me one and can't really remember much after that, although we drank it all. The next morning, I got told off by the ward sister for smelling like an old pub floor. Shortly after my dressing down, the Halewood lads turned up with KFC, gallons of Lucozade and a carrier bag full of sweets. I was over the moon with their gesture and perked up after they'd had a buzz with me, reminding me that my leg didn't look half as bad as my car did on that country lane a few months earlier.

As my leg was in traction and my blood pressure surprisingly low, I was kept in for a month just so they could keep an eye on me. I wasn't the best patient, even visiting hospitals, I usually passed out; I've been embarrassed on loads of occasions so having to reside in one was like a test of nerves for me. Anyway, I passed the test and was released only having to go back for rehabilitation and physio once a week.

If you think things couldn't get any worse; think again. Not only had I split with my girlfriend, smashed up my new car and had pins and rods hanging out of my leg like a TV aerial, I'd been burgled while I was laid up in hospital. You can imagine how I felt coming home to no TV, sound system and my collection of TAG Heuer sports watches had all gone too. I was fucking livid. I smashed fuck out of the kitchen door with my crutches out of sheer frustration and cursed the bastards who'd dared invade my home. That was all I needed as I hobbled around surveying what was missing. I put the word about and news of who'd done it and who'd marked their card that I'd been in hospital came back pretty quickly.

I ended up having to put an insurance claim together as most of my stuff had long gone and the two lads responsible had hit the road. I knew I'd catch them one day; those kind of people have to crawl out of the sewer at some point, of that I was certain.

Swimming, cycling and clubbing was now my life as my physio recommended these things, obviously, not clubbing but with my new limp, I sometimes got the sympathy vote and a few female admirers along the way. Ste and Sean, two of my pals who I'd grown up with from my Faversham Road days were glued to my side every moment throughout my recovery. As I didn't trust many people, I needed lads who knew me properly to help me out, you know, driving me round and more or less being my best mates. I'd always make sure they had a few quid in their pockets when we went for a bevvie. One reason is that I'd slope off with a bird at some point so at least they had money for the night and to get themselves home. You never know what's around the corner.

We'd been partying for months on end with no real let up; staying in for two nights in a row was classed as a break. I must have drank enough brandy and coke to last me a lifetime, not the shit one either, always XO Remy, Courvoisier or Martell. There were always a few bottles knocking around my house for the lads to party with afterwards.

There wasn't a weekend that passed without some sort of party happening in my house. Even if I left early with a girl, I'd be knocked up in the early hours by the troops and their carry outs of ale and women. I didn't always answer their whistles and shouts but on many occasions I did. There was always a buzz to be had with my pals and their entourage for the evening.

One Saturday night, having put in plenty of spade work in the previous weeks, I sloped off early with a lovely girl back to my house. When I say 'early', I mean at about 10pm which was usually when the night was just starting to get going, but on this occasion, I didn't want anybody to cramp my style. I wasn't one for hanging about with my pals when women came into the equation, I was private in that way. To be honest, the main reason was to be alone with them. Anyhow, I'd landed back at mine and put the tunes on, probably The Isley Brothers. I poured a couple of brandies and settled down on my black-and-white leather sofa.

She was a lovely-looking girl with a great attitude and the manager of a well-known women's fashion shop in Liverpool's town centre. I forgot to mention that she'd driven back from town to my house in her new, yellow Mini as she'd not been drinking – oh, and she called her car Gertrude. She really loved it and kept it spotless.

We must have somehow dozed off on the couch for a while because I was woken from my spoon-snooze by the sound of somebody knocking at my front window. It was that sharp 'tap' that could only be made by a key or a stone.

"Open the door, Lad." I could hear in a deep, drunken tone accompanied by background giggling.

"Come on, open up, we know you're in there. Come on, let us in..." They went on relentlessly, their voices getting louder and deeper with every passing second.

Now my two pals I'd grown up with could make me laugh or change my mind at any given moment so I didn't want to have a face-to-face with them. I crept upstairs and looked out of the bedroom window to see my two pals with four girls sitting on my wall making a racket. I opened the window and tried to speak softly,

"Lads, I've got company, there's no way you're coming in. Not a chance, OK?"

"Stop messing about and let us in because one of these birds needs a piss, it's either on your step or in your toilet." He was swaying from side to side with a bottle of beer in his right hand. All of the girls thought this was funny, joined in with the blag and were cackling loudly. My mates and these four, drunken, Scouse scrubbers were off their heads and bouncing off each other on my doorstep.

"You've got that bird with you, haven't you? And that's her fucking car, the yellow Mini. So you're fucking your mates off for a bird, are you? We're not gonna move from here, we're having a party on your step!" He spat out, drunkenly while giggling to his captive audience; by now some of my neighbours had made an appearance.

I looked at my watch; it was 4am.

"Fuck you and your bimbos, I'm off to bed!" I slammed the window tightly shut, closed the blinds and ran back downstairs to find my date sitting on the end of the couch looking worried.

"What's up, Hun?" I asked, sitting close to her and putting my arm tightly around her.

"Have I caused you a problem? Should I leave?" She asked nervously.

"Have you fuck, love, they're my proper mates and they're just at the bollocks, don't worry, they'll fuck off in a minute, come here." I said, as I grabbed her tight and pulled her close to my chest to reassure her.

We sat and waited for the noise to dissipate into the distance and thought that was that. It wasn't though. About 30 minutes later, we both heard laughing and music outside. It wasn't really loud, but loud enough at 5am, when usually it was only the birds you could hear.

I got up off the couch and made my way to the front door, took the deadlock off and opened it. I could still hear music as I scanned up and down the street for signs of life, when I heard giggles coming from behind next-door's works van.

Wearing only my shorts and a t-shirt, I walked towards the van and noticed my date's yellow Mini was bouncing; my two pals and four birds crammed were into it, with the tunes on. As I walked around to the passenger side, my pal's leg was hanging out the window like a discarded, shop dummy's leg.

"Lads, what the fuck are you doing? Get the fuck out of the car now!" The sight of my two, 15-stone mates rolling about inside a yellow Mini with four scrubbers was enough to put a vulture off brunch forever.

By the time I'd dragged them out of the car and replaced the door trim and wing mirrors they'd ripped off, I was joined by my now-truly-pissed-off date. She never spoke to me once, she stood fuming and silently waiting for me to finish picking up the debris from her beloved Gertrude.

She didn't see the funny side at all and left me standing in my shorts on the street as she wheel-spun away in her orgy-stained car. The following day I drove to her house and left more than enough money for the damage with a *'Sorry'* card. I never heard anything back so I assumed I fucked it up, or should I say my pals did.

I didn't have much time to dwell on social incidents and funny dramas anymore as life was becoming more serious by the day. I started to get mixed up with things that I swore I'd never touch for whatever reason, I just did it and never seemed to bat an eyelid. I am not saying I didn't think about it afterwards, because I did, and knew one day I'd rue the day I turned the corner and made that choice. My arm wasn't up my back, but I always thought I had a point to prove so now heroin was being sold in large amounts.

My older pals would keep me in check at all times, no time or space to make silly mistakes, so with me apparently going out on the ale and partying, they had a word in my ear. It didn't take long for the penny to drop and I realised they thought I'd be off my barnet and maybe let trade secrets slip. That wasn't my style, no way. I kept things tight in that respect; work and business kept well apart. Once the older lads had realised I was just enjoying myself and growing up, they started to come to my house more and more. They never used the front door as safety was always an issue, so having a back door that led to an alleyway was an added bonus. This also kept me on my toes and protected me as they would turn up at any random time to see what company I was keeping.

A wedding date for one of the older lads who I worked for was set, as was the stag do. This was a four-day trip to Amsterdam and about 20 lads had made arrangements to meet up in the smutty Dutch capital to get totally off it. Now, I didn't usually mix socially with the older lads or their pals, so it was the first time I'd met a few of them.

Everyone met up in *The Grasshopper*, just across the road from Central Station for a few pints of Amstel and of course, a joint or two. I made sure I got to know everyone and was a bit put back when I noticed Liverpool's knockout merchant and general lunatic, Tom Green, sitting in the bar with all the older lads.

I was the smallest and youngest by about 10 or 15 years, so I stuck out like a sore thumb amongst the massive-framed rowdy pack in Amsterdam. I couldn't stop thinking about Tom Green and the stories and reputation that had followed him around Liverpool for as long as I could remember. Twenty minutes later I was sitting in a taxi with him going to Rembrandtplein to meet up with more lads we knew.

He was a handful in the taxi, trying to steer the cab into an oncoming tram on the Damtrak the Turkish taxi driver didn't know what the fuck to do and neither did I. I told the lads when we arrived at the Irish bar and they all seemed to palm him off with me, as they had plans of having a buzz and believe me, you couldn't have had a buzz with this serial lunatic around you.

He couldn't handle his ale or drugs and would cause trouble in a monastery. He was fuckin' lively and the lads left him with me as they knew I was too polite to tell him to fuck off; plus he terrified me. I wasn't scared, I was terrified, it was more like he could get you into all sorts of trouble without you knowing fuck all about it or until it was too late.

We'd all eaten magic mushrooms earlier on and they were just kicking in when the older lads sloped off and left me totally stranded with a drunken, drugged-up serial lunatic and a notorious knockout merchant. I thought I was going to end up in serious trouble as we went from bar to bar and coffee shop to coffee shop searching for the lads; obviously to no avail as they'd well fucked off out of Tom's way by now.

Don't get me wrong, this fella would help you out with certain things back home, but here, in Amsterdam, he was a time bomb waiting to explode in front of my eyes. He spoke funny too. He had a way of talking that made me think he had a speech problem.

We ended up in a coffee shop about midnight having a koffie verkeerd and a spliff, when Tom decided to order two pieces of chocolate weed cake and cream. 'What the fuck was he ordering these for?' I thought, as the attractive Dutch waitress served us two portions. Tom wolfed down his space cake without hesitation then turned his attention to me.

"E r, av dis kid", Tom said, in his stuffy, nasal accent.

"I don't want it, I'm alright, thanks", I muttered politely.

"E r, just av it, e r, eat it will ya", as he pushed my portion closer to my face; by this time my head was resting on the brass bar that surrounded the dark-stained wooden bar.

"I'm alright, I don't want it", I said, as I pushed the plate away from under my nose. My head never moved as I was fucked and just need to be rid of this lunatic. I felt a tap on my shoulder and glanced up to see Tom looking at me with the cake and squirty cream in both hands, heading towards my screwed up magic-mushroom-induced face. SPLAT!

Fuck me, the twat had rubbed chocolate cake all over my face in front of everyone in the coffee shop. I leapt out of my seat while scooping the lumps of chocolate and cream off my face and realised I was right up close to this lunatic's amazed face as I shouted,

"You fucking dickhead, what the fuck did you do that for, you mong?"

He looked at me puzzled and stood up from his chair to tower over me. 'Oh shit, I'm dead, I've just called him a mong to his face', I thought, as I wiped the last bits of cake off my face. Tom gazed down on me with a strange look in his eyes and said quietly,

"Waz dat outta order?"

"Fucking right it was, the other lads swerved you and I've stayed with you all night and you go and do that, there's no need for that!" It wasn't until I'd stopped talking that I fully understood the implications of what could follow; I'd just dropped the older lads right in it. Tom looked towards the waitress and apologised and asked for another piece of cake and cream. Now what was going on in his brain? He had me worried.

Once the waitress had put the plate down, Tom scooped the new plate of cake in both hands, stared at me and to everyone's sheer disbelief, proceeded to rub the cake in his own face,

'This man is not right in the head', I thought, as he sat beside me with cake and cream sliding off his grid onto his white shirt. He wiped the cake from his eyes and said,

"Is that better? Does that even it out, Kid?"

I couldn't help but laugh, we were both dripping in chocolate and cream as the waitress cleaned up around us. I gave her 20 guilders for the mess and left with Tom, pronto. We seemed to get on a lot better after my chocolate-covered rant and he treated me with an air of respect. He kept asking me if he was behaving right and permitted me to tell him off if he got out of order. He was beginning to grow on me.

We decided (or should I say I came up with the idea and talked him into thinking it was his) to buy handcuffs from one of the many shops still open so we could terrorise the older lads back at the hotel. We headed back to our room at around 2.30am and waited patiently, off our barnets on space cake and mushrooms, for the lads to return.

I kept looking out the window, up and down the cobbled, wet, shiny road for the lads to make an appearance so that Mad Tom could do his worst with the newly-acquired handcuffs.

Around 4am, two of the older lads showed up and Tom made sure they came into our room for a night cap, or so they thought, anyway. Ten minutes into them sitting on the end of the bed and nattering away, Tom winked at me and grabbed the biggest and the hardest lad out of the two and wrestled him to the floor with his arms out in front of him. It took me a minute to figure out that Tom had somehow been able to handcuff him around the huge, metal, old-fashioned radiator below the huge window frame.

I couldn't stop laughing, as it was my older pal who always kept an eye on me and more or less talked me into being a grafter who was cuffed to the radiator. He pleaded with me for about an hour to set him free, but with Tom now on a mission, that wasn't going to happen, not a chance. I still couldn't stop myself from laughing but he wasn't happy at all and his frustration was nearly at boiling point.

Even if I could have set him free, there wasn't a chance that I'd upset Tom; the tripping, teasing, terrorist. When Tom went for a piss, my pal said,

"Lad, fuckin' stop messin and giz the key."

"I haven't got it, he's fuckin' got it, ask him for it", I said quickly, while pointing towards the toilet. Tom flushed the bog and stumbled out laughing to himself. Then said,

"So you want the key? Well I've got it here and you're not moving". He knelt down and angrily started to drag my pal's trousers off him.

"What the fuck are you doing, Tom?" My pal screamed as loudly as he could while wriggling like a fish out of water on the hotel carpet.

"Fuck off Tom – don't take my undies off!" He screamed again, as Tom was laughing and pulling off his white Calvin Kleins like he was a discarded rag doll.

"EEEEEEE, shitty undies!" Tom roared laughing, while waving the skid-marked pants right in front of my pal's beetroot face.

"Fuck off Tom, let me fucking outta these cuffs, pleeeaasse," he begged, with a look of total embarrassment scrawled across his boat race. I was still laughing and by now was in a heap on the bed, my legs kicking like a mule on crack. I couldn't control myself and nearly passed out. Fuck me, it got even funnier as Tom stretched the shitty skid-marked undies across the top of the radiator. My pal was livid and by now was fuming with me, but he wasn't bothered earlier on when he was part of the group that stitched me up with this fruitcake, so I couldn't give a flying fuck.

By now, Tom was sitting on the end of the bed telling me not to set my pal and his shitty undies free. They both needed to be aired… sometimes that's just how the cookie crumbles.

The flight home was horrible as the drug and alcohol hangover oozed out of everybody to give the atmosphere a bad taste. My pal who'd been cuffed was still fuming and I knew it wouldn't be long before he tore into me over one thing or another. He was like that, good and bad, but always wanted to be in control and thought of himself as a higher intelligence in some ways.

I knew I'd have to keep out of his way for a bit, so I'd already started to make plans in my head. Liverpool were due to play in Europe and I was going to go home and away, the long way round, that would keep me on the move and outta my pal's sights, but from that day forward, he would be known as Shitty Arse.

Away Days

I'd cover 30 miles a day on my mountain bike and was as fit as a fiddlers elbow

There were a couple of lads I'd met as a kid through footy who had started to make a name for themselves with Liverpool and Everton. Steve McManaman had broken into the Liverpool First Team Squad and Anthony Grant was making great strides with Everton reserves. I knew Steve Mc from the Walton and Kirkdale Junior League when I coached the representative team with Hugh McAuley in 1987. I became friendly with his dad too and often chatted with him en-route to watch Liverpool reserves when his son was breaking through a few years earlier.

One of the pubs I used to sell my wares in on County Road was The Netley. Steve and his pals would always be in there on

Saturday nights. He had a red Ford Orion 16i Ghia and most weekends, drove his drunken mates about without wetting his own lips with alcohol; he was pretty focused and sensible as a teenager.

Anyhow, Steve Mc would always have a ticket or two for me when I decided to travel abroad to watch my beloved Reds. The 91-92 season had a few trips in store for me and I would use these wisely to get myself around Europe undetected from watching authorities. Always safety-minded first and the rest would follow.

After trips to France then Genoa, we were knocked out of Europe but ended up having a good FA Cup run. We beat Sunderland in the final to raise the spirits of the loyal fans, as the title challenge seemed to be faltering every season. The only buzz for me was the emergence of Steve McManaman as a top-class professional footballer. It's always nice to witness good luck stories from your area and age bracket. Somehow it gives everyone a lift and fills you with a kind of local pride.

My older pals had more or less put me in charge of certain jobs which held responsibilities for many people. With these European trips now few and far between, I had to make my own excuses to travel across borders on a regular basis. I'd always go by car and ferry to avoid detection as you were able to travel without giving any personal details; well, not your own anyway.

Once a month I'd take this journey and always make the most of it with the money coming out of the expenses. My older pal who'd been exposed as a shitty-undie-wearing Scouser was a tight as a submarine's door in every way, in fact, he was that tight with money that you couldn't remove a drawing pin from his arse with a 40 ton truck. That's why the expenses got taken to the limit, plus I'd started to realise that he knew I loved what I did for a living and took pride in it, so he used this to his advantage and paid me the bare minimum.

I was slowly but surely getting on to him by now as five or six years of his constant one-way traffic mentality began to wear me down. There were times when he'd turn up and lecture me about who to hang about with and which places I should and shouldn't be seen; this control freakery was draining me but we both earned money out of each other. For now, it was ok but I was just beginning to start my own networking strategy behind the scenes. Not one person knew what I was planning, other than myself. At least he'd taught me something right. Single cell is the only way and to keep yourself to yourself.

I was still partying heavily and now firmly in to getting about the city during the week on my mountain bike. I'd cover about 30 miles a day and after a few months of Walton to Halewood on the disused Northern Line railway track and was as fit as a fiddler's elbow. This was good for doing certain bits of graft too, as rucksacks and the correct clothes gave the impression of a serious cyclist to onlookers. We'd always go in threes and took precautions as the track was a bit of a hot-spot for gangs to hang about causing mischief.

Tony Grant's name was on the lips of every Evertonian as he was getting rave reviews, which came with a bit of stick from the Red half of the city when he was out and about. I'd been friends with the whole family for as long as I could remember so his sudden fame didn't cut any ice with me, he was still that kid who borrowed my Patrick mouldies eight years earlier and his family always made me more than welcome every time I was in their house.

As he was a family friend as well as a mate, we would bump into each other in certain pubs and clubs around Liverpool and always ended up back at my house having a buzz. Most of the time we'd have to put him to bed early as he was squeaky clean and nine times out of ten we'd all be off our heads on E and weed; not Tony though. Not a fucking chance.

I watched over him like a hawk as dickhead Liverpool fans would try and persuade him into their company to take the piss out of him. To be fair, Tony could look after himself in anybody's company, but back at my house he was my responsibility and I didn't take kindly to people trying to take advantage of him.

A group of my good pals started to travel to watch him playing away for the reserves as we could have a good jolly-up along the way. Trips to Halifax, Leeds, Blackburn, Manchester, Middlesbrough and other training grounds around the country were now a regular occurrence for us in my Leyland DAF crew bus. We christened the van 'The Boogie Bus' as we cruised along motorways with The Waterboys, Earth Wind and Fire and Soul to Soul blasting on the Alpine stereo I'd had fitted. There was a table with seating for six in the back and two front-seat passenger seats and of course, a captain's chair for the designated driver, usually me as I still only trusted my own driving.

This cream-coloured van was now a vital part of my life as mountain biking in the Lake District, Snowdonia and Fort William in Scotland was becoming another regular occurrence. The van covered some miles in '93/94 and one way or another; every day was an adventure in in the Boogie Bus.

The Christmas of '93 was my first Everton Football Club party, this took place early in December as the festive period was always a busy time for professional footballers. It was a fancy dress affair and as Tony was classed as a sort of rookie, he was made to get up and sing a few badly-chosen songs by the team's captain, Dave Watson. Tony pulled it off big time while being pissed as a fart. In fact, they had to drag him off the stage and force the microphone out of his hands in the end.

With 1994 just around the corner, if Tony didn't make it as a footballer, he definitely had a chance of becoming a comedian or a grafter. Five out of every ten lads from the Sparrow Hall Estate became grafters, so that put Tony in the firing line from the start. Thank God he had a good left foot and a great attitude otherwise who knows what might have happened. Anyhow, we got on like a house on fire and bounced off each other on many nights out on the town; us both being single provided us with some great opportunities.

The festive period came and went with hardly any fuss and I was looking forward to getting busy again. January was always a quiet month for reasons only grafters know, so February picked up and I was up to my usual skullduggery, when I received a phone call that shook me to the core. On the other end of the line was an unfamiliar voice saying,

"Look lad, we've got your mate and we want a 100 grand otherwise he's getting it. I'm gonna call back in one hour with details…" and the phone went dead.

I called Shitty Arse and he answered immediately, he knew what had happened, as our mate's girlfriend had called him to say he'd been taken by police in an unmarked just car around the corner from his home.

Well, Shitty Arse and I knew it wasn't police by now and called the older lads to meet in my house to make plans. Within 30 minutes, my home was transformed into a cauldron of testosterone. Threats to every kidnapping firm in the city were being branded about and my living room converted into a hub to find our mate, sharpish. The hour had well passed and the call came into my mobile, only this time it was Shitty Undies who answered and roared threats back immediately without giving whoever was on the other end a chance to talk.

"Ya fucker, ya not gettin' fuck all!" he screamed, as he pulled the phone away from his ear while looking both worried and furious.

"They were knocking fuck out of him then, I could hear him, the cunts put the phone to his mouth while they twatted him…the fuckers." He said to the now-silent, captivated gathering of lads in my living room.

I didn't know what to think, but having heard the shout of 'Ya not gettin fuck all' roared down the blower, I began to imagine how our mate must be feeling. What had happened? Where was he? What we could do to help? Were we going to help?

With the phone call still running through my brain, I began to realise this lifestyle was threatening and profoundly serious. Now this fella, our mate who'd been kidnapped, was one tough motherfucker who never took shite, so this was so far left field for me that it gave me a wake-up call. It doesn't matter who you are in this game, you're still vulnerable to terrifying ordeals. They say that only bad things happen to bad people but I'm not having that one bit. Bad things just happen and that's that.

The phone calls kept coming, as did the amount of lads to my house. Every few hours someone would be dragged in pleading they knew nothing and in turn offered their services in finding information about our pal's whereabouts.

Daytime turned to night and night to day before I received another call. To my shock and amazement, it wasn't from the kidnappers, it was from our pal who had somehow escaped. He gave me his location and I immediately rushed to find him inside a phone box wearing only a pair of filthy jeans and a sheet wrapped around his top half.

He was bleeding from the back of his head and his wrists were both bloody as he was cuffed, but the chain had broken and only the cuffs remained on either wrist. By the time I got him back to my house, cut the cuffs off with a hacksaw blade and cleaned him up, all the lads had arrived to survey his damaged limbs and debrief for scraps of info about his abduction and abductors. This had turned into a major priority now, who marked the kidnappers' card? How did they find our mate's address? Work must have been put in to come up with the final outcome?

The only upside of the whole drama now was he was back safe with his family and to me, that's all that mattered. Throughout this entire situation, I was putting myself in my pal's shoes and wondering how I would have reacted to any of that shite, and you know what, I just couldn't imagine what it would be like to have petrol poured over you while being pistol-whipped into revealing where the dough was. He never said a word either as he was a tough cookie. This was heavy shite and it was part of my life. It was hard to swallow for my tough-as-they-come pal and to be honest, me too.

Welcome to my world.

Single-Cell Mentality

Shoulder high in finest, Jamaican ganja

Having to be vigilant became a major part of my life now as the previous few months had brewed up a few shit storms for me to deal with. In my game came problems that had to be dealt with swiftly so you could keep the machine well oiled. With Shitty Arse on my case 24/7, there wasn't much time to enjoy myself, but when I needed a blow out, I made the time. You need rest and recuperation no matter what profession you're in.

Obviously Shitty Arse would turn up at my back door with his bright red face as he'd climbed over my 10-foot back wall to try and catch me off guard in his controlling way. Mind games were his main objective when it came to me, so me being stoned most of the time just added to his perverse mind set. As I said, being vigilant was number-one priority.

We changed things around with work and I had to find more lads who'd fit the bill to carry on doing the graft, but in a totally different way. Codes were formulated and meetings were limited to once a fortnight, with the older lads to protect what we had and not give anything away. The abduction of our pal had really rattled us, but at least we'd tightened our belt so we wouldn't be caught with our trousers down.

I began to hang about with Dougie again, the kid from Sparrow Hall who I'd known for years, but for some reason hadn't spent much time with. He was a talented motherfucker who should have gone to university, but the estate mentality got a grip of him and he'd had to look after his family, otherwise he could have been anything he wanted.

We started to go out together and would be off our barnets, often putting the world to rights. We'd be regulars in The State as it was still going strong with *Rock the Casbah* and *The Whole of the Moon* still being played as homage to the past. The place erupted with whistles, horns and screams from the drug-taking clubbers when these tunes came on. It sent shivers down my spine every time I heard the first note of either song. It was like a battle cry to the ecstasy masses.

Dougie became my closest friend and I knew he was as staunch as you could get. We had a drama back in the day of the stolen cars being raced and chased up and down the East Lancs Road and Sparrow Hall, so I knew I could count on him to keep things quiet. He'd been there, done it and kept his mouth shut. I respected that.

My little mob kept our heads down and ploughed through loads of graft without causing too much fuss along the way. Money was steady and the older lads had taken a side step and left more meat on the bones for me to crack on with. Shitty Arse was still a constant thorn in my side with snide remarks and he loved to chip away at my accumulated dough. He always had a great idea that would only benefit him in the end. I should have known from the start, but I had too much respect for him to question his graft judgment. I thought of him as a father figure, when he just saw me as a cash cow. Sometimes I was his friend but only when it suited him.

As we'd worked our bollocks off, it was time for a holiday and a proper jolly up. Christmas '94 was around the corner and I'd spotted a four-week bargain in Jamaica for six people when I was walking through Liverpool town centre in early December.

I went in immediately and paid a £200 deposit and then began to phone my pals to see who wanted a month in the Caribbean for virtually fuck all. Dougie, who I'd run away with when we were kids, was my first port of call.

To be honest, he was my best mate bar none and I would have done anything for him. We went our separate ways as teenagers, yet still stayed in touch because that's what mates do. Anyway, he was a definite and said a few more of his pals would go, plus my pal from the footy away-day trips, Buster, confirmed. So that was that; one call and the Jamaica trip got sorted.

Departing Boxing Day at 1.30pm; the flight to Montego Bay was now booked and paid in full.

We wound the graft down and all got ready to head to the Caribbean sun and its beautiful beaches. It couldn't come quickly enough really as it had been a twat of a year, but at least the reward was now visible in the shape of a booklet of plane tickets and hotel reservations for Ocho Rios. It was on and I was all packed on Christmas Day, eager as fuck.

We'd managed to arrange to all go out on Christmas night and the meeting point was The State. I arrived at about 11 o'clock and it wasn't long before I bumped into the lads, who by this time were all in good spirits and looking forward to the trip the next day. To be honest, we all looked off our barnets with a spring in our step; that was obvious. Every one of us were on different birds that night, so we all ended up scattered in different corners of the club. I did my usual early shuffle and headed off to my house with a bird on my arm; it was Christmas after all.

The next morning I was knocked up at 9 o'clock by Buster who was going with us. I leapt up and rushed down the stairs all excited and unlocked the door – to be greeted by a concerned face.

"Lad, go and put teletext on", he panted.

"What's up?" I asked, as he pushed me down my hallway and into the living room, where he grabbed the remote and turned the TV on.

'Lad, ya frightening me now, what's up?" I asked sharply

"You're not gonna fuckin' believe this kid", he said, as he flicked through the telextext pages to reveal the headline,

'SHOOTING IN LIVERPOOL NIGHT SPOT: SUSPECT HELD'.

My jaw dropped when I read my best mate's name and address.

"What the fuck happened?" I shouted all over my living room. I grabbed my phone, called his parents' house and spoke to his father who answered in a quiet voice.

"He's been arrested for attempted murder. The police are here now so I'll call you back in a bit."

"WHAT? Is he ok though?" I asked quickly.

"I dunno, I'll call you back", he said, and then the phone was put down to leave the dialling tone buzzing in my ear.

Within 30 minutes, all the other lads had arrived at my front door, grimacing after hearing the bad news. There was nothing we could do and to be perfectly honest, we decided to carry on with the trip without him and maybe he'd be able to join us sooner rather than later. To be fair we all needed to be out the way in case it got heavy with the police and we got linked to any of this. We spoke to his mother and told her to let him know we'd look after him and would be in touch soon.

Knowing I had a ticket in my pocket with my best pal's name on it was making me feel a bit anxious at the airport. We looked around for any familiar or suspicious faces to see if somehow the police or customs had put two and two together. I don't know why we felt anxious and guilty, but I suppose that's just part of the game. The thought of my best mate sitting in a cell did my head in. I suppose in a way I was escaping from the situation and Jamaica seemed as far away as anywhere right now, but I'd rather have Dougie with me.

With the last few hours bouncing round my brain, it was time for my last joint before we left for Montego Bay. Off I went to the airport toilet and built a fat, three skinner to chill me out. Did it work? No, it just made me 100 times more paranoid and put my mind on red alert for the next few hours.

After a deep sleep on the plane, I was awoken by the air hostess and asked to fix my seatbelt as the plane was on its approach to land. Fuck me, this journey passed quickly and the lads all perked up knowing we'd be on Jamaican soil in 20 minutes or so. I gave Buster a nudge to move his head from the window so I could a look at Jamaica from the air as he was nearly window licking. It was 4pm and the sun was shining when the captain made his announcement:

'Hello passengers, this is Captain Holt, and I'd just like to say we're on schedule and the temperature in Montego Bay is 82 degrees, so am sure you'll all have a pleasant trip. Thank you.'

As the plane landed, we all jostled to look out of the window as there was a bus waiting on the runway to pick us up to take us to the terminal, which wasn't big or modern; in fact it looked like a glorified cow shed. There was a guy hanging about on a moped next to the bus on the side of the runway as we came down the steps. He made sure he caught our eye and made a beeline for us as we sat on the bus which was ticking over on the side of runway.

I thought he must have worked at the airport in some capacity as he was by now knocking asking us to open the window so he could speak to us. Buster slid the top window open and this black guy jumped up and pushed a small bag of weed through. When I say a small bag, I mean it would have cost about 50 quid back home, so he'd definitely caught our attention with this sample.

We smelt the weed and I looked directly at him through the window and smiled, while putting my thumb up to confirm the weed looked and smelt the bollocks. His face lit up to reveal the biggest smile I've ever seen, with the gaps in his teeth he could have stunt-doubled for Stonehenge, they were that big.

The bus started to move off the runway and the guy leapt on to his moped and followed us to the terminal building.

"Irie man", he said, as we came off the bus and entered the terminal, "Ya like de ganja?" He spoke in Jamaican patois, revealing that massive smile again, but this time we all laughed because it seemed even bigger close up.

"Have ya got any more of that?" I asked quietly so no-one would hear while we got off the bus.

"Yer man, plenty, I'll see you on de udder side", he screamed loudly, while jumping onto his moped and screeching off around the side of the building. We stashed the sample bag and sailed through customs as there was no-one there to greet us, so it wasn't long before we were on the bus and heading off.

Five minutes into the journey, we heard a horn beeping like a sick duck and noticed the guy from the runway following us with his smile now lighting up the back of our bus. His head was bobbing up and down as if he had tunes on his bright red moped. He followed us for the hour and a half journey towards Kingston until we turned into the Port town of Ocho Rios, 30 kilometres from Kingston.

Our hotel was an all-inclusive resort, fenced off with heavily-armed security patrolling and guarding the main entrance. Now this didn't look too clever as we parked outside the reception. Security had stopped our man from the airport and were now escorting him towards us while he waved his arms.

As he got closer, he was winking at us and telling security that he was our taxi driver and he only wanted to pass on his mobile number. Somehow security swallowed his story even though he turned up on a fuckin' moped; not the brightest security, hey?

He helped us to our rooms with our bags and pulled out a massive bag of weed from his rucksack and told us he wanted $20 for it. This was the finest Jamaican bomber weed I'd ever seen and as soon as we smoked our first joint, it crept up behind your eyes to twat you on the back of the head with the heaviest, but nicest, stoned feeling I'd ever experienced.

Twenty minutes later, we all looked destroyed and the guy started to get his rucksack and keys together to leave;

"Right boys, you've got my number, so don't see no-one but me for ya ganja, de name's Malcolm the Middle Man, I'll get you what you want; cocaine, crack and even de women if you want." He pushed the card with his phone number across the table.

It was about 9 o'clock now and starting to go dark, so we all decided to have a bite to eat and a few brandies in our hotel and to check out our new surroundings.

About 8 o'clock the next morning, I heard a knock on our wooden-slatted shutters on the main window, loud enough to wake me up. I pushed the stiff, white cotton sheets back and crept to the window and tried to peek out of the gap in the middle. Another knock made me jump, and by this time, the lads had woken up too. I pushed the shutters open and there was a guy brushing leaves off our huge, ground-floor veranda.

He looked up at me and my mate, smiled, leant into the bushes and pulled out a bin bag, carried on brushing with one hand and threw the bin bag into the room.

"Irie boys, I'll be back in five". We kicked the bag gently to try and figure out what the contents were and that became obvious when the bag ripped open and the smell of weed filled the air like a Dutch oven.

"Fuckin hell, it's full of weed, I fuckin love this place", one of the lads shouted. He peeled three skins out of a packet of Rizla and licked the papers' edges while he stood in his boxer shorts, still half asleep.

On cue, the guy appeared on the veranda, this time with his coat on and a black, Adidas holdall over his shoulder. We opened the double doors and sat on the wicker chairs in the morning sun as a cool breeze blew past our bodies. This guy was rummaging in his bag and pulled out a huge spliff. He sat on the edge of the wall separating the rooms, lit his joint, took two long tokes and blew plumes of what looked like rain-filled smoke clouds into the air, he paused and said,

"Ya like de ganja? Fifty dollars and it's yours". Now that meant at the current exchange rate, which would be 30 quid for a bin bag of weed then this was a great deal. We all looked at each other in total amazement as we'd not even been here for a full day and weed was in abundance. We didn't have to go on missions looking for it; weed somehow followed us from the airport, knocked on our windows at silly prices and said, 'sample me first, then buy me'.

We ended up speaking to this guy for about an hour to get the lowdown on the area. He was adamant we shouldn't go out alone as there were bandits lurking. Under no circumstance should we venture outside the fenced-off resort without a chaperone, was his direct and rather stern advice. We didn't know if he was just trying to persuade us into letting him be our paid chaperone, so we took this advice with a pinch of salt.

Later on that night, we decided to take a stroll to the port, which was about 20 minutes from our hotel. The food in the hotel wasn't the best and all the lads agreed on a fish restaurant that our new weed man had suggested earlier on.

We nattered about the possibilities of any dramas occurring and the notion of strength in numbers won over local advice, so it was decided and off we traipsed in our shorts and flip flops. Five mad Scousers thinking we knew the score and nothing could faze us, left the security of our resort and smoked our way down a few dodgy looking roads and on to a beachfront.

About 10 minutes into the journey, I noticed two lads on bikes who seemed to be following us. As we hit a gap in the road, these two fellas appeared from behind a wall holding handguns and pointed them directly at us. I noticed one of the guns was a revolver and the tallest lad out of the two was rolling the barrel and aiming it in our direction. We all looked at each other and Buster said,

"Just keep walking and don't look at them." Fuck me, it's hard not to look at someone pointing a gun at you.

I could feel the tension in the warm air as we came up the dip and out of sight. There wasn't time to think as a shot rang out from somewhere. We all ran in the same direction and somehow the smallest of the young kids was now in front of us. He aimed the gun at us and went to fire but nothing happened. He started to bang the side of the gun and point it back in our direction, but it wasn't firing; it had jammed.

Total pandemonium set in and only for a taxi driver pulling up and allowing all five of us to cram into his battered car, I'm not sure what might have happened. As we sped off all laughing with fear, not joy, the taxi driver was told to put his lead boot on and get us the fuck back to our resort.

When we sat in our resort bar contemplating our near-death experience, a few of the lads had decided to take a rain check and the talk was about going back home. Was that fuck on my mind though, nothing was stopping me from enjoying myself. I'd had a twat of a year and our recent event just made me more determined to crack on and have a better time in Jamaica.

A week had passed when Buster and two of the other lads decided to leg it back home for one reason or another. I wasn't going anywhere and neither was a lad named Tony.

I knew Tony before we came, but not that well, so this was a learning curve for both of us. Three weeks in weed and brandy-soaked sunshine for us both to enjoy and get to know each other; what more could you ask for?

Jamaica wasn't that big so you could get from one end of the island to the other in about two hours. We made a quick decision to hire two scrambler motorbikes to go and explore the island of Bob Marley.

Everywhere you went, there was some sign, sound or spliff reminding you that it was the birthplace of Bob. The reason for the scramblers was totally down to the quality of the Jamaican roads or, I should say, the lack of quality. The roads had more bumps than Stephen Hawking's skirting boards had paint scrapes. The signs on the main roads in and out of Montego Bay which read, 'Undertakers love over takers' didn't really fill you with confidence, nor did the light aircraft with bullet holes in them which lay derelict at the side of the roads; this wasn't Liverpool at all. This place was nuts but Tony and I had taken a shine to it.

There was a car on the main road driving in reverse behind us as we travelled on the road to Negril one morning. It took me a while to figure out he only must have had reverse gear working and mastered the art of doing 30 mph backwards, permanently looking over his shoulder. Jamaica was growing on us at the rate of about 30mph, backwards.

It took us two days of scrambling up and down the dodgy roads to find a hotel in Negril that had two-bedroom beach houses for hire which suited our needs. We called Malcolm, who'd stalked us on arrival, and he duly became our guide as-and-when we required him. That's it, we thought, now we can relax and enjoy the sun, sand and spliffs. Oh no, Scousers need to keep busy and get about, especially two 25 year olds with a few quid in their pockets and bin bags of weed in their beach house.

Rick's café stoned, Dunn's River Falls stoned, helicopter ride stoned and next was a trip to Bob Marley's tomb and birthplace in the Jamaican hills, obviously stoned. Malcolm was on family duties, so we called a taxi driver and headed off on our pilgrimage to Bob's place, as stoned as was humanly possible.

As we turned on to the back roads heading for the hills, Tony nudged me to let me know we were being followed by a police car. It wasn't long before we found ourselves being rinsed of all our dollars and weed by two more-stoned-than-us Jamaican coppers. These two fuckers wanted to take us back to our hotel and take what money we had left, until they got called to a shooting in the next village. Thank God for small mercies, but I wouldn't wish for anybody to be confronted by these bastards on any given day.

The taxi driver was all apologies and said he'd wait to be paid once we'd got back. That was nice of him, wasn't it? Tony nearly chinned him on the spot until I pulled $200 out of my sports sock to cheer him up. We never let the twat of a taxi driver know we had money because we both thought he had something to do with being robbed by the local gangsters; the police.

Once we reached Bob Marley's house and signed into the visitor's book, Tony and I were treated like brothers by the fellas who ran the house and grounds. It wasn't long before we smoked a friendship pipe and these guys explained that Bob Marley's father had spent time in Liverpool and therefore, we'd been treated like family.

To be honest, the real bonus was letting me leave my shoes and socks on walking round his tomb as my feet smelt like rotting corpses. Everyone else had to take their shoes off as a mark of respect, except Tony and me. Thank Jah for that.

We explained to our new-found brothers about 'losing' our money and weed and it wasn't long before he took us down a path and into a sugarcane field.

"Oh fuck, we're getting bumped again, lad", Tony said quietly, as this guy started to push aside the long stems of sugarcane. The cane cracked as we made a path and soon we came to a round clearing with huge weed plants towering above us.

"Take what you need boys", said our new brother in stoned, Jamaican patois. We looked at each and smiled nodding our heads first, then burst out laughing uncontrollably.

"What's so funny?" he asked us, snapping a huge, arm's length bud off the nearest plant.

"Fuckin hell kid, we thought you were gonna have us off, you know, just like the police did before."

"Fuck da Poleece boys, Irie, Jah-Rasta-der-fer-re-en. You wid us now, fuck da Po-lee-ce", he shouted, lighting a huge spliff to produce a plume of dark-edged smoke around his head.

Relief filled us instantly as he passed us the huge, lit spliff. After we'd sat on the rocks and smoked enough weed to knock a whole zoo out, we decided it was time to head off back to Negril.

The Zoo

Day after day there seemed to be some sort of adventure or occurrence in Jamaica. We discovered *'Pier One'* club in Montego Bay, which was an old rickety, wooden port building with connecting jetties to different bars and clubs. Amongst the dirty whining locals, two white boys stood out like sore thumbs for sure but we didn't care one bit. We met a guy at the bar called Femo, who owned a water sports centre, and he invited us to come and check out his brand new jet-skis when we had time.

The next day, we took Femo up on his offer and turned up at his beach shop-come-centre at 11 o'clock to test his brand new machines. He was busy with something but introduced us to Alan who was going to take us out on the navy blue, clear water for a spin. He told us we couldn't go outside the bay and pointed to landmarks either side and said we had to stay between the lines at all times.

After about 10 minutes on the choppy but clear blue water, we headed to the landmarks on the right-hand side of the bay. As we looked back, Alan and Femo were both waving frantically to get us to come back to the shore. Tony gave me a quick glance and shouted over to me,

"Come on lad, let's fuck off. What are they gonna do, kill us?" We both nodded and headed off at full speed to the next bay. As I looked behind me, Alan and Femo were heading towards us also at full pelt, but they were at least 10 minutes behind.

We decided to hug the coastline to get a better view of our uncharted waters and after about 10 minutes, noticed something very peculiar on one of the beaches. What looked like a huge trapeze frame and net was set up and someone was bouncing on the net as if they'd fallen. We both pointed to the bouncing body and steered our skis directly in that direction to get a better look. We got to about 50ft from the beach, when we also noticed a built-up black-and-white platform which had semi-naked people with hats and sashes on. It took a minute for me to work out that this was a game of human, naked chess. Fuck me, this was weird.

The trapeze-bouncing body was naked too and it wasn't long before we'd been joined by local, armed security telling us we would be arrested if we didn't leave immediately. Tony was shocked as by now the Bishop and Castle had joined us with their bollocks hanging out in the cool Jamaican breeze. This was weird, but we both noticed several stunning women all butt-naked and smiling in our direction; we needed to explore this beach again. As the armed guards shoved our jet skis back in the water, Tony asked,

"What's this place called, mate?"

"Da Zoo", replied the guard as he carried on deeper into the water and told us to go quickly.

Just as we'd pulled away from the weird beach, we were met by Alan and Femo who were furious at our lack of respect for their machines and generosity. After a barrage of shouting and checks of the brand new skis, we all headed back to Femo's beach shop to try and mend our new-found friendship. It took us 30 minutes and a crisp $100 bill to calm Femo down and for him to then fill us in about the weird, naked beach resort in the next bay.

'Yer boys, da Zoo is about 20 minutes away, but ya won't get in coz it couples only, it's called *Hedonism,* Femo said, once he'd calmed down and folded the 100 dollar bill into a tiny square.

Within an hour of us leaving, we'd managed to get the phone number for the Sandals' resort the locals called 'Da Zoo' in Negril. The receptionist told us that the policy of couples was only relaxed on a Thursday evening, when there was a theme party and for us to be allowed in; we would need to book in person at least 24 hours in advance.

As soon as the phone was put down, Tony and I got our passports and cash and headed to The Zoo, as it was Tuesday afternoon and Thursday's theme party was looming. Seventy five dollars each for a double room that was all inclusive was paid for rapidly with the enthusiasm of a new adventure now on the cards.

The Sandals' resort was only 30 minutes from our Negril beach house so we had no excuses to be late. Tony was eager as fuck that morning, he was up early on the beach jogging and by 10 o'clock he was showered, dressed and rushing about getting his shit together as I'd slept in. By the time I got ready and ate breakfast, it was 11am and Tony was prompting me to leave.

We arrived at 11.40 and another $50 bill persuaded the attractive check-in receptionist to alter our reservation and we checked into our upgraded room. Right, we were all set now in our superb suite and of course, the room service menu was checked out. Once we'd realised the food was all inclusive too, we sampled everything our stomachs could fit in, then headed off to explore our new surroundings.

The trapeze, which had caught our eye initially was the first port of call and luckily there was a wooden, thatched-roofed beach bar right next to the huge, metal frame and net. There was no-one around except for the barman polishing glasses and checking stock.

We got speaking to him, he called himself Fred and promptly poured two huge Remy Martins with slabs of ice and just left the bottle next to our drinks and told us to help ourselves

'Oh yea, I like this place', said Tony, raising his glass and scanning the sun-drenched sandy, palm-tree-laden beach.

After meandering down paths, tracks and sand hills, we eventually ended up back at 'Da Zoo' and prepared ourselves for the up-and-coming themed evening. Toga night was the first event and we got ourselves two seats by the bar, which just happened to be situated next to the stairs to the huge stage.

Fred the barman from the now-closed beach bar earlier on was working in the main lounge bar where Tony and I sat. Within a minute, there was a full bottle of Remy Martin, a bucket of ice and two huge brandy glasses in front of us. 'Result', I thought immediately, as I reached into my pocket and gave Fred a crisp

$50 bill. His face lit the whole bar once he unfolded the note as he walked away.

The brandy fuelled our evening to the max and it wasn't long before we decided to get involved by escorting the female, toga competition winners up and down stage stairs, then back to their seats for the odd drink, oh, and a look at their often-huge tits which were out for all to see. This was Hedonism after all.

It wasn't long before most of the toga-clad guests de-robed and left mine and Tony's chins on the floor in utter disbelief. The sight of 200 naked men and women was astonishing, eye popping and scary too. It took about an hour for everyone to leave the main bar and head off back to their rooms.

Tony and I sat at the bar blubbering drunken shite to Fred the barman for about 40 minutes, until Fred asked us,

"Are you not goin' da beach club?"

"Which beach club?"

"Da hotel beach club were da party at." Fred said, wiping the bar down with a cloth.

"Boys… da real party is wid da bubbles down below." Fred pointed to a sign in the hotel lobby with a huge arrow and 'BEACH CLUB PARTY' written in black capital letters on a white board.

We followed the arrows until we bumped into two, leather-studded, underwear-clad American women holding a choke chain with some fella being walked like a dog at the end of it. Fucking weird!

After our initial gasp, then trying not to laugh, we followed this crazy threesome to the underground beach club, to be greeted by Hedonistic madness. Wall-to-wall bondage, gimp masks, whips and chains welcomed us to this seedy, foamy-bubble-filled club.

After an hour, Tony and I had seen enough and made our way back to the main lounge and Fred. We still had half a bottle of brandy left. We'd already had more or less a bottle each, but after seeing America's version of human Crufts, we both needed a lot more. There was open sex in every nook and cranny of that hotel that night and two 25-year-old Scousers dressed like match thugs were there to witness it.

Once is enough in my book, so that box was ticked and taken off our bucket list and we departed the Sandals beach resort in Negril the following morning.

After a few days of topping up our tans, it was time for us to head home on our scheduled flight from Montego Bay back to Blighty.

On arrival, we were greeted by a Customs Officer and taken to one side for the usual, but unusual, search and dressing down of sorts by two, suited officers. I stood and stared without saying a word as they tried to make conversation with me about why only two of us remained from a party of six lads. Fuck them, I thought, they're supposed to be detectives, let them figure it out. After 10 minutes or so I was sent on my way to be greeted by Tony who just had the same treatment. The writing was now clearly on the wall, so it was time for rapid changes.

Within a week of being home, I'd sold my house, moved into my sister's in Norris Green and had a proper run in with Shitty Arse over me fucking off to Jamaica without telling him. The run in was that bad, I decided to fuck off back to Jamaica for another month, but this time alone. Was I fuck going say a word to anyone about where I was going, the news of my best mate was all over the TV by now. It had gone national for some reason and I was on the move.

I didn't arrive back home until mid-March, I'd decided to return to London and stay with family and friends in North London for a few weeks. I ended up with my Cockney pals who I'd met in Ibiza years earlier and started to make inroads into networking to another level.

They introduced me to some proper, local people who took a shine to my cheeky, Scouse humour. One door always leads to another in my game, and I always made sure it was kept open. That's how I did business, plus I needed to make a fresh start as it was as warm as a baker's oven in July for me back in Liverpool.

When I eventually arrived back home and realised that Shitty Arse was becoming the source of my stress levels rising, I had to start to make some serious decisions.

The Liverpool Echo had a headline story about Merseyside Police receiving advice and training from the New York Police Department. *Zero Tolerance* was their aim and Liverpool had been targeted as well as Manchester, as it was recently christened *'Gunchester'* by the national media. Things were about to change in my city. Shitty Arse and the police were now causing me to rethink what, where and how I should carry on.

I knew the second I finished reading the article that things were going to change forever in my world. Not only was the writing on the wall, it was on the front page of the Liverpool Echo, but the lads called this paper The Police Times, so we all knew trouble was brewing.

1995 – 2000

May 1995 was an eventful month as I'd moved into a waterfront apartment and Everton had reached the FA Cup Final at Wembley. Their opponents were Manchester United who were red-hot favourites to lift the trophy, but half of my city had other ideas.

I was still on red alert with my pal due to appear in court over the nightclub shooting, so while I sat and looked out over the Mersey towards Birkenhead, I reflected how things had turned out for me. It was a Friday evening and the sun was dropping towards the Bay of Liverpool as I looked right out of my fourth-floor penthouse apartment.

It was one of those really golden skies that when we were kids, me and Dougie (who was still on remand) would say, 'Red sky at night - Birkenhead's on fire – result'. If only he was here with me now to enjoy this experience.

The rabbit-warren of a building I'd moved into was perfect for my needs; security cameras everywhere, a lofty position to view the surrounding area, plus there was 24-hour-manned security on the entrance, of which there was only one. I'd had all the security cameras wired into my three TVs, so I could tune in at any given moment and also had a 24-hour looped recorder fitted just in case I missed anything.

No stone was left unturned regarding safety. To be honest, it was a requirement now as I'd been grafting for nearly 10 years and word travels quickly when you're earning money in my area. Although I never told anybody anything, just being a man about town was getting me noticed by the card markers of this world. I'd already had a high loss the month before which landed me a £50 grand bill for my considerable lack of judgment.

There were now a few nightclubs in Liverpool town centre to challenge *The State* monopoly of drug-crazed nights out. James Barton had opened *Cream,* whilst the old Bierkeller on Renshaw Street, Mount Pleasant, had opened up and called itself *051*. There were also loads of bars-cum-food houses opening up in the Albert Dock area, which in a way widened the scope of the city nightspots in a short space of time. With me now living on city-centre's doorstep, this new scene became a big part of my social life.

Tony Grant had broken into Everton's first team squad and was a regular visitor to my penthouse boudoir. He was more than welcome; in fact I gave him his own key as sometimes I'd be away on graft and he did love the occasional off-the-cuff party. My full-to-the-brim fridge catered for all his late-night needs when he was out and about in town.

Once Everton had beaten Manchester United with a Paul Rideout goal and lifted the FA Cup, I knew it wouldn't be long before I received a call to make sure the alcohol levels were topped up and the place was clean. I was buzzing, watching a kid from our estate bouncing around Wembley's hallowed turf with his team mates - even if it wasn't my club, I still enjoyed it.

On the August Bank Holiday, my mate, Ste G and I decided to have a weekend bender on the Garys. These were ecstasy tablets now renamed after the Liverpool FC, dark-haired centre back, Gary Ablett, which obviously rhymed with tablet. Thank God he wasn't a bad player otherwise he'd only be remembered for making the masses off their cakes most weekends and not as a footballer.

After a heavy Friday night out down County Road and then off to town dancing our socks off, we were both ready for round two on Saturday. The *051* was our destination, after a bar crawl round Mathew Street. As soon as Ste and I bopped into *051* and made our way to the bar across the huge dance floor, I noticed a girl I'd fancied for years dancing with her mates. I couldn't believe it when Ste stopped to talk to her mates and left me standing right in front of this cute, sexy, dark-haired beauty who I had the hots for. I was off my barnet so it wasn't long before I said hello and told her I'd fancied her since our schooldays.

She used to catch the bus round the corner from my house in Faversham Road when she went to school. That was where I knew her from. Her name was Lisa and after about half an hour of me trying my best to persuade her to let me take her home, she told me that she was seeing somebody; in fact he was a professional boxer. I don't half pick them, don't I?

I still wasn't bothered about her situation, I wanted her and I made sure she knew that. Lisa had a friend called Carly, who knew Ste, so we managed to get them to come back to my apartment after the *051* had finished. I sat and spoke to Lisa for hours and had persuaded her to think about her situation with her boxer fella.

Carly and Lisa left my place when the birds were singing at dawn, and to be honest, I was singing too. I'd met the woman I wanted to be with, she was everything and more, fuck me, I'd had a touch. We both had each other's numbers and decided to leave it a few days before we contacted each other.

Three weeks had passed and I went to look for a shirt in my wardrobe and had to fight my way through loads of Lisa's dresses. Yes, in less than a month we'd become inseparable and somehow without anything being said, Lisa had well and truly moved in. It just seemed natural and we both felt the same way about each other.

She was of the belief that I had a joinery company and didn't need to know that I was a grafter, really. To be honest, the joinery business was a product of the £50 grand debt that had been put on me, so I ended up owning it by default. That's how things sometimes worked when you grafted. If the money wasn't there, then something had to be handed over, so soft arse me ended up with a load of wooden window-frames. Maybe I should fit them in my new apartment so I can see people coming next time; the bigger the better.

The main thing was that I was happy and settled with someone I loved dearly. It's weird to think that I never went looking for it and found it more or less on my doorstep. After a trip to Goa in India, we decided to move into a house together in Birkdale, Southport and start a family.

A few days after returning from Goa, the headlines in the Liverpool Echo told me that my best mate, Dougie, had just received 15 years for attempted murder. It was like an anvil landing on my head from a distance. I'd been mates with him since he moved into our road in the late 70s. We'd run away together, gone to the match together, more or less lived in each other's house and now he was heading to a Category A jail. I was wounded to my core.

I obviously couldn't go to the courtroom, but I did have someone there keeping me informed, so I knew about his lengthy sentence before the headlines appeared in the local news and on Sky TV. Shitty Arse was around telling me the dos and don'ts again regarding me going to jail, or, more to the point, avoiding it. I didn't need him telling me something I already knew, especially as I was devastated over Dougie. I'd made sure he was looked after though, it was the least I could do until he got out.

I decided to settle down properly with Lisa after realising life was too unpredictable and short. It took about 18 months to sort my life out and this took me to 1997 and new pastures.

I kept grafting my bollocks off and got roped into doing more work for Shitty Arse; he wouldn't leave me alone for a minute. Every opportunity I had to earn money elsewhere, I did, without letting him know. He was always there with his one-way-traffic ideas but somehow I'd end up deeper and deeper in his tangled web. I knew I needed out, just to become my own person, really. He seemed to have a hold on me and he knew it. It really started to grate on me that I was so loyal to this fucker.

Lisa and I tried for a baby and it wasn't long before she was pregnant. Unfortunately she lost it early on in the pregnancy. She was devastated and it took loads of reassurance from me for her to get over it. I was gutted too, but Lisa needed me to be strong for her at that moment. A few months later and she was pregnant again. This time we kept it quiet, just in case, we didn't want to tempt fate.

Christmas '97 was approaching and the arrival of our first child was now on all our family's lips and the date of June or July 1998 had been confirmed for the birth. Everything went well and I kept grafting my arse off with any drugs I could get my hands on early in 1998.

It wasn't long before I'd noticed a few dodgy cars and familiar faces appear around me as I bounced around the streets and estates of Liverpool. As I was stoned to fuck most days, the situation was heightened and the gravity of my recent sightings made me morph into single-cell-protection mode. Cars were bought and scattered over the city without raising eyebrows as were mountain bikes, and the appropriate clothing to make me look like a knob-head mountain biker was also purchased and placed in the boots of the cars. All my pals thought I'd lost the plot when I told them I'd travel in the boot of their cars if they need me to go anywhere with them.

I knew what I'd seen and I knew what I had to lose if the shit hit the fan. I wasn't ready for another loss, or even worse, prison, no way. Fuck what my so-called mates at the time thought, plus I was looking out for their interests too. Me being ultra-paranoid was a good thing, I thought.

After two weeks of couch surfing and nearly smoking myself into submission, it was time to make drastic manoeuvres to avoid capture as I thought the undercover police operation was tightening its net on me. I had to resort to craziness to make the situation workable. I'd asked the lads who I worked with for help, but their comments just made me aware that no-one gave a fuck, 'Just work through it..' was the pick of the bunch. In fact, all of the comments would appear it the book of *'Fuck you, get me my money',* they'd all be in the Top Ten comments, of that I'm 100% sure.

Home life now was weird. Lisa thought I was out on site with my joinery company most of the time, so I couldn't mention my problems to her, although she knew something was wrong - coming home every other night and heading into the kitchen for a coffee and a huge five skinner was customary. The reasons for not going home all the time were that when I'd lost my followers for the day, home would be an obvious pick-up point for me. I'd sometimes stay away from home for four or five days at a time and tell Lisa I was working away. Safety first, always, that was the only way I could cope with having half a million quid's worth of tackle around me and carry on, while knowing the police had a squad on me. My stress levels went through the roof at times.

Enough was enough, one Tuesday night in March, I'd managed to get rid of all the gear and returned home to find two unmarked cars directly outside my front door. They waited for me to walk up to the front door before saying,

"So you think you're a smart arse, hey?"

I shit myself, I honestly thought they'd grab me and haul me off to the custody suite for the night. They never did though, they just let me know that they were not going to let me give them the run-around. The funny part of it was that I had £15 grand on me in brand new 50s, they'd only needed to search me and I'd have been fucked, but hey ho and all that, their loss was definitely my gain.

When I closed the front door behind me and leaned on it, I sighed long and hard while looking at Lisa lying on the couch with her huge bump now showing. It was decision time. I went up the stairs to check I had my passport and placed 10 grand under Lisa's side of our double bed. When I came back downstairs, I sat next to her and explained that I'd have to go away for a few weeks. She never moaned once but she did raise concerns over her wellbeing once I'd gone. I told her not to worry, that my sisters would be there to check on her, plus there was money for her under the mattress. I made of point of not telling her how much there was as any woman would spend the lot. I also knew that when she realised there enough to last her for a good while, it would ease my absence.

The next morning I was up early to pack a rucksack with a few clothes, said my goodbyes and drove to Manchester Airport without knowing my destination. I couldn't even be arsed to pay attention to my recent followers as I had distance on my mind, five grand in my pocket and my coded, red telephone/address book on me.

Once I'd left the car in the long-stay car park, I made my way to the check-in area to check the departures. One destination jumped out at me on the departure board - *Toronto*. Suddenly things started to click in my head. I knew one of my sister's old flames lived out there somewhere and I had his brother's telephone number in my red book.

It didn't take long before I was calling my sister's ex in Scarborough, Toronto. I woke him up and it took him a while to figure out who I was. He was buzzing when I said I wanted to visit and told me to call back in five minutes.

His name was Tony and he used to have a serious problem on the Nasty (heroin) when he lived in Walton, Liverpool. He had to move otherwise he would have ended up on the street corners with the other junkies back in 90/91. The only money he had with him was what he'd grafted out of his electricity meter from his Council flat. He landed at his aunt's door with a pocket full of 50 pence pieces and now he owned his own decorating company in Toronto. I was greeted by the news that Tony's wife was Head Stewardess with Air Canada and a First Class ticket would be available for standard price at the Air Canada Information Counter. What a result. How fucking jammy am I? The Gods had spoken and given me a champagne-laden journey to Toronto when the night before I was shitting my pants outside my own front door.

The journey was an alcohol-fuelled one, with plenty of first-class food available, which made it pass quickly. The air hostesses made me feel more than welcome as if somehow they knew I was a friend of Tony's. To be fair, everyone was friendly with 6ft 6, blonde-haired, blue-eyed and hilarious Tony.

Cast Away

In New York with John Power

I was greeted by Tony and his pal, Mike, who told me there was a surprise waiting for me back at his house, which was about a 40-minute drive from Toronto Airport. There was remnants of snow all around, especially on the mountain tops in the distance as we made our way down a five-lane highway.

As we approached Tony's house, I was still guessing what the surprise might be but my pleas fell on deaf ears. It wasn't long until I'd entered the kitchen and saw two lads from Sparrow Hall standing in the corner sipping cans of beer, that the surprise was sprung. I had no idea that these lads had also made the trip to Toronto.

"What the fuck are you doing here?" I laughed, giving them the customary bear hug.

"We've been here for a week; fishing, shooting and getting stoned 24/7." Kevin said, passing me a lovely joint of some locally-grown bud. I'd known Kevin since I was a kid. He'd always have a spliff in his mouth, no matter where he was. The other lad was Danny, he was related to Shitty Arse but he was on the button regarding Shitty Arse's controlling nature.

Danny and I always got on like a house on fire, so I knew he wouldn't start reporting back my every move to his totalitarian relative. I still couldn't believe that they were here and Tony's brother, Carl, wasn't; so we decided to chip together and pay for his flight and give him some spends so we could have a proper jolly up. Within two days, there were six drunken, stoned and adventure-seeking Scousers sitting in Tony's Canadian kitchen; plotting our next moves.

We'd noticed in one of the local Toronto papers that the band, *'Cast'* were playing a major venue in the city. Now, Cast hailed from Liverpool and the lead guitarist, Liam Skin Tyson, was from Walton and Carl knew him pretty well. We tore the article out of the paper and noticed it was happening that night. We got our shit together and headed off to Toronto looking for the radio station, as they were doing an acoustic set to promote their gig in the evening, even though it was sold out.

The radio station was located easily enough but they wouldn't let us in, so we parked our arses in the coffee-house directly opposite.

It wasn't long before we noticed a bit of a commotion outside the radio station. We jumped up and went outside to shout to the fellow Scouse lads being mobbed on the opposite side of the road. I couldn't believe it when they immediately dropped what they were doing and ran across the road to buzz off our arrival. I knew Skin, the guitarist, but never really bothered him about his talents or fame, so I was amazed when he made a beeline for me and gave me a massive hug and handshake.

"Fuckin hell lads, what are you doing here?" He asked, with a huge grin on his face.

"We've come to see you play tonight, Skin." I replied rapidly, pulling a ready-rolled bud joint from my jacket pocket.

"Have you got weed, lads?" the rest of the band seemed to ask simultaneously, as they noticed me and Kevin sparking up on the sidewalk outside the coffee shop. The smoking ban had just been implemented in Toronto so there were plenty of people smoking outside, which gave us some cover to openly blaze up.

An hour later, we were all sitting on Cast's tour bus outside the city-centre venue smoking our balls off and acquiring more hard drugs for the night ahead. By this time I was friendly with all the band's entourage and I'd taken a shine to Pete, the bass player, who seemed to be on my wavelength.

John Power was the main man in the band, but he seemed a bit standoffish; well, I suppose the band was his baby and he needed to protect his interests. Anyway, the lads had got comfortable on the tour bus and were enjoying the banter flying about.

The concert came and went and we had a proper buzz until the early hours of the next morning. The following day, the band had a day off and were due to head off to New York via Buffalo. I had such a good laugh with them that I persuaded Danny, Carl and Kevin to head off to New York to meet up with them again. The Mercury Lounge, New York City was our destination.

The train journey from Toronto to New York via Buffalo was as rowdy as fuck. Danny and Kevin argued from the get-go about anything and everything. Carl and I decided to move about 20 seats down as it was getting a bit embarrassing at times.

Heads turned, tuts were frequent and Carl and I cringed quite a lot. We obviously had our own stash of bud on us, so when I shouted back to the arguing fuckers that Border Patrol had stopped the train, they redirected their bitterness towards me and didn't believe it. Now I wasn't having it at all and shouted back at them,

"Well, 10 fellas with navy blue jumpsuits, guns, dogs and *'BORDER PATROL'* emblazoned in bright orange across their chest and backs have just stopped the train and are now getting on, ya silly fuckers." Fuck me, Danny and Kevin started a blazing row as Kevin had popped his head out of the top window and noticed the Border Patrol too.

He tried to tell Danny, but he wasn't having it at all and decided to bounce an apple off Kevin's massive head just as the centre doors opened in our carriage to reveal two stunned Border Patrol officers, with their hands on their holsters. 'Oh shit, this can only go two ways', I thought immediately, as the officers moved swiftly and meaningfully towards the rear of the carriage.

'"What seems to be the problem here, folks?" asked the officer, in a slow American accent to Danny and Kevin, who by now were as quiet as mice. I jumped up and explained we'd been travelling for days and the difficulty was due to tiredness, plus I'd personally make sure there'd be no more problems. It seemed to work and after they'd checked our passports and made sure we all knew that the consequences for troublemakers would be a night or two in a Buffalo jail. That made all of us shut up on the spot. Not for long though, the silence was broken five minutes later when Kevin exploded on Danny over the apple-throwing incident; he wasn't happy.

I had another two hours of this before we arrived in New York. The worst part of it was I'd had to dump the stash of bud back at the border once I'd seen the dogs on the side of the train track. I only had about enough for two joints hidden where the sun don't shine, as back up.

The arguing kept us all feeling uncomfortable. By now, everyone on the train was getting thoroughly pissed off with this constant slanging match. There was a gorgeous-looking, short-haired woman who'd got on a few stops after Buffalo, sitting right in front of me whose eyes were rolling every time Danny and Kevin piped up. She was fiddling with her phone and handbag on the table right in front of me and I noticed a small sealed bag of bud in her side compartment to her bag. 'Is right', I thought to myself, 'a weed smoker.'

Now anyone who smokes weed seriously always likes to help fellow smokers out in their hour of need. She knew Carl and I were friends of the two rowdy fuckers, but she never said anything to us about it, so I thought it appropriate to say something to break the ice, especially as I knew we had something in common.

"I'm sorry about our two mates arguing all the time, but they've had two heavy days and nights partying, I'd just like to apologise on their behalf."

"That's ok, it's not your fault." She said, in a distinctive New York accent.

"So you're from New York then?" I replied.

"Yeah, where are you boys from?"

"Liverpool, England", we both replied.

"Wow, I thought you boys were from Ireland or Scotland, that's a strange accent, I like it", she said, smiling and rummaging through her handbag again to find her phone. By now, Danny and Kevin had kicked off again, this time it was about Caesar and the Roman Empire. To be fair to them, they were both very well-read, not your usual estate-fodder mentality; these lads knew their stuff.

We introduced ourselves to the New Yorker and she replied with a gentle handshake and said,

"Well, I'm Helena, as we've now met, I'd like to say your two fuckin' friends are annoying."

"Yeah, we know that Helena, and as we said earlier, we apologise on their behalf", I said, looking around at the now-quiet Danny and Kevin. They'd noticed that we had started talking to Helena and decided to come over and investigate; then most probably to argue.

Danny was first over and offered his hand and introduced himself, to be greeted by a sarcastic and rapid,

"Go fuck yourself, Caesar". It was brilliant and put Danny in his place in a millisecond. Carl and I nodded and offered our hands for high fives, to which Helena duly responded with loud slaps. Kevin opted to say nothing and just sat close to us, trying to earwig the conversation. Danny headed back to his seat to lick his ego wounds as Helena had given him a proper mouthful of common-decency etiquette.

On the approach into New York, we had gained Helena's respect and she agreed to take us for 'dime bags' of weed from her neighbourhood over in Queens. This was going to be a weird experience.

The amount of homeless, living in makeshift shanty towns under railway bridges on the outskirts of New York was a total shocker and by this time, the mood had changed and Danny and Kevin had landed back on Earth from their time on Planet Bollocks. Helena gave us directions to Queens and her mobile number and told us to call her once we'd checked into our hotel, which was apparently uptown. We said our goodbyes to the attractive-and-welcoming Helena and headed out of New York Central Station to Madison Square Garden and beyond.

Lexington Avenue was a seriously long avenue; in fact we walked for nearly an hour until we came to the junction on 53rd and Lexington. As we stood outside our hotel, I looked up to the skies to try and catch a glimpse of the top of our hotel, which seemed to touch the edge of low cloud lying above us. Once we'd checked in, we jumped into the elevator but had to get out on the 40th floor to get in another elevator to our 47th floor, four-bed, luxury suite.

Danny was immediately off into the bathroom and came out off his barnet. He must have had some Charlie stashed somewhere because the froth around his mouth made him look like a rabid dog. The rapid change in his demeanour, behaviour and his jaw angle made us all wonder what the fuck had just happened. It was like Clark Kent going into the telephone box and coming out dressed as Superman, only Danny had turned into an over-opinionated, drug-crazed lunatic.

He switched on the massive TV, raided the mini-bar and plonked himself down on the huge, comfy armchair, with the look of a medicated, institutionalised patient all over his face. Kevin and I headed for the window to do the customary look-out-of-the-window ritual and surveyed the new view and surroundings.

The ant-like scene moving around, 47 floors below us seemed a million miles from our spliff-smoke, filled suite. We smoked the last two joints and had a few expensive, mini-bar beers, while Danny chirped on about the death rate in New York (only because that's what was on the local news at that time). Kevin and I decided to make the trip downtown to Queens and catch the 'J' train to meet up with Helena so we could top up our weed levels.

We explained to Danny that Carl was going to keep him company while we headed out. As soon as we'd stopped speaking, Danny leapt up on the armchair ranting and raving about the recent spate of drive-by machete attacks in Queens. He spat froth whilst crazily repeating,

"Lads, you might get killed, the response time for shootings was minutes as the local thugs have resorted to drive-by machete attacks to defeat the response time. Lads, it's fuckin heavy you know, I wouldn't go."

By this time, Danny was highly self-medicated on Charlie, weed and beer and was at times speaking another language. We needed weed and that was that; fuck the death rate, fuck machetes, Kevin and I were heading downtown to grab some bud, but also to get away from the now-overpowering Danny.

We followed Helena's handwritten directions and landed in a huge concrete square outside a train station in Queens. It was lively as fuck, with activity on every corner; we must have looked totally alien to the locals as we made our way to the phone box on the far side of the square. We spoke to Helena, who said she would be about 15 minutes or so and told us to sit outside the station.

While we walked back, there was a screech of car tyres and police sirens rang out. Within 20 seconds, all hell had broken loose with a gang of black lads and four police cars in the far left corner of the square. Before I could say anything, Kevin had turned on his heel and was walking rapidly into the eye of the trouble.

"Kev, what the fuck are ya doing?"

"I'm gonna see what's happenin' lad", he replied in a cocky way, whilst seemingly gaining a spring in his step, Liam Gallagher-esque.

"Are you mad? Are you FUCKING MAD?" I bellowed, grabbing hold of his forearm with both hands, trying to pull him in the opposite direction. Now bear in mind we're two Scousers out of our comfort zone trying to score weed on foreign soil and there are police everywhere with loaded guns. Then there's the environment we've ended up in, Queens New York, gang territory and volatile.

It wasn't long before we'd managed to grab the attention of three black lads wearing vests, bandanas and baggy jeans. They came over and looked us up and down while sucking their teeth at us. Kevin was too busy observing the ensuing scuffle with the police to notice the attention we'd attracted. When he turned around and they were about three feet away from us.

"Alright lads, we're on holiday from Liverpool, we're Scousers," Kevin said quickly, as if just being from Liverpool was a sort of walk-over. Fuck me, they didn't look impressed.

"What the fuck you sayin' boy?" The tallest lad said, with these black eyes that had somehow rolled down his face to gaze down upon us with a look of intent.

"It's ok lads, we're going", I said, to ease the tension, grabbing Kevin's arm again to keep him close to me. Out of nowhere came Helena to the rescue and totally took the danger out of the situation.

"Fuck me, Little Caesar, are you still causing fucking trouble?" Helena reeled off to Kevin, while acknowledging the three black lads with a nod and a discrete wave.

"Come on lads, follow me", she said, with a huge smile on her beautiful face. "You sure like confrontation, hey?" she mumbled to Kevin.

I wasn't going to let Kevin answer that as he most probably would have said the wrong thing, so I intervened with a brisk,

"Thank you, Helena," and changed the conversation to our hotel on Lexington Avenue rapidly, while giving Kevin a look as if to say, 'Shut the fuck up, you muppet.'

She took us to the local convenience store, which was more like a sealed vault. There were items for sale if you could manage to see through the thick, metal-barred Perspex counter. We walked to the back of the shop and Helena knocked on a black metal door. The shutter came down immediately to reveal a stoned-looking black face with dreadlocks. We never heard what Helena said to this fella, but she put her hand out to us and said,

"Guys, give me $50."

Kevin already had the money in his hand and passed it over, quickly. As soon as she'd handed the money over, the shutter was slammed shut for about 30 seconds, then it flew open and the Rasta guy pushed five, small dime bags of some sort of bud across the flap to Helena. We took them from her and opened one of the plastic, press-seal bags to unleash the aroma of some strong-smelling weed into our nostrils. This was good shit, oh yeah, we'd had a belter of a result.

We gave Helena another $100 and asked her would she take us back for 10 more bags. She obliged and before we knew it, we were sitting in Helena's tiny New York Queens apartment with her boyfriend, Paul, smoking our newly-acquired stash. We spent about an hour chatting and invited them to the concert in the Mercury Lounge later that night to meet the rest of the lads, plus the band.

Helena refused on the spot, citing Danny, or as she called him, Caesar, as the main put off. To be fair, she had a valid point, I didn't really want Danny to be forcing his opinion on every Tom, Dick or Harry around New York. Anyway, we said our thankyous, goodbyes, swapped details, then headed off to catch the J train back to see the lads. In a way, we both had a sense of pride and fulfilment returning with the weed.

The concert was an unbelievable experience as we were treated like superstars by the staff at the Mercury Lounge, and the fans too. Cast were on form and we partied late into the night; well, Kevin and I did as by the time we returned to our hotel earlier on, Danny had turned Carl into a car crash with the amount of Charlie they'd ironed out. Their loss was our gain as it was much easier for two of us to blend in. Danny would have cramped our style if he'd been there anyway, so it turned out to be perfect.

We made sure the band lads had enough weed as they were heading to Oregon as soon as they'd packed their kit onto their silver tour bus. Kevin and I were the last two people to leave the venue. We jumped onto the tour bus rotten drunk and blagged the driver to drop us off over the other side of the Hudson River, which was closer to Lexington Avenue.

After a 20-minute journey, we said our drunken farewells to the band and their crew as we almost fell off the bus into a busy New York street. It was 4am, but this road was oozing life and noise. Kevin was trying to persuade me into carrying on with our party in some unknown venue in the city that never sleeps, but I had other ideas. I was fucking starving and in need of hot food, while Kevin just wanted more alcohol. We argued for about 10 minutes until it got a bit heated, in fact, we ended up in each other's face, I wasn't going to just leave him but I wasn't going to go bouncing around New York City at 4.30 am on the prowl.

Out of nowhere appeared a yellow cab on the opposite side of the road with the window down. Kevin and I were about to come to drunken blows, when we heard a Scouse accent,

"E r lads, ger in 'ere, I'll take you for a bevvie and food." We both stared at the cab, when the driver's door opened and a tall, slender fella waved his arm at us and said, in broad Scouse , "Come 'ed lads, I'll take you, I'm from Bootle, where are you from?"

Fuck me, the New York yellow cab driver was from Bootle. We bounced over to the taxi laughing our drunken heads off. What were the odds of us bumping into the only Scouse taxi driver in New York? Pretty slim, but we were now heading to his local, late-night haunt for food and refreshments.

He introduced himself as Terry from Marsh Lane, Bootle, which is in North Liverpool and a stone's throw away from Liverpool Docks in Seaforth, it's not too far from Norris Green either. I had a full English breakfast at 5am and Kevin had two cans of Carlsberg lager, while we chatted to Terry. We got a few cans to go and Terry said he'd drop us off free of charge as we'd given him a dime bag of our finest bud to help him through the night.

The next morning felt like someone had freeze dried my brain and defrosted it with a blowtorch. Kevin, Carl, Danny and myself headed for Central Station to catch the train back to Toronto hardly saying a word to each other. It even hurt my brain to make conversation with the lads. Fragile was my middle name on the train journey to Toronto that day.

C-Section Day

After a week of rest at Tony's and another few days fishing in an Indian reservation, it was time to pack up and head home to see my pregnant Lisa.

April, May and June was as hectic as the months before I went to Canada. The graft was as heavy as ever and I'd finally paid the outstanding bill for my silly mistake months earlier. The joinery/kitchen company was busy and now needed extra time and money for it to grow. As it had come to me through a problem, I needed to tend to it at all times so that I could make my money back that I'd lost.

The birth of our first child was just around the corner, so my single-cell graft mentality was taking centre stage in my mind. Shitty Arse was still on my case 24/7, he'd really started to grate on me now, but nothing was going to distract me from being there, wholeheartedly for Lisa and our child.

June 28th 1998 was nominated as Caesarean Day. Seven hours into some heavy labour, Lisa was asked some straightforward questions from the midwife;

"Do you know your name, do you know where you are, do you know what day it is?"

"It's fucking Caesarean Day!" Lisa screamed out all over the hospital room. She kept screaming,

"Get this fucking baby outta me noooowwwww", she shrieked, grabbing the gas and air every 10 seconds or so to ease her pain.

Two hours later, we were the proud parents of Paul Michael, who weighed in at 9lb 4ozs. Mother and baby were both fine and before long, Lisa was flat out and I was on my way to wet the baby's head with my brothers and friends. The next day was a bit fuzzy due to the late night, but another night of alcohol and head wetting was arranged with all the lads in town as England were playing Argentina in the World Cup, so with mother and baby fine; off I went.

That night was special for two reasons; obviously the birth of my son but also the birth of another Liverpool centre forward, Michael Owen. He scored a goal that made the world sit up and take notice, oh, and all the Evertonians too. They knew that he'd terrorise them for years to come, and so did I. What a night.

The news of HMP Altcourse opening on the fields and wooded area where I grew up and even ran away to when I was a child was a downer to me. I loved going over to the Annex and the old Jack Sharp golfing driving range in Fazakerley when I was a kid. Now this was going to be semi light even in the darkest of winter months, not to mention all the razor wire, CCTV, patrols and Welsh reprobates roaming the approaching streets and roads – it was a prison for young offenders; Cheshire, Warrington and Welsh criminals. It was classed as a Category B jail but it still didn't help me come to terms with a prison being built on my playground. I was gutted. I was visiting Dougie in prisons up and down the country and to be honest, I hated those places and it made me more aware that I didn't want to end up in any of them. I'd had a near miss a few months earlier with the squad on me and that was still fresh in my mind.

Skunk was now the drug of choice for me. I was smoking my bollocks off every day to the point where it was making me ill. Stress levels were through the roof as I'd had a massive fall out with Shitty Arse and some of his pals, so skunk was my salvation. I was on the SS diet; smoking and stress. Everyone who saw me said I'd lost loads of weight, but I thought I looked fine.

Mountain biking was my fitness kick, nearly every day. I rode everywhere stoned and stressed out, eventually, it would take its toll on me - sooner rather than later too. I had an episode where I passed out and came around freezing cold, but dripping with sweat; it freaked me out big time. I tried not to mention it to anyone as I was embarrassed to fuck about it. They became more frequent and even heavier in the most unusual places; the cinema, my pal's car and in a bar round town one night. The final straw was when I had one in my house.

Lisa was in the living room when I felt it coming on me, so I slowly made my way to the hallway where she couldn't see me and gently sat down with my back resting on the wall. The feeling rushed through my body, only this time my dad was clearly in my mind telling me off. Dad told me not to hang about with Shitty Arse and was specific about other mates of mine. It was like he was there with me; a proper dressing down was going down in my mind.

Suddenly I could hear a voice and saw an outline of a head. My breathing was heavy with my lips pressed together blowing a flow of air out. I panted like crazy until my hearing came back and it was Lisa's voice I could hear.

"Are you ok, come on, just take deep breaths." My vision returned, a bit fuzzy, but it was back. I could feel the sweat rolling off my forehead and down the side of my face and I was shivering profusely.

"Wow, I'm sorry about that", I whispered

"What have you got to be sorry for luv, don't worry, you're ok now", Lisa replied.

Once I'd finally recovered and made my way into the living room, I explained to Lisa that my dad was with me when I passed out, it was totally freaky.

A doctor's appointment was made for me by Lisa immediately once I'd explained it had been happening for a while now. Needless to say, the doctor just said I was fainting and some rest and recuperation was on the cards. He also asked me what line of work I was in, so the 'kitchen business' was my customary reply. Obviously I couldn't tell him I was a drug dealer, as if …

With the words of the doctor ringing in my ears, it was time to ring in some lifestyle changes. I'd picked up the guitar a few years previous, but never really took the time to learn to play properly, so now was the time to pick it up again. My Yamaha, 90-quid guitar was dusted off and tuned in ready for another attempt of me maybe knocking a few tunes out in the months to come. A pal of mine from my Sparrow Hall days, Simo, was the best guitarist I knew, so once I'd learnt a few chords, I decided to pay him a visit.

Simo was a talented fucker who played nearly any instrument you put in front of him, so me landing on his doorstep with seven chords on an acoustic guitar nailed was a minor achievement compared to his skills. To be honest, I was only doing it to chill out a bit more, the thought of me being serious about playing was furthest from my mind. I was 29 years old for fuck sake and just wanted something else in my life; my family, Liverpool Football Club and graft was all I had.

The graft was nearly killing me with the stress levels going through the roof and I needed something for me. My graft consisted of dealing with about six other lads who all had their own families and every night, I would worry about slipping up and putting them in a position of losing their liberty. My uneasiness festered into more worry and then I'd light up a spliff and the worry would quadruple. Instant worry; just add water – in my case, skunk – and you've a recipe for illness and sometimes, depression. The guitar became an antidote to my anxiety and I was loving it too, even though it was the bane of Lisa's life as she had to put up with the scrutiny of my practicing.

'1999; I was dreaming when I wrote this so sue me if it goes too fast, cos life is just a party and parties weren't meant to last'. The Prince song was getting played on every radio station as the millennium was just around the corner. The lyrics for that song also

seemed apt for my life at this time as my decade-long relationship with Shitty Arse was at rock bottom; in fact it was a nasty parting that I'm sure left us both with a bitter taste in our mouths.

Enough was enough, with all the years of mental torture I'd suffered at times, my tether was no longer in sight. The party was over and now the battle started. Everyone who grafted knew I was an earner so I wasn't bothered about lack of work because I knew there were lads out there who knew what I was all about.

Changes were brewing across the board now; home, work and pleasure. Gerard Houllier was Liverpool's manager and had provided the squad with a stealthy attitude and given all the lads something to sing about. Lisa agreed to move house and I'd met a new firm of lads who wanted to work with me.

The fella who previously owned the joinery/kitchen company had brought these lads to me as he owed them, too. We seemed to be a match made in heaven from the beginning, everyone was happy and earning money.

The last thing I needed right now was any aggravation or hiccups as Lisa was just about to give birth to our second child. On the morning of 5th October 1999, in Southport Hospital, Elizabeth Ann Kathleen entered our lives by way of a C-section weighing in at a healthy 9lb 6oz. I wasn't allowed in at the birth but I was the first person to hold her. I was love struck the moment I laid my eyes on her, she was the most beautiful thing I'd ever seen.

The Smell of Petrol

The summer of 2000 brought another house move due to the kids' illness. They had been vomiting every morning for the previous six months. After a protracted and arduous screening programme, our doctors worked out that they were allergic to rape seed which was grown and harvested in the surrounding fields.

Blundellsands in North Liverpool was a perfect choice, as I'd found a four-bedroom, town house that backed directly out onto the beach. The sand hills were now only 50 yards from my back door and the views of the Liverpool Bay and the Welsh mountains behind the Wirral peninsula were fabulous. I couldn't have asked for anything more really, the doctor said,

"Move the kids to somewhere where the air is clean and fresh." In my mind, there was no better area to bring our kids up.

Blundellsands was a middle-class area with some great schools and facilities dotted around. Loads of Liverpool FC players lived nearby and there were plenty of famous names from music, acting and media who socialised locally.

Due to the new graft I'd got myself involved in, most of my time was spent travelling to Amsterdam and Brussels. The lads Peter the Joiner had introduced me to more-or-less allowed me to take full control of their graft, this meant plenty of responsibilities and if the shit hit the fan, you know who'd be in the firing line. Yes, me.

When I wasn't running around Europe, I spent most of my time in the now fully- functional Ruby Studios on Dale Street, Liverpool town centre. My guitar playing was improving but I was nowhere near the standard of Simo, who was frighteningly talented; at least I had a benchmark that was achievable as long as I put the practice in.

With Christmas and New Year around the corner, I treated myself to a Gibson Les Paul gold top and a Takamine limited edition acoustic guitar. That was me happy going into 2001, although Lisa was getting properly pissed off with my constant practice, practice, practice; that's what Simo drilled into me. My fingers would be throbbing with the hours of chords, notes, hammer ons and finger stretching scale exercises. This still never cut the ice with Lisa and it wasn't long before I was barred from playing my guitars at home. She locked the door where my guitars were kept and I was told the consequences of me entering that room would end in a violent manner. She was like a rabid dog. Well, I suppose I could have a few months off while I got back to graft.

When I told Lisa I'd have a break, she made me swear not to go back into the now-locked downstairs room. Her threats were sometimes furious and definitely made me take note, so I did on several occasions; this being one of them.

Football and graft took centre stage now Lisa had put the blocks on music. Gerard Houllier's new-look Liverpool squad looked resilient and strong, with Gary McAllister adding a pinch of class into the mix. Plenty of 1-0 wins were popping up and that gave us optimism in the UEFA Cup and FA Cup. Without looking like world beaters, we seemed not to concede many goals and with Fowler, Owen and the up-and-coming, Steven Gerrard, we always looked like grabbing a goal or two along the way. The shouts of 'Hou let the dogs out, Hou, Hou, Hou', would rattle the Kop to its musical core when we dragged out results from nowhere. I was going to as many games as I could but sometimes graft would pop up to dictate my whereabouts, but occasionally, it coincided with games abroad, which was always a bonus.

There were always a few tricky situations that seemed to be popping up with these new lads I'd been grafting with. I thought I'd gotten away from the mind fuck games that Shitty Arse would play, but apparently not, as these lads were at it too.

Some of my older friends were keeping me informed about who these people really were. In fact, I was being told to tread very carefully and watch my back. As I was earning plenty of money and thought I knew what I was doing, I took the advice with a pinch of salt. Not to say I didn't absorb the information, because I did, it just seemed like who in their right mind would fuck up one of the best earners they'd ever had? We earned serious amounts of cash daily so who would want to mess that up?

Around mid-April I decided I was in need of my guitars, so I rooted out the key and unlocked the downstairs spare room. Lisa had only gone and smashed my Fender 12 stringer to bits and somehow cut every string on my newly-acquired guitars. No wonder she didn't want me near that room and made me swear to leave it be for a while.

Nearly three months had passed since she'd flipped so I was gathering she'd forgotten about it as she'd mentioned fuck all to me. When I called her to let her know I was sifting through my guitar debris, her tone was not that of the previous rabid dog, but more like an apologetic mouse. To be fair, I did take the piss and stay up until the early hours, plus I was always in the studio, so I didn't go mad. I did, however, dine out on the apologetic-mouse attitude that Lisa had adopted once she'd realised what she'd done three months earlier.

Simo was in the studio every day and developing the ideas we had for songs. My time was now split in three directions; family, graft and music. I started spending all my spare time in the studio and got to know some of the other bands in the building quite well.

Tramp Attack were a group of talented lads who had the room opposite ours and The Bandits was another new local set of lads trying to make it on the music scene. They were a great bunch and would always be in our room as we always had the finest-quality skunk. Gary Murphy was the driving force behind The Bandits and always told me they were going to make it; he was ultra-confident and it showed. He couldn't half smoke my fucking skunk too, I didn't mind though as we seemed to take a shine to one another.

I loved people with drive and ambition, it made me tick, so I took to Gary instantly. The rest of the band were sound too, John, the lead singer, and Swee, the drummer, would bounce into our studio like it was their second home; that's how it was, very welcoming. It wasn't long before Tramp Attack split up and Dave McCabe, who seemed to be the cheekiest of the group, formed a new band called the Zutons.

Another band had moved directly above us who hailed from Hoylake, across the Mersey. They called themselves The Coral and it wasn't long before they followed their noses and ended up sitting on our leather sofas, drinking coffee and smoking the finest bud around. Our sense of community was first class amongst all the bands, except for Dave McCabe who had a youthful Huyton 'I don't give a fuck' attitude. I just let him get on with it, he didn't bother me so I hoped he wouldn't piss me off either.

Don't get me wrong, we let on to each other on the stairs and in the clubs and pubs we drank in, but that was as far as it went. Abi, Russ, Sean and Boyan, the rest of the Zutons, were, on the other hand, very polite, approachable and spent plenty of time in our studio having a smoke and socialising. Most of the lads were football fans and tales of past glorious victories often filled the studio, to Simo's dismay. He fucking hated football and only idolised '10cc', the 70s and 80s' Rochdale band.

Liverpool FC had reached both the FA Cup and the UEFA Cup Finals in 2001. Cardiff was the venue for the FA Cup Final as Wembley was being demolished. After we avoided one of the giant-killing episodes against Wycombe Wanderers, our opponents were our North London rivals, the Arsenal.

Dortmund, Germany, was the venue for the UEFA Cup Final and our opponents were the virtually unknown Spanish side, Alavés. The matches were to be played within four days of each other so plans had to be made and tickets obtained pronto. There would be at least seven of us making the continuous journey from Liverpool to Cardiff and then on to Dortmund.

After rallying the footy troops and hiring two motor homes, Tommy, Benjie, Spanner, my nephews Alex and Antony, two of Tommy's mates and myself headed down the M62. With the smell of skunk constantly in the air, we made our way to the first leg of our footy adventure; Cardiff Millennium Stadium.

Arsenal were favourites as they'd been on fire throughout the season and Thierry Henry had terrorised us every time he played. None of that dampened our spirits though. We arrived in Cardiff about midday and once we parked our motor homes, we made contact with our mates and headed off towards the sea of red and white that had partly covered Cardiff.

The Millennium Stadium was packed to the rafters and our seats were fantastic. It's a pity the game wasn't fantastic in the first half as Thierry Henry had missed a hatful of chances and we didn't look like we'd even bothered to turn up.

Arsenal went 1-0 up, to groans of anticipated defeat. Antony and Alex, both looked devastated and had their heads in their hands with 10 minutes to go.

"Paul, this can't happen, it's gonna fuck the rest of the trip up." Alex said, shaking his head in disbelief.

At this point, we won a corner and to our utter delight, Michael Owen popped up in the box with an equaliser. As we all crowd surfed and made our way back to our seats, the atmosphere turned into a cauldron of song and optimism. There were only minutes left when Patrik Berger played a long ball for Michael Owen to chase. He was electric and managed to make his way into the box and somehow still have the legs to finish. WOWWWW! I nearly lost consciousness as Alex, Antony and myself bounced up and down screaming at the top of our voices.

This was Alex's first proper final and as I watched the referee put the whistle to his mouth to confirm our victory, my attentions turned to Alex. His face was a picture which hadn't yet been painted and put into an art gallery. I grabbed both of the boys, holding back joyous tears and joined in with 'You'll Never Walk Alone' and continued our celebrations while the team paraded the trophy around the stadium.

As we walked down the steps and out of the stadium, I had a feeling that I'd just witnessed the FA Cup and the Millennium Stadium robbery; the great FA Cup robbery.

"How the fuck did we just win that?" I asked Alex and Antony. There was no reply as we couldn't stop laughing on the journey back to the motor homes.

Once all the lads had made their way back, it was time for round two of our football odyssey. Tommy had picked a few souvenirs from Cardiff which decorated our Talbot motor home on the journey to Dover to catch the ferry to Calais. He'd somehow acquired a banner that I only saw on the pitch when the Liverpool players celebrated; it read 'LIVERPOOL FC, FA CUP WINNERS 2001'.

The Arsenal fans didn't take too kindly to our banner on the motorway, but we didn't give a flying fuck. About an hour into our journey, Tommy asked did anyone feel as if the suspension on the motor home seemed weird.

'What do you mean weird?' I asked.

He was driving and bounced in his seat a few times and said with a huge grin on his face.

"Well, I don't know about you, but am fuckin floating lads, this suspension is gonna float us all the way to Dortmund after that result."

Everyone started to jump up and down, singing footy songs. Our bus was bouncing towards Dover with the air still filled with skunk combined with the taste of victory.

We'd planned to drive to Amsterdam en route to Dortmund, so once we'd crossed the Channel, I took control of the steering wheel and made my way to Clog Land. We didn't arrive in the Dam until the early hours of Monday morning and everyone was asleep. I didn't wake them as I stocked up on food, weed and alcohol supplies, then I headed off towards Zandfort.

Zandfort was a small coastal town with beautiful beaches about 40 minutes from Amsterdam, it had a Butlins type of resort which was perfect for us all to freshen up - we could only do so much in the motor homes and showering wasn't one of them. Next to resort is the Zandfort Race Track which was the venue for the Grand Prix many years earlier. It was about 4am when I parked up in the open, somewhere on the grounds of the race track. Everyone was fast asleep as I just needed a quiet spot to plot up. Spanner had driven the other motor home in our convoy, so after a skunk joint and a cold Heineken, it was time to get our heads down.

The screeches of high-power touring cars racing round at about 9am woke us all up. We'd only gone and parked in the middle of the fucking track. It took me about two hours to blag a steward to let us out of the heavily-guarded track which Ford had hired it to test their touring car team.

Of course, we didn't leave empty-handed, we had to somehow take souvenirs and mementoes of the touring team. Alex and Antony traipsed around the track with me for an hour while I mooched for free gifts, well, when I say free, I mean stolen, that's standard. Our next stop was going to be Eindhoven as we'd been contacted by some of our pals who were going to meet up for a 'Gaucho's' steak later that night. Now I'd travel to the ends of the earth for a Gaucho's steak, so a two-hour motorway journey was a drop in the ocean to eventually let my nephews into the Gaucho's secret.

After restocking the motor homes with food, ale and the finest quality coffee shop weed, we hit the road and made our way to Dortmund. Spirits were high, and so were we, once we'd delved into the selection of world weeds. It's amazing how different types of weed can give you different buzzes and complement certain situations. Just like a good wine can make certain food taste better on the palate, certain weeds can change the meaning of an innocent conversation into a real-life drama in a second.

It was raining when we arrived in Dortmund on the Wednesday morning. It was match day and there was red and white dotted about the place. The stadium was our first port of call as we only had three tickets between us and the word on the grapevine was tickets could be bought at the stadium.

We parked a stone's throw from the stadium where the red-and-white, travelling army had set up camp, too. Once our door opened, the waft of skunk alerted every pot-smoking Liverpool fan in a 50-metre radius. Alex and Antony were clad in red and white, but there was no need for the rest of us to wear our colours as our eyes were red enough. If that wasn't enough of a dead giveaway, we all seemed to stumble onto the gravel car park.

Tickets were everywhere and we only had to move 20 feet from the car park before we all had one. We could enjoy the day now, even if it was raining. We headed for the usual biggest square in the city, which always attracted the masses. The Germans were on it to fuck and put on live entertainment in the square to try and occupy our wandering minds. Alex and Antony had enough of me and my pals getting stoned, pissed and rowdy and kept asking to head back to the stadium. I knew what it was like to be near your dream destination as I made my way back with Alex and Antony, singing Liverpool songs.

We entered the ground an hour before kick-off and scanned the 80,000-capacity arena from our seats up high behind the goal to the right-hand side of the dugouts. The match-day programme was perused and the electric atmosphere was absorbed. Before we knew it, the teams were on the pitch and the match kicked off. The atmosphere seemed to make time fly and Liverpool went into an early lead.

Gerrard, Owen and our German defender, Markus Babbel, had given us a 3-1 advantage and what seemed like a winning position. Alavés seemed to have other ideas and it wasn't long before they'd pulled it back to 3-3. Our emotions were up the fucking wall as the game went one way, then another. Robbie Fowler scored a belter fourth for us and sent us crowd surfing, but that was short-lived. Alavés had only gone and equalised again, 4-4, the UEFA Cup Final was 4-fucking-4 and my nerves were shot.

The referee blew the whistle for full time, leaving us gasping for breath and wondering what excitement was around the corner. Alavés had a man sent off just before full time and that should give us the upper-hand in the Golden Goal period of extra time. Whoever scored first were the winners, that was UEFA's new rule in the competition and now Liverpool and Alavés lay on the UEFA dissecting slab like lab rats. Next goal's the winner, it's what we played as kids in Faversham Road 20 years earlier; it was pulsating stuff.

Five minutes into Golden Goal time, Alavés had another player sent off and Gary McAllister put the ball down to deliver a free kick into the Alavés box. Would you believe it, the free kick seemed to miss everyone but somehow end up nestling into the back of the net and sent every Liverpool fan into sheer delight and relief. There was about 40,000 Liverpool fans in the stadium, but it felt like 80,000 once all the singing and celebrations started. Alex and Antony were buzzing and couldn't stop smiling on the way back to the motor homes.

On the journey home from Dortmund, we had a bit of an incident on the Dutch border which was dealt with by humour. We couldn't give a fuck really as we'd somehow robbed the FA Cup and sneaked the UEFA Cup to add to the Carling Cup won earlier in the year. Once we were allowed to leave and head home, we had a run in with a pigeon on the motorway. It flew across our motor home but never quite made it. It smashed into the left hand upper corner and cracked the windscreen. When we pulled over to survey the damage the pigeon had left a greasy outline of its last living body shape on our windscreen. It was exactly the same shape as the Liver Bird, it was like a sign from above. We couldn't stop laughing as we continued the journey home.

Back to Graft

Money was rolling in and, apart from my family, nothing else mattered. My new work pals were making my proper friends edgy and I was still being warned about their dubious nature. Stories about different people were ten a penny, but I always thought there were three sides to a story; their side, your side and the truth, which would be somewhere in the middle. I needed to make my own mistakes anyway, not on purpose of course, but you have to grow up, and mistakes are a part of life. Give me a man without mistakes and I'll give you a slap around the head and tell you to 'leg it'. There's no such thing.

A couple of months of solid graft came to an abrupt end when my not-so-new working pals had fixed a meeting way off the beaten track. I turned up beaming with life and asked them what the new graft was. I'd been enquiring about finding some sort of farm building to start a new line of work and they'd found the perfect site with the perfect owner. With that in mind, I bounced in the back of their car with my Big Audio Dynamite CD in hand, to be greeted by smiling faces and handshakes.

We drove up to what seemed like a few outbuildings on a working farm and parked up on the black, stony car park. The two lads led me into a huge barn for me to be greeted with a smash on the back of the head that nearly knocked me unconscious. Before I got my senses back, I was dragged like an animal into the corner of the darkened barn. I could hear walkie-talkies in the background, so my initial thought was police, but that notion was soon put to bed. I was dragged to my feet, handcuffed and my face sprayed with CS gas from close range.

My eyes, nose and throat began to burn like fuck, then I was doused with petrol and punched in the back of the head with a knuckleduster. My legs buckled but I stayed on my feet while I tried to tuck my head into my shoulder and wipe my eyes. I could still hear the walkie-talkies, then a light was shone into my face to reveal a snub-nose revolver about two inches from my face. Fuck me, this was serious. I could only see the gun through squinted eyes, and that's when the talking started, or should I say shouting.

"Fuckin' grab his hands, will ya!" One of these bastards hissed furiously, while dragging my coat collar sharply to knock me off balance. I fell to my knees and was pulled back up with all three of these fellas up close to my face.

"Right, we wanna know who's got the fuckin' money and tell us what names you've got them under in your phone." I couldn't make out who was doing what as a mixture of CS gas, petrol, blood and fear had impaired my vision and seemed to be buzzing round my head.

"What the fuck are you doing this for, there's no need?" I blurted out through petrol-spurting lips. "I thought we were supposed to be mates." I said repeatedly, trying to engage them in talking instead of treating me like some Al Qaeda commander who'd burnt their family alive. The feeling of fear dissipated into numbness and shock as more petrol was poured over my head to stop me from talking.

"Right, here's your fuckin' phone, so who owes the most money?" One of them shoved the bright screen of my graft phone into my face.

"I can't see, I can't see, you'll have to wipe my eyes", I pleaded with them, as I wanted this to be over with. The burning was even more intense now as the petrol had got into the deep gash in my head. The stinging pain just added to the perilous cloud that had engulfed my space. I was fighting for survival. That's when I was hit in the side of my temple with fuck knows what, all I knew at that point was that my whole life flashed by in a nano-second. It hurt, it hurt so badly I couldn't feel anything but I could hear them shouting constantly.

"Who owes the most money, tell me now … you've got five seconds then I'm gonna start cutting your fuckin fingers off one by one, then you won't be playing any guitar." I was kicked in the chest by the sole of a shoe, which threw me backwards.

"Go and get the secateurs and we'll cut this fucker's fingers off now!" I heard that loud and clear.

"Wipe my fuckin eyes and I'll tell you who owes the most …. PLEASE!" I screamed as loud as I could. Before I could say it again, I could hear the handle of a metal bucket clinking beside my head. *'Whoosh'.*

This odd sensation shocked me instantly as I realised it was water and not petrol. As the water dripped off my battered face, the burning sensation subsided. It's a shame the beating didn't stop too, that just went on and on until finally all the numbers had been extracted from my phone.

It still wasn't over though, they made me call them without giving anything away and I arranged for the money to be picked up. By now, my vision had returned and one of the lads was looking at me with his shoulders shrugged and palms turned up as if to say, 'Sorry, I can't do anything.' That was the point when I began believing I was getting out of there alive and he was my ticket.

I'd been in his house only three days earlier as his brother was on the local music scene. I knew him well and now he was part of my living nightmare. Suddenly, a voice came over the walkie-talkie and the other two left the barn leaving me alone with the fella I knew.

"Lad, what the fuck is going on here, you're gonna have to get me outta here, please, you know this is wrong, please help." I pleaded.

"Lad, I'm sorry, I'll take you back home, but you've gotta give them the money, quick", he said, in a fast, nervous, whisper. Just as he stopped speaking, the other two came back into the barn and picked up the secateurs and passed them to the fella I knew and said,

"Cut one of his fingers off." He looked at me and stepped forward to take the brand new cutters off the other two fuckers and he said,

"Look lads, if ya want, I'll take the gun and him now and go and get the dough for yas. I won't let this fucker outta my sight and I'll deffo make sure he doesn't see anyone or mention anything, what do you think?"

CRACK! I was knocked to the floor by a single blow to the back of my head. I scrambled back to my feet using my shoulder on a bale of hay for leverage and noticed blood dripping off the end of my nose and splattered on the two fuckers who'd gone to town on me. Utmost on my mind at that particular time was when this was going to stop. They took the other fella to one side for what seemed like forever.

After about 40 minutes in the barn of nightmares, they moved towards me, dragged me into glorious sunshine and put me into the front seat of a VW Golf, still handcuffed. Once the door was slammed shut, I knew I was leaving there alive.

One huge sigh of relief travelled out of my body the minute the fella I knew sat in the car and said,

"Look lad, this has got nothing to do with me, they've just asked me to help them out, it's nothing personal mate, honestly." I didn't really want to say too much after that as shock had a grip on my total being. I knew what had just happened and I had to come to terms with it.

My so-called pals (who I'd been warned to keep away from) had turned on me in a big way. He came out with some cock-and-bull story about me trying to pull the wool over their eyes, but they couldn't have been further from the truth. These people were just utter, greedy bastards who couldn't stand seeing me with bucket loads of money which, from the onset, they'd earmarked as their own. These horrible, two-faced cunts would deserve every bit of bad luck that came their way.

The funny thing was though; I wouldn't be causing them any grief myself. Plenty of my proper pals wanted to make an issue of it when I eventually told them, but enough was enough for me and I said 'no' for the first time in a long while. Every fucker in the city would know my business in a day or two if I retaliated, including the police, that's if they didn't already know. It was time to draw a line under it, wipe my mouth and have a profoundly serious think about where the fuck my life was heading.

I was father of four kids; I didn't see Emilly much and never saw Dayne but I could start now and make a go of one big family. It was weird how, as soon as the shit hit the fan, I reverted to my own flesh and blood. Where did that come from? I'd always been pretty selfish and in my hour of need, I turn into 'Father of the Year'. I needed to give my head a serious wobble.

Shame, embarrassment, pride and all the emotions I could muster went through my head for the next few months. I'd been left more or less penniless except for what I had put far, far away for a rainy day. This seemed to be that rainy day, so plans were made to retrieve my nest egg and start to make other plans. Lisa was just about to start her nursing degree and that meant all hands to the pump where the kids were concerned. Obviously I didn't mention anything about the barn horror show; that would have rocked her boat into sinking. I just had to try and soldier on with only a handful of close people knowing the truth; the truth being that I never deserved what came my way but sometimes, that's just how the cookie crumbles.

Music to the Rescue

Gary Murphy AKA Doddcilla from 'The Bandits'

Music was the route I chose to save my soul. The studio was fully operational and Simo had written a load of belting tunes, which encouraged us to properly form the band, which eventually became 'Blue Ruby' - 2002 was going to be the year where I finally got away from heavy, stressful graft and make a new career for myself. It wasn't a well-planned procedure, more of a 'suck it and see' approach.

Blue Ruby was now the main focus. Music took control of me and I went with it, anything that took my mind off the previous drama was a bonus and being part of this creative learning curve was uplifting.

I more or less moved into the studio and didn't come home until the early hours of the morning. After a couple of hours' sleep, I'd get the kids up, dress and feed them and take them to school. A cuppa and another few hours' sleep and I'd be back to the studio about midday to do the same.

This continued for a few months and didn't please Lisa too much. Some of the lads who I used to graft with would pop in for a smoke and coffee to have a catch up. They were more or less just making sure I was okay and would always raise the barn drama issue for one reason or another. It didn't take too long for them to catch on to the idea that I didn't want to revisit the past, especially not that incident. They were amazed with my earner choice as no mention of me learning the guitar was ever brought up in previous conversations.

The Coral, the band above our studio, had broken through and they were being tipped for big things. Top-of-the-range tour buses would be a common sight on Dale Street to take The Coral lads to and from their sold-out gigs. They were always in our studio and made us all welcome as guests at any of their gigs. Jay, Ian, Nick, Lee, Bill and Paul were all decent too, you couldn't have wished for a better set of lads to make it. Jay Melia was their roadie, I'd known him for years; in fact, from my Jackie Scott, the County Road florist days in 1989/1990. We had many a good night out on the tablets off our heads, dancing to Inner City and Soul to Soul; now we danced to a different beat.

Deltasonic was the Liverpool-based record label that had discovered and nurtured the band early on. The owner and kingpin was Alan Wills, a drummer with a band called 'Top' back in the late 80s and early 90s. Everyone thought him a bit strange, but I didn't and we hit it off from our very first conversation. I couldn't tell you what he thought of me, but I just liked him instantly. It wasn't long before we would meet up at gigs with our partners. Alan's wife, Anne, was lovely and somehow projected Alan's beliefs and desire to greater heights with her unbounding support.

With Anne and Alan's encouragement ringing in my ears whenever I spent time with them, it wasn't long before I became ultra-positive towards my music. You have to have a particular attitude to open the doors of influential musical movers and shakers. Credibility was always used, along with style, influence, vibe, and a real street-image when you spoke to any A&E person. I spoke to as many as I could at local gigs with Alan and Anne.

Alan was focusing his attentions on to 'the Zutons', as they became a tight, live band with a great vibe and local fan base. With all this happening within spitting distance of our studio, it wasn't long before Blue Ruby started to create a certain mystical vibe around the thriving Liverpool live music scene.

This seemed to snowball rumours to different record labels, management companies, publishing companies and other bands. We hadn't even played one gig and somehow articles appeared in local papers with stories of little substance, but nevertheless, great publicity.

Not only had I been taking in everything that Alan and Anne had been saying, I was now getting advice from Tim and Paul Speed. They owned Elevator Studios, Princess Building (the building we had our studio in) and they had their fingers on the beating pulse of everything musically fresh in the city and beyond. I spent many a night bending their ears for information, contacts and help in getting Blue Ruby a possible record deal. I seemed to have a gift for schmoozing and forging lasting relationships with music-minded people and I loved every minute of it as I simply transferred my drug-dealing networking into the music business.

The Coral were hitting dizzy heights and kept gaining momentum with the Indie scene masses. Their tour manager, Neil, was a belting fella who often came into our studio for a coffee and a joint and always made sure that there were guest list spaces for Blue Ruby. They were playing in Rock City in Nottingham one Friday night, when I received a call from the lads from the band saying they were low on weed and did I know anyone who could help them. I fucked them off jokingly and said, 'I'll see what I can do'.

Two hours later, I was outside Rock City with Gary Murphy from The Bandits looking for a way in to surprise the lads with some of the finest skunk. I'd tried to call all the lads but no-one answered then I noticed an open window on ground-floor level with thick, frosted, bathroom glass. I could hear voices coming from inside but I didn't give a fuck cause once I was in, I would be able to throw a few names about that wouldn't get me kicked out.

As soon as I put my foot into the small, but big-enough-for-me-to-squeeze-through gap, it all went deadly silent. I found my footing and wiggled down on to a table filled with laptops and wristbands, I noticed Neil, his face in shock following my every movement on to the wooden table. Once I'd hopped off the table onto the stone floor, I looked around and noticed the sign on the inward open door; 'PRODUCTION OFFICE'. As the three shocked women and two burly security guards gasped, I said,

"Alright Neil, where's the lads?" whilst taking my phone out of my jacket pocket.

"They're in the changing room two doors down and what the fuck are you doing here?" he asked, with a smirk on his face. He knew quite well why I was there.

"Bandit's outside, you'll have to go and get him in." I said, as he tried to explain my entrance to the stunned staff at the venue.

"Nothing like a grand entrance, hey?" I said, while we walked towards the dressing room.

The lads were buzzing when I opened the dressing room door with a bag of skunk now tucked under my armpit. If I could smell it, it wouldn't be long before they could, too. Neil went to fetch Bandit while the band and I rolled joints rapidly and chuckled about my unusual entrance into Rock City.

After the brilliant gig, we partied in the venue until the early hours and came up with one of the best nicknames ever. Gary 'Bandit' Murphy was a great kid, but he had a look of both Ken Dodd and Cilla Black. After several beers and numerous joints, I christened him 'Doddcilla'. Fuck me, he took it well as everyone joined in with the name calling. The love child of Ken and Cilla sat there and took stick all night off The Coral lads and myself. One nil to Hoylake, well, it was deflected goal from my drunken humour but nevertheless a picture was painted forever.

It was the middle of 2002 and after a few more months of solid rehearsal, it was decided that *Blue Ruby* would play live at the Bandwagon Night held at the *Zanzibar* in Liverpool town centre. There was three bands on and we had the middle spot; between *Odega* and a London band called *The Libertines.* The venue was full to the brim 40 minutes after the doors had opened at 8 o'clock, there were lads I knew locked out and constantly called my phone in an attempt for me to pull some weight. I was shitting myself, after all, I'd only been playing for a couple of years so this was an even bigger thing for me. Simo, Tom, Mark, Ste and myself all took to the small stage to announce the arrival of Blue Ruby on to the live music scene in Liverpool.

The cosmic 50s and 60s throwback tag that had been bandied about in the musical press was certainly not our stamp. Our songs were pop tunes with a Council estate view born from real life in Sparrow Hall. Ian Dury meets 10cc was our aim. Anyhow, the gig went as well as I could have hoped, with The Coral, Zutons and Bandit lads in attendance. It was one of the most nerve-wracking experiences I'd ever had.

A few days after the gig, word had got out to everyone in the know and meetings began to be set up. The gig had sparked the flint that was the initial hype and now we had fire; the Blue Ruby flame was burning bright. Electric 6, Alabama 5 and The Coral lads had asked deal or an album done and tour offers were on the table. I was ecstatic when I heard all the fuss; job done on my behalf.

George Williams managed Odega and was on the phone asking whether he could come and meet the band and listen to our top-secret demo tracks. Now I'd never met this fella and my nature was always to say 'Yes' and wonder about it afterwards. After playing a full, live set for him in our studio then chatting for about 30 minutes, it was decided that we'd get in touch with him once we'd all mulled over future possibilities. George spoke like he'd been educated in some far-away, public school; but there was a hint of Scouse in there somewhere.

I walked him back downstairs and helped him out of our heavily-secured building; then I leapt back up the stairs to find out what the band were thinking. For some reason, they had a bad taste in their mouths about him. I thought he was a nice fella and I'm not one for keeping people hanging for long, so I contacted George there and then and arranged to meet him in the pub next to the studio on Dale Street. I got straight to the point once we'd settled down to our bevvies; mine a pint and George's was a gin and tonic; of course, what else would he drink?

Honesty was a policy when business was the issue so George was told the truth with no hard feelings. After a few more drinks, we were getting along as if we'd known each other for years. His sparkling appearance and tanned skin made him look like an Old Bailey QC returning from Barbados. It wasn't long before he said he had to leave and take his Bentley Turbo to his other half as she'd be waiting impatiently. He looked a bit taken back when I insisted he should have another round. I am not one for, 'It's your round' when you're enjoying yourself and you've got money in your pocket. I always just get the ale in and don't bat an eyelid about whose round it is, that's the way I am.

"Paul, I can't get you a drink back as I only had £20 cash with me this morning, I've already bought two drinks and had a sunbed at lunchtime, so that's me, cash strapped and they don't take plastic in here. That's the price of vanity hey, two drinks and a sunbed." George said, in his posh accent. I couldn't stop laughing and rocked back in my chair roaring out loud.

"The price of fuckin' vanity." I said, swigging my last bit of beer. "Fuck me, George, you're an absolute belter." I chuckled endlessly on that 'price of vanity' shout. That was it instantly, I thought, 'I'm staying in touch with this fella cause he's as real as they come, plus he makes me laugh.'

Another live gig was set up for the next Bandwagon Night at the Zanzibar; only this time, there was a buzz floating about the city that Noel Gallagher had heard our demo and liked it. Was this just another rumour on the hype front? No, it wasn't, as by now The Bandits had got themselves a deal and had been supporting Oasis. We didn't give many copies of our tunes out, but Doddcilla had one and passed it on to Noel one night on tour. Anyhow, two days before the gig, I called Paddy Shennan from the Liverpool Echo and dropped a hint at Noel possibly showing up. The next day there was an article, only small, about 'Noel's favourite band'. Oh yeah, it fucking worked.

On the night of the gig there were thousands outside the Zanzibar, it was only held 250 max, so the police had to be brought in to manage the crowds. It was unbelievable to watch them swell minute by minute from my vantage point at the upstairs, arched window. All the lads were buzzing, plus we had one extra member now, Austin Murphy who we'd poached from Odega.

I knew Austin's dad, Paul, who was my accountant, it all seemed to add up and Ozzie, as he was known, was multi-talented musically so he fitted in perfectly to Blue Ruby. The night was 'Electric' and Noel did show up and afterwards I got into a bit of football banter with him for about half an hour, it was hilarious. Our brinksmanship was beautiful and gave our on-looking pals palpitations at times, as most of them were not as footy mad as me. The main thing is, I made an impression, as did he on me, that was a brilliant gig and all our friends, family and groupies believed we were going to make it.

The thought of the past dramas were beginning to look like an episode I'd look back on with a sense of relief once I'd cracked the music business. Well, that's how I hoped it would turn out. The hours spent in the studio were becoming a major issue with Lisa and I had to juggle family life with Blue Ruby. I wanted to be as far away as possible from graft so sacrifices were made and that brought an old issue back to haunt me. The stress, skunk and rock-and-roll lifestyle were making me have my funny turns again. I fainted a few times in the studio and if it wasn't for Simo being there on one occasion, I could have choked to death. I didn't mention it to Lisa, but she always knew by my skin, I'd turn the colour of boiled shite for a few days. It wasn't pleasant at all, but I just carried on with my dream relentlessly.

The Bandwagon night always featured up-and-coming bands and became a focal point in bands or acts gaining kudos. The Music, The Libertines, the Coral, the Zutons, The Bandits, Miles Kane, Candy Payne, The Jones' and plenty of other names passed through the doorway of the Zanzibar. Blue Ruby played a gig there with The Zutons headlining late on in 2002. I didn't really pay Dave McCabe much attention, but because we were on the same bill, I had to make contact at some point of the gig. During the sound check, I was by the doorway talking to Tony who ran the venue, when the phone in the main office rang. Tony answered the call, then came back out to carry on talking to me then shouted Dave McCabe from the stage area. Dave bounced over Frank Gallagher-esque and said in his dead Scouse, cocky way,

"What's up, Toe?"

"Sony have just been on the phone saying they're sending two A&R fellas down and can they go on your guest list?" Tony replied, in a matter of fact manner. Dave parted his hair and looked down on to the guest list that was on the counter in front of Tony and said,

"You did say Sony, didn't you, Toe?"

"Yeah, deffo Sony."

"Fuck 'em, if it's Sony, then they've got money so make the fuckers pay and I'll put two more of me mates on the guest list instead." Dave said, whilst nodding his head like a militant rebel disobeying orders.

"No worries mate, I'll tell them when they get here, Dave," replied Tony, with a casual smile on his face. I was fucking buzzing at Dave's reaction and immediately changed my attitude towards him. I reached out my hand in agreement with his no-nonsense attitude.

"You'll do for me mate." I said to Dave, laughing my bollocks off. Some people would give their right arm for the chance of A&R coming to their gigs and Dave McCabe was fucking them right off in superb Scouse style, just because they hailed from Sony. From that minute, I became Dave's friend and that night was spent with Dave in our studio until the early hours of the next morning having a proper buzz. I even got him to own up to ripping our gig posters off the walls outside our studio and the Zanzibar; the cheeky fucker.

Time blended with a hint of skunk always in the air when anything concerning Blue Ruby was happening. Whether it was meeting a journalist, A&R rep or some management company, the skunk was an integral part of our make-up at that time. Rob Swerdlow was one of the most successful managers in the country and was sniffing around trying to find out what all the fuss was about. It didn't take me long to meet up with him and see what he could do for us.

Image and age were Rob's main concerns; he hinted at more of a publishing deal than a record deal. The catch was, he wasn't really interested in us as a band; he just liked to keep up to speed with anything new or musically fresh in Liverpool and kept his finger firmly on the pulse just in case something popped up. Gary Murphy and The Bandits were being looked after by Rob and when he mentioned the skunk and Class A's were causing problems with certain bands, I knew the writing was on the wall for The Bandits. They'd got a three-album deal but went mad on the drugs and the partying. Skunk had become the heroin of the Noughties and it got a grip of the nation in a big way. There wasn't a band around that didn't have one, two or more members on some sort of drug; that was standard, really.

The Coral asked us to support them on their next tour round Britain; obviously we said yes. It was due to start in November 2002, with the first date in Manchester at the Academy and then on to Middlesbrough, Glasgow, Aberdeen and then back to Liverpool on an eight-day tour. We were buzzing, but I'd be lying if I said I wasn't shitting myself. I'd only been playing guitar for a couple of years and now I was going to be playing in front of thousands of music lovers.

A local journalist, Kev Mac, got in touch and became an adviser to me, as I had also taken on the unofficial role of manager. Kev had worked for the NME and had plenty of contacts and good, sound advice for us as a band trying to make it. He guided us towards radio stations and set up loads of Press-related meetings that gave us some decent coverage in the local and national papers. I knew

George Shepton who was the tannoy voice/DJ at my beloved Anfield from when I was a ball-boy back in the early 80s. I sent him a sort of Press package with a handwritten note explaining I was a ball-boy years earlier and put my contact details on it. To my sheer delight, he contacted me to let me know he loved the songs and he would be playing them at half time at the up-and-coming Premier League match on Sunday which was also live on Sky TV.

Everything looked rosy and Blue Ruby had a chance of making it. Franny Jeffers, the former Everton and then Arsenal player, had even said in an interview that his favourite band were Blue Ruby. Tony Grant had sent him our CD, he loved it and apparently passed it to Thierry Henry who loved it too. We had famous musicians, footballers and journalists all saying the right things about Blue Ruby's tunes, the future certainly looked bright.

In my seat in the Kop at Anfield on the Sunday afternoon of the match listening to George Shepton talk about our band was spine-chilling and wonderful. When he played his favourite tune off the demo, *Bassline*, I could barely contain my elation. My phone went fucking mental from those watching at home on TV who could hear it in the background. It was a proud moment for me, this was my spiritual home where I poured out years of emotion to will my idols on and now 45,000 fans could hear me and my pals. It was weird and beautiful at the same time. Not only did George play it half time, he also played it once the final whistle went. While my idols walked off the hallowed turf, we could hear the lyrics, 'We'll be making bullets out of cool chords', in the background.

The next few weeks were fucking hectic, stressful and filled with phone calls about Blue Ruby. The tour was fast approaching and with me as an interim manager, the strain was noticeable on my face. A publishing company tried to persuade me to convince the band, or more to the point, Simo, to sell some of our songs. He was ultra-protective about his songs, but to be perfectly honest, I'd actually been an integral part of the conception of 95% of our work. By rights, I had as much say as him, and that's when it all began to look very, very one-sided.

We weren't a democracy and I had a decision to make. No way was I making an off-the-cuff decision; I was riding it out until I see the end of the tunnel. I fucking loved what I had been a part of and created, this had saved my soul from certain destruction. I kept all my opinions quiet and never let it get in the way of possible success. It was the achievable goal I'd set and that's what I was going to give 100% dedication to - success somehow. The funny thing is that Madonna's lawyers got in touch to buy the rights to some of our songs and Simo said,

"No, we'll make those songs a success ourselves." Wow, that was a big refusal in my mind, but as I said, I'd keep my opinions quiet for the time being, at least.

A tour bus was waiting outside Princess Building, Dale Street, Liverpool, to pick a band up to take it to a venue. It wasn't there for one of the other 19 bands that had rooms in the building; it was there to pick up Blue Ruby. A few lads out of other bands had asked to come along to help, but only one lad made the trip. Ste

Weevil from the band, The Bo Weevils, had become a pal of mine and so I made sure he had a bunk in our 400 quid-a-day tour bus. We had enough skunk and ale to last us a month as we knew The Coral lads would be spending plenty of time on our bus, too.

Manchester was the first gig and after a few sound problems, it turned out fine. The 2000 plus crowd on the night took to us pretty well, even though we were two Scouse bands in Manchester. Glasgow Barrowlands was the next gig and the huge net that covered the front of the whole stage was a troubling sight when we first sound checked. I asked the Coral about it and they told me it was to stop the cans and plastic glasses from hitting us while we played later on. Fuck me, I thought, I wasn't expecting the welcome we got when we opened with our first tune; it was electric, overpowering and by the end, wet!

It wasn't until after the gig when Jay the lead singer was fuming that I found out the contents of some of the plastic glasses. Piss. Jay was soaked to his skin with a cocktail of sweat, beer and Scottish piss. The funny thing is, apparently it was a sign of appreciation when they fling their piss all over you. Jay wasn't having that though, and neither was I, the fuckers. Middlesbrough, Aberdeen and Liverpool all went down a storm, our main aim had been to raise awareness of Blue Ruby. The feedback was great and we decided to have a break from gigging while we concentrated on recording an album. Job done.

By now, Alan Wills was flying with Deltasonic and asked us to do all the pre-production of all his up and coming bands. As he was a friend of mine, we always came to an arrangement regarding cost; that's what mates do. Simo and the other lads would always have something to say about me still running the day-to-day affairs with everything concerning Blue Ruby and its growing reputation. Lisa was nearly at the end of her tether as I was letting the music control my life. She'd not known about my previous line of work, but at least money was coming in then. Now there was next to nothing and I was running really low on my excavated stash of savings. In fact, I could only comfortably last for another six to eight months, then that was it.

The time spent in our studio recording the 10 tunes we'd picked to put on the record was starting to look ridiculous. Simo was a talented motherfucker, but also self-centred and a stickler for doing things his own way. There was only so much I was going to take and with Lisa on my case 24/7, I had to make some serious decisions.

I got in touch with Peter Coyle formerly of the Lotus Eaters and explained the situation in detail. He was my encouraging mentor from the start and knew how much I wanted this but he'd also been there and done it in the music business. I respected his opinion greatly, so once he'd told me not to let it rule me, it was the moment of reckoning. The towel was getting thrown in on the Blue Ruby chapter, but not on the music business.

Some contacts had become friends and I wasn't going to let that go to waste just because I wanted to leave the band. I didn't just leave abruptly, I was more calculating than that. I stayed around until June/July 2003 and after sitting down with my kids one Sunday morning, it was as clear as the hot summer's day outside my window what was needed. Family had to come first, I was 34 and just about starting to grow up properly.

The following weekend, Alan Wills had heard the news of my total departure from everything Blue Ruby and invited me to go to Finsbury Park, London, to watch The Coral support Oasis and Madness. When he turned up to collect me that Sunday morning, I had my son, Paul, ready to go with me. He wouldn't leave my side as I'd not been home at the weekend in ages. Don't get me wrong, I always took him to the Liverpool matches, but I'd usually drop him off at home and either head the pub or studio. With him clinging to my leg that Sunday, I knew I had to be there for him. I had to start being a proper father to Paul, Elizabeth, Emilly and Dayne.

The Finsbury Park gig was a superb experience. Paul was on my shoulders on the stage in front of an 80,000 plus crowd as The Coral and Oasis wowed the crowd. After the gig, the look on Tim Burgess' face from The Charlatans when he found Paul mooching in his portakabin back stage will be with me forever. Paul was only five years old, but had managed to get past security and tried to leave holding two bottles of Stella and a bottle of JD. The Coral lads made young Paul an honorary member on the spot when Tim Burgess came to our table as cool as you like, sat down and in the broadest Manc accent,

"Fuck me, you don't half train Scouse kids to rob from an early age, lad." The laughter was non-stop and even Alan Wills had a chuckle about it with Paul in the car on the way home.

The rest of the summer was spent being a family as Lisa had taken a break from her studies and I had totally switched off. When the kids returned to school, I became a stay-at-home dad who made sure the kids came first. Two weeks into the school term, I was asked by one of the teachers to wait behind after school. My initial thought was that the kids done something wrong.

The teacher passed me a small yellow note book with my son's name on the front and asked me to turn to the first page. 'SUMMER HOLIDAYS' was the handwritten title and underneath it read,

'Dad's band, The Coral, played in a park far away.

He took me on the big stayge with lowds of peopol'.

As I looked up from reading the book, the teacher was smiling and asked if it was true. "Yeah, we went to Finsbury Park in London, why?" I asked.

"Well, when I asked Paul about it, he told me it was your band and that they always come to your house."

"Well, yes, they do come to my house, but it's not my band, they're friends of mine", I told the now goggle-eyed teacher, Miss Jones.

Once I explained how I knew them, she asked whether I could possibly come in and teach some of the younger classes the meaning of beats and rhythm at some point. Of course I said yes.

After three reception class sessions that turned out to be a total success, the Headmaster called me to have a meeting with him one Friday afternoon.

Mr. McQueen was a softly-spoken, religious man and made me welcome when I turned up for this unexpected meeting. He wanted me to come in and perform for the music class as it was some sort of project for the school that term. Obviously I said yes, again. A date was arranged and I went about my business in planning a small gig for about 50 kids. How wrong was I?

A week before the school event, Mr. McQueen called me back in to explain that it was now the whole school in the main hall and not just the musically-minded students that I'd have to entertain. I needed back-up, quickly. A few phone calls later and some favours called in and I had one of the finest, talented bunch of lads to help me out at my kids' school. Three LIPA (Liverpool Institute for Performing Arts) graduates, one Nigerian pop star called Shabba, Ste, Mark and Austin Murphy and I all turned up anticipating a low-key event. Wrong again; the children had made their own shakers out of household items and the noise once the curtains went back on the huge stage was deafening.

We kicked off with *Jungle Book* songs and then on to 'Hey Ya' by Outkast. Shabba, who just happened to be in LIPA when I was picking the lads, took centre stage and had the kids in the palm of his hand. The band just jammed out beats and Shabba MC rapped over it with sheer quality. The children's faces were a picture and so were the teachers who were dancing by now and seemed to be enjoying it as much as the kids. When we finished the gig, every one of the band was shattered, but all said it was one of the best ever. We'd all played in front of thousands of music lovers, but this was off the scale, the sense of fulfilment was overwhelming and it took us all hours to come down from this unparalleled high.

Bringing the kids to school the next day was a huge difference to the previous times I'd taken then. I was getting called 'Sir' by the children and they all thanked me for entertaining them. Even my own kids seemed impressed with their father's new-found, schoolyard fame.

A few days after the concert, Mr. McQueen called me again to ask me to pop in and see him whenever I had the time. I went the following Friday as I was unwell a few days after the concert, after having another funny turn again. When I entered his office, he had a box at the side of his bookcase filled with folded pieces of paper that he immediately picked up and plonked it directly in front of me.

"Well, Paul, firstly, thank you for arranging and performing for the children, we all loved it so much, and in the box are letters from the children for you and your band."

"Wow, that's fantastic", I replied to the Headmaster, who by now had picked one of the letters out and began to read it.

'I'm proud to go to this school because no other school would arrange a concert and let us join in. All my friends who attend other schools are jealous right now. I love Ursuline. When is the next concert, soon I hope'. Thank you. Melisa Yates-Brown

Oh my God, I began to well up with emotion as Mr. McQueen picked another one and started to read out loud again. It was weird and overwhelming, to the point where I made myself deaf to Mr. McQueen's words. I had to, otherwise I would have blubbed all over his office. I've travelled the world dealing in heavy shite, had guns pushed into my face while being terrorised and 400 letters from honest children had brought me to my knees. I had to fight back my emotions in Mr. McQueen's office that Friday afternoon. This was life at its best and what I wanted forever. How was I going to achieve it though?

My graft days were behind me but there were always offers of work from pals who I'd grafted with in the past. It was 2004 and my money situation had nearly caught me up. Dougie had been released from jail and it was only right that I should try my best to look after him. Once I'd made sure he was comfortable and redesigned the downstairs of my house to accommodate my pal who needed somewhere to live, I was running really low on cash. The thought of having to get back on the graft train was turning my stomach; I wanted to be creative and not a social-demolition guerrilla.

With the last bit of spare cash I had, Gary Bandit persuaded me to start our own management company and take a new career angle in the music business. The Mouse Company was set up in offices provided by George Williams, who'd left music management and headed down the publishing road. He gave us the office space for free and provided any assistance that was needed.

We'd open the office during the day and run about Liverpool town centre at night visiting local bands that needed help. Our best find happened to hail from my own family. Years earlier my nephew, Shaun Walsh, had asked us to perform at a family party. He was only six years old at the time and performed a dance routine he'd taught himself in his bedroom to Michael Jackson's 'Smooth Criminal'. I was gobsmacked and told him if he could sing as well as he could dance, he was going to be a superstar. Anyway, two weeks into starting the company, my sister called me and asked me to listen to Shaun singing down the phone. As I listened not really paying attention, I could hear Michael Jackson singing 'I Want You Back'. I couldn't hear my nephew at all. When the song stopped, I said to my sister,

"That wasn't Shaun; that was Michael Jackson, what happened?"

"No, no, Paul, honest, it was Shaun".

"Fuck off, Sue", I said quickly, in a dismissive way.

"Paul, on our dad's grave, that was Shaun singing." Now my dad's grave was a huge shout, so by now my ears had pricked up.

"Put Shaun on the phone now", I said to the now-excited, Sue.

"Hiya, Uncle Paul, did ya like it?"

"Yeah, that was deffo you singing?"

"Do you want me to do it again, Uncle Paul?"

"Can you do it now down the phone for me with no backing track?"

As soon as I'd stopped talking, Shaun began to sing. Bloody hell, I thought, as I pulled the phone away from my ear so Gary could hear. Within 20 minutes, Gary and I were in my sister's house asking Shaun questions about what he wanted to do; a wish-list of sorts. Appearing on TV and singing at Liverpool Football Club were Shaun's top two requests; he was eight years of age and had an air of stardom written all over him. He blew Gary away and we both went right for our phones to contact everyone we knew who could possibly help.

The next few days were spent in Elevator Studios getting a decent demo CD so we could move forward with Shaun's wishes. Once the demo was finished, it was time to make his dreams come true. Wish number 1 – TV. Phone calls made to the BBC Studios in London resulted in us emailing Shaun's demo tracks on a Tuesday afternoon. Two hours later, we had Shaun booked on the *'Dick and Dom in Da Bungalow',* for that Saturday's live show. The BBC Production Team had organised travel and accommodation within hours and seemed really excited about Shaun's impending, live appearance. We moved swiftly in the right direction and objective one was more-or-less in the bag.

Saturday couldn't come quickly enough. Gary and Andy, Shaun's dad, travelled to London for the live show with Shaun, while I stayed with my kids, Paul and Elizabeth in my sister's house in Fazakerley to watch it live. Shaun sang 'I Want You Back' apparently in front of four million viewers. The phone went berserk once he'd finished performing as I'd sent a text to all 304 contacts in my phone; some contacts had nothing to do with the music business, but getting the word out was my aim.

The next few weeks were spent discussing offers from every Tom, Dick and Harry regarding Shaun's future. As he was family, I didn't want one single penny of any money he earned, even though I'd put my own money up to fund it. Family's family and that was that.

Rob Swerdlow (Lily Allen, The Kooks) Mark Hargreaves (Sugababes' Manager) and many more came to my house enquiring about Shaun, but he was still only a child and needed to be protected. The Production Team which worked on Dick and Dom had another show that was called *'Let Me Entertain You',* with Brian Conley and an unknown female Irish host, Christine Bleakley. They contacted us to see if we wanted to go on that and there would be a substantial fee involved. Offers just seemed to be pouring in and Shaun was the richest kid I knew. The Brian Conley show was a total success and someone had uploaded on to the new internet site, YouTube; it went viral in a matter of weeks.

The strain was now heavy on my purse strings so I had to consider other ways of making money quickly. Offers of graft were still on the table but it meant moving to another country and staying away for three months at a time. The beast that was graft was raising its greedy head and showing me a road I thought I'd never travel down again. What was I going to say to Lisa? How could I explain three months away at a time? I know, I thought, I'll tell her I've got a job as a tour manager. That's how easy the thought process was once I'd realised money would help me out in the short term. The long term was in the future, so that didn't matter to me now. I was in the moment, trying to survive; everything else could go and fuck itself as I was being sucked back into crime.

I had to leave all the musical knowledge on the shelf as I dived back into the world of graft. The barn drama was revisited daily in my mind, which then made me overthink situations, conversations and my blood boil at times. Skunk was being smoked twice as much as I'd ever used it, to add that into my equation at this was like pouring petrol on burning petrol, while being covered in petrol. I must be fucking mad.

Gary Murphy kept the Mouse Company running while I went and found the money to keep my family ticking over. I ended up moving to Amsterdam and then on to Belgium, where I settled into some heavy graft. I became stressed out to my limit as I was dealing with the same type of people who'd tortured me in a barn years earlier. I must be fucking mad to dive into doing this sort of graft again. It was the same old story for me, I always said yes and never said no. What the fuck was wrong with me? Why didn't I just explain to Lisa that my situation was life threatening? I'm sure she would have understood, but I was brought up with lads telling me not to tell your partner anything as it could come back to hurt both of us. My head felt twisted at times, but pride, upbringing and loyalty had seen me through this far, so I soldiered on, with no-one knowing what was going on in my head. After all the troubles I'd been through, I finally thought I'd made a new life in music and the money dragged me back into the chasm that is graft.

With the arrival of the 2004/05 football season just around the corner, Liverpool had appointed another foreign manager in the form of Rafa Benitez from Spain. To be perfectly honest, I didn't know much about him, only that he'd come through the coaching ranks at Real Madrid and managed Valencia. I could remember Valencia coming to Anfield a few years previously and giving us a total football lesson, so that's all I had to go by.

Xavi Alonso, Luis Garcia and Djibril Cissé were new arrivals to my beloved Football Club that pre-season, so all we could do was wait and see what happened in the Champions League. Gerard Houllier had left a strong squad behind for Senor Benitez to thrill the red masses. Who knew what was around the corner, as long as it wasn't a bar, I'd be okay.

Dead For One Minute

"Get in there, you beauty!" Andy Gray screamed as the ball hit the back of the Kop End net in the dying minutes of the Olympiacos, Champions League match. It was late 2004 and that goal secured us a place in the knockout stages of the competition to every diehard Liverpool fan's utter joy. I was gutted I couldn't go as I was in a Spanish bar somewhere on the outskirts of Marbella sorting out graft.

The sight of Steven Gerrard running towards the Kop with both hands simultaneously punching the air like a Formula One car's pistons, sent me jumping for joy in a bar full of expats and Spanish onlookers. There was only me screaming as the lad I was with was a crazy Evertonian. He just kept nodding and saying,

"I knew you fuckers would score in the last minute, I fuckin' hate yers", with a bitter-blue expression all over his scrunched-up face.

I told my mates earlier on in the season that I was going to all the home and away games I possibly could. My son, Paul, was now a fully-fledged Liverpool fan who loved going to the home games along with my nephew, Alex.

February 2005 and Bayer Leverkusen were our next opponents. I went to both games; the away leg was a buzz as I was driven via Amsterdam again. You couldn't go to a match in Northern Europe without figuring Amsterdam into the logistics; that was a Scouse standard - you'd stock up on everything needed in the travelling fans' unwritten guide book and off you'd pop down the road, contented.

With all the travelling, juggling life and music stuff with Gary, Lisa and Alan Wills along with the graft headaches, my body wasn't right. Skunk was still top of the menu while I tried my best to keep everybody happy.

It didn't take long for me to have another funny turn and end up in a hospital bed in Fazakerley for a few days, while tests were carried out. For one reason or another, the doctors weren't happy with my condition and ended up giving me a tilt test. I was told by the nurses it was no big deal and nothing to worry about. Lisa was with me all the way through the tests as her knowledge was a sounding board for my concerns. To be honest, she just thought I was fainting and it was down to the weed and I was getting no sympathy from the now-fully-qualified, Nurse Ratched.

They wouldn't let Lisa into the room while the tilt test was taking place, so two doctors and a young nurse had the task of preparing me for it. Sensors were placed on roughly 20 different positions while I lay immobile in the windowless, cold, pale- blue hospital room.

Four massive straps were tightened; two round my legs and two on my upper body. I couldn't move much now as the young nurse brought a clipboard with a disclaimer form towards me to sign. How the fuck was I supposed to sign the form while I was strapped to this bed like a lab rat? It was starting to freak me out now.

No-one mentioned anything that could go wrong and now it was making my stomach churn. The thought of having one of my funny turns was now in the pit of my gut and rising quickly. The reason for this tilt test was to induce passing out so they could monitor my every effect before, during and after. There was nothing funny about it, to be honest as the doctor explained; I would be raised until the bed could tilt over and fill the chambers of my heart. I began to feel queasy.

"What's the quickest anyone has ever passed out during this test?" I asked the doctor standing on the opposite side of the room, holding the control for the machine. "Usually about two minutes into the initial tilt." he replied, in a matter-of-fact tone. "Well, I am going now," I said, as my mouth dried up and within a second I had passed out.

"Are you okay? Just breathe…" were the next words I heard as my vision was slowly coming into focus and I felt myself panting heavily.

"Are you okay, Paul? Can you hear me?" asked the other doctor, who was now bent over my cold, sweating body, looking into my eyes with a small light.

"Yeah, yeah, I'm all right. What happened?" I asked in a voice that felt like a whisper. I could feel my whole body was cold and sweat was running down the side of my forehead as my senses began to sync up. I pouted my lips and blew air out of my mouth while the nurse offered me some water.

"Yeah, please." I said. As I turned my head to the right, I noticed the nurse had blood seeping from three small flesh wounds on her arm.

"Wow, what's happened to you? Are you okay?"

"I'm fine, how are you?"

"Okay, why is your arm bleeding?" I noticed her NHS name tag which read, Helen Pritchard. She leant over me and whispered,

"Fuckin' hell Paul, I've only started as a qualified nurse this morning and you've just flat-lined for 28 seconds, so never mind my arm, are you deffo okay?"

"What? Flat-lined?" I was trying to fully absorb what Nurse Helen had just told me.

"But your arm, how come it's bleeding?" I asked again.

"When you passed out and we got the bed level, you broke one of the straps with your arm, then grabbed me and wouldn't let go. I shit myself, Paul, on my first day too!" Nurse Helen said, as she began to check the sensors all over my body. I could hear the two doctors talking near the door, they were looking for Lisa who was supposed to be waiting for me outside.

It took Lisa a full hour before she eventually turned up to be told that I was being rushed to Broadgreen Hospital to be operated on later that night. She was as flabbergasted as I was when they told me. I asked if there was any alternative because the thought of surgery was not on my agenda at all. Once Lisa had talked to the doctors, she relayed the conversation back to me in layman's terms. They wanted to fit a pacemaker quickly. Fuck me, I was only 35 years of age and the thought of a pacemaker made me feel like a fossil.

Lisa was telling me the options available and there was light at the end of the tunnel as the doctors said they'll wait until the cardiothoracic specialists came to see me the following morning. I was wheeled to a ward on the fourth floor of Fazakerley Hospital with five other fellas. I must have been the youngest by at least 30 years and was fitted with a wireless set of sensors and told to relax for the night in this ghoulish ward.

Throughout the night I was woken up by worried nurses who worked the graveyard shift. They kept checking my sensors as my heartbeat was apparently slowing down to worrying levels. The next morning, I was woken up by Dr Davies, the Cardio specialist and Lisa, who turned up bright and early to bring some goodies to eat.

Once the doctor had checked my charts and spoken to the nurses, he came up towards my head to look into my eyes with a small light.

"Now, I need you to be truthful and tell me if you are on any drugs, prescribed or others?" He said firmly.

"Well, I smoke skunk daily, but I don't do any other drugs." I replied.

"And what about exercise?" He asked, as he rolled his eyes towards the clipboard in his left hand.

"I run, cycle and class myself as pretty fit for my age, really."

"And what do you do for a living?" He peered over the top of his gold-rimmed glasses then stopped writing on the clipboard. How the fuck was I going to answer that question? I couldn't tell him that I was an international drug dealer who travels across Europe making deals with stone-faced killers, lunatics, revolutionaries and people who'd kill your whole family if you fucked up and brought trouble to their door.

I also couldn't tell him I'd been bouncing round Liverpool for the past 20 years with bundles of cash, from a grand up to a million quid or more, trying to avoid detection by the police and local, armed, dog-like gangsters who want to rip you off. Just like I couldn't tell him I'd had run-ins with fellas who'd burn you alive if deals didn't go their way. That's my world with frosted icing sprinkled all over some of the shite that's happened in my life. I'd buried that deeply in the back my mind and didn't want to find it ever again, not just for one reason, for several reasons. So what was I going to say to the specialist who wanted answers? Should I tell him the absolute truth; that I'd only ever met three lads in my line of work that I truly liked and respected wholeheartedly, and by the way, that's a ratio of about 0.3%.

That's how stressful my life had been for the past 20 years at times and you wonder why I smoked weed? So I could escape and drown my thoughts in numbness. Should I tell him that? No. So what do I say?

"I'm in the music business and I'm on the road a lot", was my reply once I'd realised that Lisa's bubble would have burst and most probably put our relationship on to hot coals if I'd told the truth. So after a 10-minute discussion, the doctor decided to put me on beta-blockers to regulate my blood flow. That was music to my ears, as I definitely didn't want a device inserted into my chest cavity with a wire to my groin.

The doctor decided another five days on the cardio ward and then off home for some R&R, well, that's if I could get some peace. To be fair, Lisa looked after me as I was now a bit short-tempered due to the doctor telling me to give smoking weed a total miss. The nightmares were relentless a few days after getting home from hospital. Every night I had the darkest dreams that woke me up sweating like I'd been drenched in macabre water.

Istanbul - The Best Night of My Life

Cunningly disguised in Istanbul

It wasn't long before I was out of the house and enjoying a trip to Anfield to watch a Champions League quarter-final against the Italian giants, Juventus. There was plenty of media coverage as they were our opponents back in May 1985 when 39 football fans died due to a wall collapsing. As I approached the main stand, the sight of the black-and-white-striped jerseys brought memories of that fateful day in Brussels, flooding back.

The majority of the Juventus supporters turned their backs on our efforts to build bridges that night. The Ultras made their point loud and clear to the packed-to-the-rafters, Anfield; no violence, it was just a protest of sorts.

The atmosphere was palpable with more than a hint of some super-charged electricity. Sami Hyypia opened the scoring with a great goal early on in the first half and Luis Garcia added a wonder goal to take us to half time with a 2-0 advantage. The second half produced a goal apiece to send Alex, Paul and myself home buzzing with a possible semi-final to look forward to.

The next leg in Turin was a tense affair on and off the pitch, but when the game ended at 0-0, the thought of a semi-final with Chelsea was mind-blowing, especially as we'd play the first leg at Stamford Bridge.

By now, everything I did had to be thought through with my health in mind, so when I had to up sticks and travel back to Amsterdam to meet up with some of the other grafters to sort a problem out, I did it reluctantly. Usually, I'd be buzzing to take the trip, but my stress levels had to be managed these days. The only up-side was that I knew The Zutons were on tour across Europe, so I figured their tour dates into my logistics and headed off with my guitar as a cover for my illicit journey.

When I'd completed my running around, sorting the 'graft problem', I made my way back to central Amsterdam to meet up with Dave McCabe and the rest of the band.

The 'Melkweg' was the venue for their Dam gig and was a sell-out, but all I knew was that I'd be on the guest list. What I didn't cater for was that the band wanted me to introduce them on the stage to the packed Dutch crowd. It was the first time I'd been to Amsterdam without being stoned and as I'd only had a few beers, I was on the button and up for it. Wow! I thought, I'm supposed to be keeping low-key and I'm in front of 2000 people acting like the warm-up guy. Not only that, it wasn't too long ago I was being told to take life easy or I'd probably be in serious trouble, health wise.

But I'm one of the mad-as-they-come jammy fuckers who just doesn't care and lives for the moment. Not mad in a violent or lunatic manner, but in a way that my thought process seems to work in a crazy, warped way; especially as the next day I was in Berlin with the band as they played a gig at the Artefact PRC Quatre. After another wild, drunken night, it was time to head off back to Liverpool. The tour manager said I could travel back with them on the tour bus. I wasn't going to argue with that, so I managed to come back into the country more-or-less undetected.

I was home a few days before the second leg of our Champions League semi-final with Chelsea at Anfield. The first leg was a 0-0, tit-for-tat affair, with Jose Mourinho playing out his usual war of words in the national press after the game. All I knew was I had three tickets for Alex, Paul and myself slap bang in the centre of the Kop.

There was a special sense of belonging amongst the Liverpool fans in the days leading up to the match, especially as Chelsea were favourites to go through. I wouldn't have had it any other way to be honest, nor do I think would any Liverpool fan as it added to the recipe, drama and possible two-fingered salute to Mourinho's boys.

Our usual routine was to take up our seats about 10 minutes before kick-off, but this was no usual match, so we ended up in the ground an hour before. It was packed to the rafters and the noise levels had reached new heights as the pitch-side European TV elite prepared for the match.

The sheer weight of colour made it feel like you were part of an epic battle that would define borders and nations. There's always something special about night matches at Anfield; they seem to come to life beneath the floodlights in a way that only those who've been there can truly comprehend. This was a huge occasion and all the thoroughbred, Liverpudlians knew what was needed to help our cherished team across the finishing line; unconditional, 100% support.

The wall of sound that greeted the players on to the pitch muted the Champions League anthem into the background. The whole stadium was on their feet from the get-go; with no exceptions.

When the whistle blew for kick-off, you couldn't even hear your own breath as the singing absorbed everything in its path. On paper, Chelsea, were the better team, so when the ball bounced towards the goal after Milan Baros was flattened by Petr Cech, all the crowd thought 'penalty' and sending off, as Luis Garcia hit the ball towards the Kop end goal. The referee had other ideas as the ball bounced and William Gallas tried to hook it from the goal line.

Garcia thought the ball had crossed the line, as did every Kopite, so the celebrations went stratospheric in a heartbeat. Goal! Goal!

Chelsea players surrounded the referee, who by now was heading back towards the halfway line. The excitement nearly made me pass out as Paul and Alex jumped and hugged me senseless. Every single Liverpool fan took that goal and it wasn't until half time that the debate raged about whether or not Cech should have been sent off, should we have had a penalty instead and then therefore played the rest of the game against 10 men? As the players took to the pitch for the second half with the score line at 1-0, all that mattered was to see this through until the end.

The noise levels and singing were at heights not heard at Anfield for years, the hairs on my arms stood to attention with electric excitement as the second half got underway.

Chelsea tried to break our solid back line, but Carragher, Riise and Hyppia kept them at bay until the last 10 minutes. Jose Mourinho threw the kitchen sink at us, but every supporter behind the Kop goal threw it right back in their faces.

Gudjohnsen came close in the dying seconds, but it looked destined for Liverpool to go to Istanbul on May 25th 2005. As the 42,500 Liverpool fans whistled, sang or screamed, I'm sure every one of us was clock watching too. It was agonising following the ball and referee at the same time, while keeping an eye on the clock too. The ref finally blew and all hell broke loose with crowd surfing, jumping up and down punctuated by hugs and screams of jubilation.

George Sephton, the tannoy announcer, played 'You'll Never Walk Alone' immediately on the final whistle, with everyone joining in. Tears poured down my bright-red cheeks in a fast-running stream. I tried to wipe them away with Alex and Paul's red and white scarf that was now held aloft like an offering to the God of Football during the show of brilliant colour and song.

Walking out of Anfield with my head ringing, ears buzzing and heart beating furiously was a heavenly feeling. My son was there with me to witness this; how lucky was I to have that moment to share forever? Alex was like a son, so having them both with me was mind-blowing. How fucking lucky am I? This would be my fourth European Cup Final with my team and by hook or by crook, I was going to take Paul and Alex to Istanbul.

The looks on their faces on the way home in the car when I said where we were going took me back to 1981, when my brothers told me I could go. That feeling ran through my bones and found its way into my son's and nephew's being in an instant; I could see it. What a fucking night.

My preparation for the Istanbul final was meticulous. If I was going to take my six-year-old son, I wasn't going to miss any opportunity of making it into a trip of a lifetime. This might not happen again, so I had to make the most of this for Paul and Alex.

It was 10 o'clock on the morning of Monday 23rd May in Manchester Airport with what seemed like thousands of lads who I'd either worked or partied with, it was a great way to start our

European adventure. Paul and Alex had decided to wear their colours to show onlookers their loyalty lay with Liverpool FC.

The departure lounge was a Who's Who of crazy reds from all walks of Scouse life. If I was a betting man, I would have put my house on every one having some sort of tackle (drugs) on them. That's just standard, you're not going to go traipsing round Turkey looking for Gary's or beak; you just take your own.

Once we'd boarded and taken our seats, it was obvious that our journey would not only be powered by aviation fuel, it was going to be aided by humour and recreational drugs too. When the plane settled into its flight path and the seatbelt light was turned off; that's when the fun started. Apparently you're not supposed to smoke on planes anymore; well, no-one told the majority of passengers on this chartered flight to Istanbul. Never mind the smell of tobacco, that was the least of the cabin crew's worries as the smell of skunk, filled the plane.

The crew's attempts to quell the epidemic that swept the cabin were fruitless, in fact, it was pointless too as the Champions League party had started prematurely. It was funny though, I knew I had my young son with me and it's wrong to allow him to be around that, but hey, it wasn't anything he hadn't smelt before.

To be fair, he didn't care what was happening as he played his computer game while watching the on-board movie with headphones on. Alex kept nudging me as the stewardesses wandered by telling lads to put their joints out, otherwise the plane would be turning back. After a few announcements by the Captain trying to stamp his authority on the smoking situation, the rowdiness quietened down, only for it to pick up an hour later. The flight crew knew they were pissing in the wind so they gave up and stopped serving alcohol for the rest of the flight. That didn't do much to stop the rowdiness either as the duty-free bought in Manchester Airport was cracked open and passed around freely.

Turkey made sure our welcome was one of brute force and rapidity due to the sheer number of travelling supporters. The Airport was lined with Police and Military personnel on our arrival at this huge airport located an hour outside the city. After our escorted trip, we finally crossed the Bosphorus River and headed into the metropolis; Istanbul. A few drop offs at hotels scattered across the city and 10 of us were left on the coach as it pulled up at our five-star hotel in the bustling trendy port area.

Armed guards either side of the entrance raised issues with Alex and Paul, but I reassured them there was nothing to worry about as we walked through the heavily-guarded lobby of our hotel. Once we'd checked in and done the customary scan out of the hotel window to discover the huge swimming pool surrounded by palm trees, it was time to check Istanbul out.

Tuesday morning was spent by our pool while we enjoyed the beautiful weather that beat down on the leaves of the huge palms. There were about 40 Liverpool fans around the outside bar, with local TV crews trying to gauge the atmosphere of the up-and-coming final.

After making a few calls on my mobile, it was decided that we'd head to Taksim Square to meet up with some of my pals who'd also made the trip. The usual huge square was the destination of the masses of travelling supporters. To be honest, it was one of the biggest squares I'd ever visited and there were groups of Liverpool fans far and wide, but no sign of any AC Milan fans, not a single one.

Paul was searching for any rival fans as it was his first European final and foreign supporters must have seemed like aliens in his young mind. I'd mentioned on the plane that we'd swap a scarf so Paul had brought his spare with him just in case we bumped into any rival supporters; so Paul was on red alert in Taksim Square. His other scarf was packed away with my clothes back in the hotel; that was the one I'd wiped my tears of joy with when we beat Chelsea; no way that was getting swapped.

Now, I had a bit of a problem to deal with that involved our hotel. When I was booking it, I'd called a friend who worked for LFC to inquire where the team was staying and once I'd had the heads up, I went online to book our own suite before the initial avalanche of bookings ensued. I'd kept this a secret from Alex and Paul the whole time, but the number of security on the Tuesday evening in our hotel raised eyebrows from Alex, who's on the button, he's a bright motherfucker. I had to keep dodging the team with constant phone calls to my friend, a ticket tout, checking on their whereabouts, plus I'd told Alex that there were loads of media staying there. Paul wasn't an issue as just being in Istanbul was good enough for him, so he wasn't fully aware of his surroundings, but I still wanted to keep it a secret. I had a plan from the onset and I was trying my hardest to stick to it.

On the morning of the match, I sneaked us out of our hotel with relatively little fuss and without Alex and Paul being aware of their idols only four floors above us. We headed to Taksim Square in a yellow taxi that seemed to dodge in and out of the smallest gaps in the traffic. These cabs were everywhere, thousands of them that appeared to run on washing machine engines, lined the roads of Istanbul, with the majority of them full of Liverpool fans heading to Taksim Square.

The sea of red, white and yellow was plastered all over the now-throbbing central square. Banners hung from every available space as we weaved through the meandering sea of colour to meet up with my pals. Every 10 seconds I bumped into someone who I knew and it didn't take me long to find my pals from the Zutons, The Coral and Gary Murphy. We had all decided to wear our colours as it had been a long time since we attended a European Cup Final (now Champions League) so the sight of everyone, and I mean everyone, in red looked amazing. I felt part of a fanatical movement and having my son there meant so much as I'd been in his shoes in 1978 at Wembley.

The band lads were playing gigs for Sony, the match sponsors, in the hospitality area surrounding the Atatürk Stadium, which was situated about 30 minutes outside the city, so they left at midday to sound check. I ended up meeting some young lads I knew from Norris Green, who kept asking me to come to find some filthy women. Firstly, I was with my son, so that was a no-no, secondly, I wouldn't do that to Lisa so their pleas fell on deaf ears.

These lads tried to pick my brains about where the bands would be playing as they knew I had my finger in the musical cake, as well as in the drug sandwich. I told them there was a huge Fan Zone outside the stadium and I'd see them there a few hours before kick-off. The zone had a massive stage that Gary Murphy had a hand in arranging. He persuaded Pete Wylie to perform and told me I could jump up to give them an extra voice on the microphone if I was up for it. Anyhow, the lads from Norris Green all vanished into yellow taxis to look for filthy women of the daytime, as we carried on meandering through the sea of red.

The amount of banners people had spent time making was unbelievable. I knew we had a tradition of sorts with witty, colourful banners and especially when we reached major finals. Back in 1977, I remember my sisters covered in red-and-white material while they sat on our living room floor, hand-stitching a banner for Joe Mac and our brother, Rob, who were heading to Rome for the final again Borussia Mönchengladbach. *'Joey Jones eats Uniteds and munches Gladbachs'*. That was made in *my* house by *my* family with love and an affection only Scousers could exude onto fabric. You get the picture; we love our banners and put something of ourselves into them.

With all that in mind, we scoured the Square, gazing at the tapestry of faith, humour and fanatical dedication. There seemed to be thousands of banners and flags which had made the long journey to Istanbul, some brilliant and some not so good. There was one that must have been about 50-feet long, 3 foot high and read; *"SuperCroatIgorBiscanUsedToBeAttrocious".* It was draped over a balcony in the corner of the Square and it took a few scans to realise it was another witty banner about our present day tongue-in-cheek icon, Igor Biscan, who also gave his all for Liverpool Football Club; it was fucking genius and made us all chuckle as we wandered around the now-totally red square.

Someone must have taken a bed sheet from their hotel room with *"This is a Sheet"* written on it in black marker. It stood out like a sore thumb and for me it was the best of all the banners.

Paul and Alex wanted to head towards the Stadium just to be certain we all got there in time, so to make doubly sure, we left the heaving square at 3 o'clock and joined the hordes of fans in a yellow convoy.

It took about 40 minutes for us to reach what looked like the other side of the moon. It was a rocky, hilly area, with the Atatürk Stadium dumped in the centre of it. What a strange place to put an 80,000-seater stadium; in the middle of nowhere.

The game wasn't kicking off until 10pm and we were there for around 4 o'clock. We had six hours to spend on the dark side of the moon. All the yellow taxis stopped on the road leading down to the stadium, while the masses of Liverpool supporters traipsed across this rocky outcrop like soldier ants towards the huge Fan Zone behind the stadium. The look on Alex and Paul's face when we reached the Fan one was one of relief and sheer excitement.

Being on beta-blockers, I'd not had a drink in Istanbul, although I could have a few as long as I didn't go mad and start rolling joints again. My mind was free and gave me time to absorb the atmosphere with no distractions, alcohol free and not a joint in sight. You could tell Alex and Paul had noticed I was refusing drinks, because usually I'd be lounging in some smoky bar off my head; but not this time.

There weren't many fans at the stadium at this point, so I made a few calls to the band lads who were playing in the hospitality tents. It must have been about 5 o'clock when they called back to find out where we were located.

"I'm behind the huge stage in the fan zone", I said.

"Fuck me Paul, so are we, shout out so we can hear ya", Jay from The Coral said. "Yooooow!" I screamed and could hear laughing behind me as Nick, Lee and Jay had popped up like the shopkeeper in Mr. Ben.

It wasn't long before Gary Murphy and Colin Murray, the Radio One DJ, joined us soaking up this ever-increasing crescendo of excitement. The lads were playing in the tents at 7 o'clock and the fan gig was starting at 6.30, so after a walk around the stadium, we parted company for the time being.

The sound of the Turkish compere yelling, *'Get off the stage, it's going to collapse!* - will stay with every Liverpool fan who heard it, forever. It was supposed to sound alarming, but it didn't, it was comical.

I'd already been on the stage half an hour earlier with Gary Murphy, Pete Wylie and others singing the customary, 'You'll Never Walk Alone' and 'Heart as Big as Liverpool'. I ended up putting on a red false beard thinking no-one would realise it was me, but a few lads I knew got right on to me. They appeared to be astonished, they didn't know I was into music; they had me down as a Norris Green grafter. The looks on their faces was priceless.

Paul and Alex had gone walkabout around the various tents and missed most of my stage antics, but we all heard the, *'Get off the stage, it's going to collapse'* shout. To be fair, it was sort of my fault as I'd invited the lads who recognised me singing on to the stage to join in. That was the catalyst, before too long the stage had been rushed with drunken, singing Liverpool fans.

As the sun went down and darkness fell upon the Atatürk Stadium, the atmosphere turned into an electric, red vortex as we entered the stadium an hour before kick-off. The crowd was pulsating with red-and-white clad fans trying to get into the venue. There was absolutely no need for tickets as the Turkish system was fundamentally flawed and the Scouse masses knew how to take advantage of this situation.

Paul, Alex and I had no problems weaving our way through security, police and ground staff undetected in a daisy chain fashion; no need to show any ticket either. We had gained entry into the stadium and it was now time to find our seats, as Paul and Alex were getting agitated. On our way round the inner concourse, we bumped into the lads from Norris Green who'd been searching downtown Istanbul for filthy Turkish women.

Alex took Paul to get a match programme, while I chattered to the lads who were all off their heads on Class As.

"You're not gonna believe what's happened to us, lad", said Ronnie, who I knew from the Youth Club days in the late 80s.

"I just watched yas all vanish into a yellow plume in the Square looking for brass", I replied, laughing.

"Fuck me, kid, we asked the taxi driver to take us for women and he pulled up outside some seedy, dark-windowed bar type of gaff and told us to go in there and he'd wait for us….it was only a fuckin' belly dancin' yard, kid, the silly Turkish cunt…trying to stitch us up." Phil said, with his jaw wobbling like an Antarctic explorer's bollocks exposed to the elements.

"So we jump back in the taxi and told him we wanted a fucky, fucky…ya know, suck and fuck." Phil said, with his eyebrows dancing off his forehead.

"Ah, yes, yes, yes, okay, I take you there", said the taxi driver to Ronnie and his mates in broken English.

So this beaut takes us another place about 20 minutes across town and told us to go inside…so we all bounce into this yard lookin' for our nuts and fuck me, it's only a titty (lap-dancing) bar.

"Lad, we were all fuckin' fumin' and steaming by this point, we flew back to this divvie still waitin' outside with a grin on his kipper and told him again. We want fuckin' proper sluts, not tits an arse...so I made a hole shape with my fingers and pushed another finger through it to indicate sex, and he said, "Oh, sorry, yes, yes...I take you...sorry, sorry."

"So this has been an hour now with this taxi driver and we're all rotten drunk, steamin' and now fumin' as he drove us down some country lane and into the middle of nowhere. To be honest, I thought we were gonna get mugged, when he pulled up at the side of this country lane, got out of his taxi and indicated for us to get out of the car. This fuckin taxi driver has only bounced round to the front of the car, put his hand on bonnet and dropped his kecks to his ankles and invited us to fuck him..." Ronnie said, laughing that much that frothy spit was spurting from his mouth.

"You're havin' a laugh aren't ya?" I replied, open mouthed.

"Am deadly serious, lad, this Turkish taxi driver thought we'd asked to fuck him and took us down a country lane and dropped his kecks pronto, haaaaaa, for real." Ronnie spurted out all over the concourse. Just then, Alex and Paul came back and Ronnie shook my hand and said,

"Can you believe that, lad? Unbelievable."

"I'll see you later, lad." And with that, Phil vanished into the constantly-moving red crowd. I couldn't stop laughing and told Alex what had happened as we made our way to our seats.

Six Minutes of Sheer Joy

Steven Gerrard with Paul Jnr

The pre-match ceremony came and went in a flash of tens of thousands of cameras and the match was about to kick off. Our seats were high up to the right-hand side of the goal we were attacking. As I peered down at the AC Milan fans, who made a mosaic of black, red and white, I noticed that Liverpool's support was about 75% of the stadium; we outnumbered them massively.

'This must surely give us an advantage', I thought, as 'You'll Never Walk Alone' reverberated around the stadium.

A couple of minutes into the game, Milan got a free kick and Paulo Maldini, the Italian legend, was on the end of it to give them an early lead. You could feel the energy drain out of the crowd at that moment, the moans and groans amongst the Liverpool fans was noticeable. Paul gave me a look of youthful disgust, while Alex shook his head constantly and said, "This ain't a good start".

In the next 40 minutes, Milan's midfield pairing of Kaka and Pirlo destroyed us and put two chances Hernan Crespo's way. He was pure class and finished them both to put Liverpool 3-0 down at half time. Shock had grown legs, trampled all over every Liverpudlian's dreams and made them into the finest-tasting Italian wine which the Milan fans sipped at the half time break.

'This could turn out to be a total embarrassment if something doesn't change quickly', I thought, as I grabbed my phone from my shorts pocket - 52 missed fucking calls in a two-minute period, all the blue-nosed bellends calling from back home buzzing off our sheer humiliation in the first half. I couldn't take it, not one bit, so I launched the phone down onto the running track down below. When I looked around, Paul was taking his Liverpool shirt off.

"What are ya doin'?" I asked.

"I'm throwin' me shirt with ya phone", Paul said, with a tear rolling down his cheek. I was mortified, I froze solid, not a word would come out. I knew how he felt but I just couldn't bring myself to say anything to my sobbing six year old.

"Why did you bring me here?" His voice was angry and quivering.

I was totally shell-shocked.

"I'd rather be home playing with my Lego", Paul said, through floods of tears. By this time, I'd grabbed hold of his shirt and composed myself enough to address his plea.

"Look son, it's cost a lot of money to get you here and no matter what happens, everything will be okay, so there's no need to get upset." I said, calmly and quietly.

The fella who sat beside me noticed Paul's tears and knelt down beside him and said,

"We'll win this son; you've just gotta pray for it and sing." Paul looked at him, confused but it made me think. In an instant, I began to ask my dead father for some divine intervention. *'Please dad, can you just call in one last favour up there and help your devastated grandson out, PLEASE, whatever it takes, I'll suffer the consequences, can you help me out?'* I muttered under my breath while I looked up to the star-studded night sky.

By this time, Alex had fixed Paul's shirt and lifted him on to his seat to give him a better view.

"We're all gonna have to sing", we said simultaneously. Within seconds, the crowd around us all noticed Paul was upset and rallied round like fighting troops. Scarves were raised aloft and 'You'll Never Walk Alone' was sung like never before. The song caught on quickly as every Liverpool fan felt the same way as Paul. Within 30 seconds the whole Liverpool contingent was on their feet, singing our anthem with such emotion that it changed the mood in the stadium. As I looked around, there were grown men with tears rolling down their faces, singing at the top of their lungs.

I'd never felt like this ever before, singing the words to our song. It touched my soul like never before; the spirits of the 96 and all the fans who'd passed were with us.

The players made their way on to the pitch for the second half with every Liverpool fan on their feet still singing. Alex touched my side and passed me his phone.

"It's Lisa, she wants to make sure Little Paul's okay," he said. I told Lisa he was fine now but I'd thrown my phone away due to Evertonians pestering the life out of me at half time.

Like the rest of her family, Lisa is an Evertonian, but her son was a crazy Red like me. She told me she was watching the first half in the pub with her mates and had to leave when the third goal went in.

"Every time I listen to the match on the car radio, you win, so I've left the boozer and I'm driving round Liverpool's deserted streets now, praying for you." Lisa told me.

I tried to pass the phone to Paul, but he didn't want to speak to anyone. To be fair, we were still 3-0 down at half time in the Champions League Final and facing potential total meltdown.

"Gotta go babe, second half kickin' off now, oh….. and don't go back to the pub, we need all the help we can get luv, tarra." I said quickly, then turned my full attention to Paul and the match.

Didi Hamann came on for the second half and Rafa Benitez changed the system giving Steven Gerrard more of a forward role. In my mind it was damage limitation until Stevie G headed a belting goal early on in the second half to give us all a sight of hope. Liverpool's possession grew, as did the confidence of the players and supporters who all stood singing in the Atatürk Stadium. Within a few minutes, Vladimir Smicer scored another; a daisy cutter, which rapidly changed everyone's mood.

Paul was bouncing like a red-faced Tigger in front of me, I waited for him to calm down before I picked him up and placed him back on to the seat he'd been standing on, so he was now at eye level with me. Just as I wrapped my arm around his waist, Gerrard burst into the box after Jamie Carragher had went on a rampaging forward run.

"PENALTY!" Every Liverpool fan in the whole world shouted simultaneously, as Gerrard was upended by Gattuso. The referee pointed to the spot and Paul, Alex and myself went into another bouncing huddle, spinning round in ecstasy. Fuck me, we had a chance of pulling this back in six minutes, we'd found a 'get out of jail free card' or maybe my prayers, like thousands of others, had been answered.

We celebrated like we'd scored as Xavi Alonso placed the ball on the penalty spot at the other end of the stadium. Alonso was a class player, so everyone thought it was a given that he'd put the ball in the back of the net. I grabbed tight hold of Paul and Alex as Alonso hit the ball to Dida's right-hand side. Dida guessed the right way and parried the ball back on to the advancing Alonso, who rammed the ball into the roof of the net.

All hell broke loose as screams roared out of every Red, not just only in the ground, but around the globe. It was more disbelief than joy as six minutes earlier I'd watched some fans leave the ground because they couldn't handle it.

"Where the fuck were they now?" I thought to myself, as we began to sing our heads off. This was a great escape of epic proportions, you couldn't write shit like that for a far-fetched movie; the stuff of dreams, but it still wasn't over, far from it. I thought back to half time and the phone-throwing incident, which made me giggle now thinking of gutted Mancs and Evertonians; there's not much between the two of them really, so I'll refer to them as Manctonians from now on.

With 15 minutes of normal time remaining, Milan had gained the upper hand with possession and Dudek and Carragher needed to be at their very best to deal with it. They never let us down in that department.

The clock ticked as every Liverpool fan sang their hearts out trying to encourage one final miracle to go our way. The referee blew the whistle and now it was going to extra time. Whatever happened now, we all knew we'd done ourselves proud, the whole world would be watching this comeback of all comebacks.

With heads and scarves all held high, the singing reached anthemic heights during the tense, extra-time period. Jamie

Carragher showed unbelievable strength, courage and desire to block several goal-bound Milan efforts, as did Jerzy Dudek. In the dying seconds of the second half of extra time, Dudek pulled off a double save from Shevchenko that had goal written all over it.

Paul was holding on to me for dear life when the ball dropped to Shevchenko, one of the world's best players. When the ball flew over the bar, it was greeted like a goal as it would have been curtains if it had gone in. The referee blew his whistle on open play and now it was a penalty shoot-out to decide the 2005 Champions League Final in Istanbul.

Paul grabbed hold of my coat collar and said,

"We'll win this Dad, we will, we will ya know, Dad," as he put his head on my shoulder. I grabbed hold of him and I could feel his heart racing as my ear was now on his chest as we scanned the stadium for maybe the last time.

After a few minutes of players rushing round, especially Jamie Carragher who'd got hold of Dudek and was advising him on the penalty antics of Bruce Grobbelaar back in 1984 in Rome, when he put the Italians off to earn us a penalty shoot-out win. Carra waved his arms and moved from side to side to get his point across to the puzzled goalkeeper.

Serginho was the first penalty taker who, to our sheer delight blazed it miles over the bar. Didi Hamann strolled up calmly and slotted the ball into the back of the net to send us all delirious. For the time being, we had an advantage in the match. Pirlo was next and also missed to send us all ever so closer to our fifth European Cup. Cisse was next for us and he made sure of his pen and put us into a 2-0 advantage. Paul, Alex and I all started to look at each other with conviction now; we honestly could win this...

Tomasson was up next for Milan and scuffed his shot into the net to give Milan a gasp of hope. Vladimir Smicer was next up for us and he buried it to his great relief. He grabbed his Liver Bird badge and kissed it as he made his way to the centre circle to join the rest of the team, all linked together.

Now we were 3-2 up with Shevchenko walking towards Dudek's goal with the ball in his hands. This was Milan's last penalty, so they needed to score to give them any chance. Paul, Alex and I all did our own huddle of sorts as Shevchenko placed the ball on the penalty spot; he hit it towards the centre of the goal and Dudek saved it with his feet. OH MY GOD! The place erupted into a writhing mass of red and white, with people from 10 rows away somehow now beside us.

Ten seconds later, we were ten rows down celebrating with any supporter who was free; when I mean free, I mean for some reason they weren't in a mass huddle of their own. I could hardly breathe as excitement had taken over my body. I held Paul as if my life depended on it and looked up to the stars and thought I could sprout wings and fly right out of this stadium if I prayed hard enough. That's how strong the spiritual feeling was - somehow Liverpool Football Club had won the fifth European Cup in its history and now got to keep it, it was ours to keep forever. Put that in your Manctonian pipe and smoke it.

Paul and Alex were absolutely drained of emotion by the time we left the stadium. That was after we'd taken part in the best winning celebrations I'd ever seen. The sight of Stevie Gerrard lifting old Big Ears will always be in Alex, Paul's and my soul, no-one can change that, ever!

Hero Worship

Jerzy Dudek with Paul Jnr, Alex, myself and his Champions League medal

After an hour-long, sweaty coach ride from the stadium to Taksim Square, we joined in with the red masses taking in what had happened fully. Stories of people leaving at half time were floating about as everyone shared their own personal experiences of that crazy six minutes that changed all of our lives. Another hour was spent moving from one group to another swapping stories and I noticed it was getting late; in fact it was nearly 3am. In a heartbeat, I grabbed Paul and Alex and hailed a yellow cab to take us to the hotel.

Fifteen minutes in a jalopy taxi and we'd arrived outside our hotel to be greeted by armed guards who were stopping all cars from entering the grounds. I lowered the window, paid the driver and lifted Paul by his arms out of the window. Alex was looking round in amazement as TV cameras and crews were everywhere. It was at this moment I told Alex and Paul we were staying in the team hotel.

The driver wouldn't take the lock off the doors until he'd checked the money but by now, Alex had lowered his window and wormed his way out with a grin a mile wide.

"No way, are you messin'?" Alex said excitedly. Just as he finished speaking, bright camera lights revealed Jerzy Dudek 10 feet away, with a Polish TV crew interviewing him. Paul's jaw dropped as he noticed Dudek, he wriggled out of my grasp and headed full pelt towards him with his arms out.

"Jerzy, Jerzy, get in der, Championa, Championa, Championa, Liverpool!" Paul screamed out as he grabbed hold of him. Paul had ambushed the interview and Dudek grabbed him and lifted him up with one arm while high-fiving him on live Polish TV. It wasn't long before Paul realised Dudek had winner's medal around his neck and reached out to touch it. Alex joined them next, while I got my camera out to try and get a few pics of this moment. Dudek ended up putting Paul on his shoulders and dancing towards the hotel entrance with us all singing, *'Championa, Championa, Championa, Liverpool'.*

There was plenty of hustle and bustle and passport checking in the lobby. We never had an issue as somehow the security just left us to dance in with Dudek unchecked. I know it didn't matter anyhow, but that lead us right to a huge room at the back of the hotel. Alex and Paul were gobsmacked as all the players came over and said hello, especially when Steve Gerrard made some quality time for them.

We partied until 7am without really getting tired, adrenalin is a wondrous thing when you really need it. Going to sleep with Paul lying next to me that morning was hard as my body was still buzzing with excitement and sheer, utter, bamboozled joy.

A Flight to Treasure

Our flight home was not until 9pm on Thursday, so we arrived at the airport at 5pm trying to avoid any problems. The airport was in utter chaos as thousands of Liverpool fans had missed previous flights. There were huge tents set up to deal with the influx of supporters pre-boarding; this didn't work. Lads were just getting on to any flight they could, just to get out, and the authorities facilitated this openly. Fucking hell, this was turning into 'every man for himself'.

I grabbed Paul and Alex and rushed to the boarding gate to join in with the chaos. As I was waiting in a queue, I noticed a pal of mine who ran a totally-red boozer called 'The Anfield'. His name was Gary, but his head was in his hands and never seemed to move. I thought something had happened to him as I approached him through the madding crowd,

"Gary, Gary, what's wrong? We've just won the Champions League and you look lost, what the fuck's up with ya, mate?" He raised his head and shook it from side to side without saying a word and then slowly lowered it again. His pal was sitting next to him and stood up, grabbing my hand and whispered in my ear,

"He left at half time."

"NO FUCKIN' WAY!" I shouted, really loud, and then I roared laughing. In fact, I couldn't stop laughing and everyone around joined in. Instantly I started to sing,

'He left at half time, he left at half time

In Istanbul, he left at half time'

Everyone nearby joined in and within 20 seconds, so did everybody else in the boarding area, to Gary's utter shock. I wasn't being nasty, as Gary's a mad Liverpudlian, I was trying to lighten his mood. What's done is done, but I still couldn't believe he was one of the half-time unbelievers who'd scarpered.

We fought our way through and found Duty Free to try and get some goodies to take home as mementoes from Istanbul. I wanted to buy a few bottles of champagne for when we got home as Lisa had Sky-plussed all the pre and post-match events.

Chaos ensued throughout Duty Free as thousands packed the small concourse, I caught the attention of a woman serving and she tried to help me, only to be dragged away by her co-worker. She left a full case of Dom Perignon Rose champagne on the counter in front of me. I had to take it, it would be un-Scouse not to. Wham bam, thank you ma'am, and we vanished with six bottles of the finest. I even went back in and bought a bottle of black Cassis liqueur to add to it.

By 8pm we had boarded a Manchester-bound flight, singing our heads off throughout the rowdy journey. It was the same as the inward flight as skunk and Class As were in abundance. I thought it only right to pass two bottles of champagne around, while I polished off two on my own. I'd hardly consumed a drop in the whole four days so I'd earned it really. Paul fell asleep an hour into the flight, he was exhausted.

I'd saved the other two bottles so I could sit and watch the recorded match in the comfort of my home. This moment had to be shared with all the family, so Elizabeth, Lisa and Paul all joined me on the couch with some pizza and free champagne the next day.

It tasted of victory x 5!

Charity Begins at Home

With the songs of Istanbul ringing in my ears throughout the summer of 2005, I tried to relax as much as I could and push on with the Mouse Company. Gary Murphy was by my side every day as bands and artists had to be checked out at any given moment. I believed we could change the face of the music industry and start something exciting, fresh and growth-worthy in Liverpool. You have to dream to achieve.

Every budding musician wanted some connection with our city, so why not tap into that channel? LIPA (Liverpool Institute for Performing Arts – The Paul McCartney School) was also attracting the crème de la crème of European talent which was available to tap into as we both had our fingers in numerous pies. It was all around us if we wanted it badly enough. All we had to do was sing from the same hymn sheet and we'd do okay out of this.

I was still running about sorting high-profile gigs out for my nephew, Shaun, who was now a child celebrity. The BBC were forever on the phone booking him for shows or in-house charity balls, he always performed to the max and was breathtakingly good for his age. That kept me busy and moving me towards my objective: to try and get out of the drug game and start a new life.

One of the mothers in my kid's school approached me on the yard one morning and asked me to get involved with a local fundraiser. I was told that one of the kids who attended the school was seriously ill and it could prove fatal, so I immediately said yes.

It wasn't until a week later when I met Pat, one of the organisers, that the issues and event were made clear. They wanted me to pull my musical strings and get one of the local top bands to perform on the night. Pat had heard that the school events which I'd organised were a total success and pleaded with me to make this a success too. The main reason for the event was to raise money for the family who'd had to leave their jobs to attend to their sick child's every need. Of course I was going to help.

Pat hounded the life out of me every time I saw her at the school gates, in a nice way; however, it was intense.

"Have you sorted anything yet?" She asked twice a day for three solid weeks.

"Don't worry, Pat, everything will be okay, just leave it with me, once I get 100% confirmation, I'll let you know instantly, okay?" was always my reply, it must have burnt Pat's head out.

I'd called The Zutons and Coral management team as soon as Pat asked me three weeks earlier to find out their itinerary. I knew they were both free on the night but it's hard work pinning musicians down, especially two successful touring bands. Both bands had said they would play and told me to let them know closer to the actual day.

The party was now only three days away and everything else had been sorted. The family whose event it was were mad Liverpudlians, so I'd asked George Sephton (the voice of Anfield) to compere the evening and Shaun was also performing. The PA system was hired as was a van to carry the band's instruments to and from their rehearsal rooms. The Lord Mayor was also attending as a special guest; it was only in a small church club in Netherton, Liverpool. The venue looked like something out of *'Kes'*, wooden slatted walls with a huge glitter ball with several missing sections, hanging from the ceiling. It even had a picture of the Queen hanging behind the stage taking pride of place for everyone to see.

On the morning of the event, Pat was on the phone at 8 o'clock trying to ease her anxiety over who was going to play in the evening. Now, I'm one for surprises, so I kept her hanging on knowing that both bands would be turning up later on. I told her not to worry and just make sure that her end was boxed off. To be honest, I didn't want to let it get out that a top band was playing in a local club because it could attract the local youngsters and possible headaches.

The logistics to pick up The Coral and The Zutons was proving to be a nightmare until Philly Carragher, Jamie's dad, called and offered his services. I'd been speaking to him in the sauna at the local gym and he offered to help once I told him the family's situation. I took him up on his suggestion and he helped out in getting the show on the road and on time too.

Frank Cottrell-Boyce who wrote the screenplay for *'24 hour Party People'* had also called asking whether he could attend with his children who went to the same school as the sick child. News travels fast and it wasn't long before my phone was like the 'Bat Phone' – red hot.

My head was up my arse all day making sure everything was going to run smoothly, so I didn't see Pat until she arrived at the club. Her face lit up when she saw the equipment set up on the small stage.

"Who's playing, who've ya got to play, Paul?" she asked excitedly.

"The Coral, The Zutons and Shaun Walsh, plus I've got George Sephton to compère the evening for us." I said calmly, but really I was buzzing inside as I'd actually pulled it off.

The Coral had just finished supporting Oasis and would normally cost 20 grand for the night, and I'd just got them to do it for goodwill. It was the same with The Zutons and Shaun was on £1500 a time from the BBC, this was turning out to be a proud moment for everyone involved.

Within an hour, the club was packed to the rafters and the show got started with Shaun Walsh, followed by the Zutons, finally The Coral perfectly rounded off the musical side of the night. The family couldn't thank me enough and were amazed that I'd managed to get the bands to play. Tears rolled down their cheeks while they thanked the band lads, George Sephton and Shaun at the evening's end.

The auction on the night raised tens of thousands for the family, so it was a total success. In fact, Pat was that pleased with my efforts she asked for my hand in marriage, not seriously, but it meant a lot to both of us, successfully pulling this off. Every single family member of the young child personally came to thank me for helping them out, the satisfaction was enough for me and the added praise filled me with hope.

A few weeks later, I was contacted by a mate of Gary Murphy who worked for Liverpool Football Club. His name was Tom Cassidy and he wanted me to help him out with the music side of future special events at Anfield. I was buzzing when I put the phone down Anfield was my nirvana.

Tom explained the sort of events he was putting on and when he told me it was to celebrate our fifth European Cup win, my mind started to dance around, just like I danced on the Wembley steps back in 1978. I attended the December event to gauge what it was all about then put my networking skills into play to come up with a realistic plan of who would play live. This looked exciting, I was buzzing.

I'd also had a shot across my bows in December when a pal I grafted with got word to me from Walton jail. The message wasn't a good one either, the SOCA (Serious Organised Crime Agency) squad had been asking questions about me when he was being interviewed. That's not fucking good at all, here's me trying my best to get away from that shite, but it just wouldn't go away.

If I was to tell you that I didn't give a flying fuck about this message, then I'd be lying through my back teeth. It doesn't matter who you are, when the police come knocking, you shit yourself. We've all been pulled by bizzies and had narrow escapes from being nicked, but it still leaves everyone with 'wobbly foot' - that's when your foot shakes on the clutch just after being told you're allowed to drive after being pulled over. Well, this phone call gave me a wobbly brain, it fucked with my plans as I'd kept a finger or two in certain pies for insurance purposes. Don't get me wrong, I wanted nothing more than to leave the graft but I'd grown accustomed to a certain lifestyle which needed to be maintained at times.

My Oasis

It was the beginning of 2006 when the tax man invited Lisa down to discuss her and her family's tax issues. Some of the questions seemed strange and sparked concerns from me. Obviously, I couldn't say too much to Lisa as she still knew fuck all about what I did, but I did mention it on the quiet to a few of the lads I grafted with

It was there and then I made the decision to be ultra-observant about all my actions and reactions. Here's me on one hand leading a normal life and on the other hand, I'm acting like a single-cell militant drug dealer just so I can exist; good job I'd stopped smoking skunk because that would have seriously given my head a massive wobble.

My life just seemed to float from one extreme to another as I tried to redress the balance of power within myself. Every time I took two steps away from the drug game, it wouldn't be long before I found myself on the backward escalator which dropped me off in the middle of shite. One minute I'm with an up-and-coming band giving them advice on how to make strides in the right direction, then I'm meeting with fair-weather graft friends who want me to do this and that. Why don't I just grow a set of bollocks and fuck the drug game off? Why? Why? Why? You know why I didn't turn my back on it; for two reasons – money and my inability say 'no'.

I was sitting at home watching MTV during February when Liam and Noel Gallagher were being interviewed. They were asked about the national football team and basically disrespected the whole squad, except for Jamie Carragher.

"You don't hear stories about him in the press, do ya?" Noel replied to the interviewer. "All the others and their birds are plastered over the tabloids, but Jamie Carragher isn't, he's the only one we can relate to", said the Gallagher brothers as they nodded at each other.

I was buzzing to hear the Mancunian superstars bigging up Carra and was right on the phone Philly, who I'd kept in touch with after the charity concert and frequently bumped into him at the gym. Ten minutes later, Philly, he called me back to inform me that Jamie was a huge Oasis fan and was proud as punch to hear the news. Within five minutes of that conversation, I'd called James Skelly of The Coral, who'd just finished touring with them and asked him to contact Noel or Liam.

Jay Skelly was buzzing because he was a massive Liverpool fan and got in touch with Noel rapidly. Within an hour, Noel Gallagher had called Carra too. He'd arranged a load of guest-list tickets for Jamie and his pals to go to Sheffield Arena to see Oasis play live. Jamie and his family were over the moon with the outcome. It wasn't long before phone calls about the upcoming gig from Carra started.

"Paul, how many tickets did you say we could have for the concert?"

"Why, what's up?"

"It's just that I need double what you said…I'll pay for them though." Carra said apologetically.

"Leave it with me, Jamie, I'll get ya back in a bit."

After a few calls, everything was sorted and Jamie was buzzing with the outcome. I decided I wasn't going to go the gig as I didn't want to look like a geg-in, that's just not my style, my place was at home with my kids as Jamie and his pals all made the journey across the Pennines to see Oasis a few days later.

Gary Murphy ended up going and was phoning me throughout the evening like an on-the-spot reporter telling me about their five-star treatment. Noel and Liam had really pulled out all the stops and gave them their own private box, as well as having a private party sorted after the gig. I earned some great brownie points for sorting this out, the whole Carragher family were buzzing meeting up with the Gallaghers.

The music side of things was starting to take up most of my time. The events at Anfield just kept coming and Shaun Walsh was singing at all of them, he started to get a great reputation as he was a regular on 'Dick and Dom in Da Bungalow'. The BBC production crew were constantly booking him and we'd often meet celebrities when we were at the London studios; Alan Hansen, Gary Lineker, Al Murray and Tracy Beaker were all just some of the celebs that made a beeline for Shaun when we waited around in Shepherd's Bush.

On the last ever live show of Dick and Dom, we bumped into David and Carrie Grant. The first thing he said to me was, 'I can tell you're Scousers, but I need to know if you're Red or Blue?'

"We're crazy Liverpool fans", I replied to an excited David Grant.

"That's good, because so am I, in fact, John Barnes is my cousin", he batted back quickly.

"Oh, and by the way Shaun, you're a superstar, how long have you been singing?" David asked Shaun, while rubbing the top of his head.

"Since I was six", Shaun replied politely.

"Well, I'm glad that you're both Liverpool fans and I'm thrilled at hearing you sing live this morning. How old are you now, Shaun?" said David.

"I'm ten."

"Here's my number, call me in a few weeks and we'll meet up." David said, placing his business card in my hand. After a five minute conversation about our beloved Liverpool, David's wife, Carrie, appeared and dragged him off to catch their taxi.

Two days later, David's business card was burning a hole in my pocket. I couldn't wait two weeks to get in touch; that just wasn't my style. I ended up emailing David on the third day and invited him to Liverpool to watch a game with me. A few days later, he contacted me and gave me his personal numbers so we could keep in touch. He wanted Shaun for a project in London the following week, which led to us meeting up again and we arranged to go to the next match at Anfield together.

It was May 2006 and Liverpool had reached the semi-final of the FA Cup at Old Trafford; our opponents were Jose Mourinho's Chelsea. I invited David Grant, but he was busy, so I ended up going in a mini-bus with the lads from The Coral.

The ground was heaving as my usual match-day companions, Alex, Paul and I took up our seats in the main stand. John Arne Riise opened the scoring and Luis Garcia scored an absolute belter to take us into the FA Cup Final with West Ham in a few weeks' time. The journey home in the mini-bus listening to Buddy Holly was brilliant. Didier Drogba was a thorn in our side throughout the season, so we changed every possible word in every Buddy Holly song to take the piss out of the London-bound Chelsea fans, who were parked next to us on the roads out of Manchester. No-one really expected us to win comfortably, that just made the victory even sweeter on the way home.

A few phone calls to Philly Carra and a text to Jamie gave me an idea of a sort of 'thank you' to Jay from The Coral for helping sort out the Oasis trip for Jamie. I made all The Coral lads come the Salisbury boozer in Marsh Lane, Bootle; reluctantly though. They weren't really heavy drinkers, plus they all lived in Hoylake which was at least a 45-minute drive away. What I didn't tell them was that Jamie Carra was going to be coming back for a few drinks to celebrate with his friends and family. Ten minutes into trying to keep them in the boozer, in walks Jamie all suited and booted and walked to the bar where we all stood. The Coral lads' jaws all dropped and Jamie said,

"I fuckin hate that Drogba, he's just kicked fuck outta me all game, I need a beer – now." Nick Power (keyboard player) kicked my foot and nodded as Jamie had noticed Jay and started to chat to the band about music, football and Didier Drogba. That was my cue to put some Buddy Holly on the jukebox to liven up the bar celebrations.

That season wasn't a bad one for LFC either, as we'd managed to reach the FA Cup Final where our opponents were West Ham. We also managed to finished fourth in the Premier League to qualify for the Champions League again.

The FA Cup Final was another adventure for Alex and Paul as we travelled to a recording studio in South Wales with The Coral, where we stayed the night before the match. Apparently it was the studio where Oasis' first album was recorded; a maze of rooms and corridors in the middle of nowhere and we spent the night singing, drinking and eating barbequed grub.

Star Struck

It took us about an hour to make our way down back roads and country lanes into Cardiff on the morning of the final. I'd arranged to meet David Grant, Dave McCabe, Russ Pritchard and Philly Carra for a few drinks, so I was plotted up nice and early with Alex, Paul and The Coral lads. The sea of red, white, claret and blue around the Millennium Stadium was fantastic. The banter was friendly as most people thought Liverpool would walk it. Once we'd bumped into everyone we wanted to see, it was time to head into the stadium.

It didn't take long for the first goal to go in and it wasn't good for us. Not long after that, we found ourselves two goals down. This was turning out to be a proper downer. Paul was hanging on to my arm throughout the first half with a face on him. Luckily Djibril Cisse pulled a goal back to give Paul and every other Liverpudlian hope at last.

The second half started off just like the first and West Ham scored another early goal to give them a two goal cushion. Stevie Gerrard pulled one back for us, but time seemed to be slipping away. It looked like nearly-relegated West Ham would win the Cup as underdogs and I knew every Evertonian and Man United fan would be buzzing their socks off.

Paul was asking me to leave a few minutes early from the end as he was pissed off. We were into the 93rd minute now, with only 60 seconds left, when the ball fell to Stevie Gerrard about 35 yards out, ooosh!! He belted it low like a rocket into the corner of the net and the Liverpool end of the stadium erupted into a sea of swarming, swaying bodies. He'd only gone and pulled us out of the shit again. We were dead and buried minutes earlier and now relief, belief and excitement grew rapidly.

The Ref blew and it was down to extra time. Most of the players on the field were totally knackered, so the extra time period passed by without much incident. Penalties? How much more penalty drama could Liverpool fans take? It seemed like every major game we played ended in some sort of dramatic, over-scripted climax.

West Ham missed a few but we were on the button and Pepe Reina made some great saves to send all the Liverpudlians home buzzing. Another trophy and more great memories shared with Paul and Alex. A few drinks with David Grant, Dave McCabe, Jay Skelly, Nick Power and Philly Carra afterwards ended obviously in song and we'd all arranged to meet up on 25 May for the anniversary of Istanbul back at Anfield.

Tom Cassidy from Liverpool Football Club was on the phone to me on the Monday after the Cup Final asking to help him with the Istanbul anniversary. He wanted me to try and get some of the first team players to turn up, as only ex-players came to the previous one.

I pulled out all the stops and eventually persuaded Jamie Carragher to attend, along with David Grant, the Coral, the Zutons, Starsailor and Dave Kirby; a great Scouse playwright and poet. Tom had worked his bollocks off to get things sorted, so you can imagine how anxious we both felt on the morning of the party. All our hard work was now on the line as 300 guests expected one of the best nights of their lives.

At 8.30 that night, Shaun Walsh started to sing his version of 'You'll Never Walk Alone', setting spines tingling. None of the paying guests knew Jamie Carragher was attending, so when he appeared through bright red doors holding the Champions League trophy, the whole place went mental. Flashes from cameras lit the room up like a firework display; screams of joy and scarves being hurled around ignited the guests into Johnny Cash's 'Ring of Fire' chorus hook … "de, de, der, der, der….de, de, de, derr". These moments in my life just seemed to get better.

I took a deep breath and stock of my surroundings. I was in the biggest suite in the Centenary Stand in my beloved Anfield with a present-day Liverpool legend, alongside some of the most talented musicians of the day. I'd actually had a hand in making this happen and I was fucking loving it. The night couldn't have gone any better and the party carried on to John Aldridge's bar in Liverpool town centre until the early hours of the morning. What a night!

Madness still engulfed my time as one day I'd be having serious meetings with professional business people and the next I'd be balls deep into graft. I couldn't get away from the graft no matter what I tried to tell myself. I made a decision to try my utmost to make a serious go of the music business.

Another Chance to Escape the Drug Game

An opportunity came about from a guest at the Istanbul Anniversary dinner. He worked for a major telecommunications company and invited me to their head office to sit in on in-house training and look for angles that I thought could work. This fella believed in me and was impressed with my networking and social skills. With his faith in me and my scheming brain, it didn't take long for an idea to spark me into overdrive.

It was originally featured around a festival and it was now morphing into a totally different beast with a major phone company backing me. Meeting after meeting ended up with more meetings and I eventually ended up having to invite David Grant, Gary Murphy and a major development company on board to take it forward seriously.

David Grant took the idea to new levels and before too long we needed advisors on ethics and morals. So I was having discussions with business people about ethics and morals after I'd been dealing drugs for years and I'd managed to worm myself into a situation where I was bordering on hypocrisy. In fact, it was 100% hypocrisy with bells and whistles on.

I carried on with it and called the venture *'Your Band'*. By now, somebody at Government level was interested through David's contacts and they wanted us to introduce an identity card scheme. I even contacted Philly Carra to see if Jamie's business partners wanted to jump on board; this was looking tasty now. Philly eventually got back to me and said we'd meet up after the World

Cup in August or September as it was only early stages in development.

One of my pals who I grafted with had decided to go to the World Cup and left me holding the fort for him. I knew the ropes so it wasn't a big deal, but it just meant I was back on the frontline with major graft responsibilities. With the news of the lad in jail who'd marked my card and the tax man sniffing around, I approached everything with caution.

It didn't take long before it went tits up and someone got nicked on the road moving tackle around. That shook my plans to the core and the 'Your Band' venture had to take a backseat as bodies had been nicked and money and drugs had been lost. That meant questions had to be answered - and fast.

My pal was on the phone from the World Cup which didn't help matters; my belief was that phone calls got you nicked. Trying to have a conversation when the shite has just hit the fan is hard, you need to tell them outright, but you can't. They want to know what's going on now, they're not arsed about security as the need-to-know-now syndrome kicks in and everything else goes out the fucking window. I tried my best not to break the rules I'd led my life by for years.

The worst thing about it was that lads I hardly knew were knocking at my house trying to make sense of who, what, where and when the nicking happened. I must be fucking mad, what was I playing at?

Drugs, lads I didn't know knocking at my front door, everything you shouldn't do, I was now doing. I thought I'd be free from the drug game by now and be a legitimate member of society, that's what I was hoping and now I had muppets knocking at my door asking questions. For fuck sake!

Domino Effect (Tumbling Down)

The following week, another problem popped up and more or less had us all scratching our heads. Someone else had been nicked and that triggered a sequence of events that ended up in another three people being nicked; it was looking bad.

An in-house inquest was issued resulting in all sorts of conspiracy theories. All I knew was I was properly in the thick of a massive pile of shite, no matter which way you looked at it. It was time to get rid of all the communications again and shut up shop until we could try and make sense of the debacle.

A week's camping in South Wales and then peace and quiet at home with the kids watching the World Cup was like a shot in the arm. We had a proper buzz in Cardigan Bay and the kids loved every minute of it. In fact, I promised we'd go back at the end of September. While I was sitting at home watching Granada Reports, I receive a call from an unknown foreign number. This was on my own personal phone, so I panicked at first and didn't answer. Two minutes later, it rang again. I paused, stared at the phone and pressed the receiver button.

"Hello?" I said, tentatively.

A Scouse voice replied, "Is that you, Paul?"

'Who the fuck is this?' I thought quickly... "Why, who's this?" I replied, frowning and taking the phone away from my ear to look at the number again. As I put the phone back to my ear, the voice said,

"It's Philly Carra."

"Fuck me, I was wondering who the fuck was calling me from a foreign number. What's up, mate?" I said, with more than a hint of relief in my voice.

"Jamie's worried about his medals; Jerzy Dudek's house has been burgled. His haul of memorabilia and Champions League medals have gone. Can you go and get all Jamie's medals, England caps and footy shirts from his house and keep hold of them until we get home?"

"No problem, I'll go now, mate." After another lengthy phone call from Carra himself, explaining the elaborate code system to deactivate the burglar alarm, I felt an incredible sense of urgency. Once Jay had informed me where his spare keys were, I went and picked them up rapidly. I was buzzing that he trusted me to help him out, I hadn't known him that long but the main reasons were that I lived locally and I knew his dad pretty well.

It wasn't long before I was putting all Jamie Carragher's medals, trophies, caps and autographed opponent's shirts into bin bags. Somehow this just didn't seem right, how could I put these treasured items into bin bags? It was wrong; really wrong.

I decided to call Jamie and came up with a plan of taking the most important ones and I'd stay in his house until he came back from Baden-Baden. I couldn't believe I was looking at Paolo Maldini's signed AC Milan shirt from the Istanbul final. That shirt represented to me and tens of thousands of Liverpudlians, one of the best nights of our lives and I was holding it and about to take it home.

I ended up staying in Jamie's house until he returned from the World Cup and kept all his beloved trophies, medals and shirts safe.

Over the rest of the summer, I spent most of my time with the kids and took them on another camping trip to Lake Windermere, whilst Lisa cracked on with her new nursing job.

Our relationship was a bit rocky as I was out of the house all the time. As soon as she returned from work, I'd have to scarper off to see someone, somewhere. I couldn't help running about as the problem with the graft was weird. Questions still needed to be answered and my pal who went the World Cup decided to extend his break and stay out the country for longer. I would have done the same if I was in his shoes, the only thing was though is that I was in my own shoes and I needed to deal with these problems now. It was up to me as I was the only person around who knew the ropes.

The Shit Hits The Fan

The 2006/07 football season was around the corner and a welcome distraction from graft politics. I set a goal of going to as many games as possible, both home and away. Paul was always asking to go on away trips too. Which eight-year-old footy fan wouldn't want to go everywhere with their team? So I made some promises to Paul and plans for pre-season games and the up-and-coming 2006/7 season.

A local-ish trip to Wrexham was sorted and David Grant even made the journey to Liverpool, where we had made plans to have some meetings about the 'Your Band' venture. It was still moving in the right direction, but now it had some weight behind it due to David's involvement; plus the phone company, O2 were willing to jump on board.

David ended up staying in Liverpool for a few days so I had to look after him and keep the graft side of things totally out of sight. I would kick myself if somehow David got wind of my other life. I really wanted a clean break and getting something stable and legitimate on the go was my absolute priority.

I knew it could all change any second as every time I've achieved anything in my life, somehow it's dissipated into nothing. That was the pattern, that's why my fingers were permanently crossed, I always touched wood, looked for another magpie if I only saw one and constantly prayed silently, asking my dad to watch over me.

With all things rosy in my life now except for the graft aspect, the footy season was underway and a trip to Sheffield United that ended up 1-1 wasn't a bad away day to get us off the mark. Paul, Philly and Alex all made the trip with me across the Pennines to Sheffield and on the way back home; we stopped at Hillsborough to lay some flowers. I couldn't go to Sheffield without paying my respects and even today, half a lifetime later; it still chokes me up and sends my mind back to that fateful day.

The next away match was a game against PSV Eindhoven; Paul was at school so Lisa decided he couldn't go, but I was 100% going. Another trip to Holland, it was like my second home. Even though I lived only a 35 minute drive from Wales, Holland was more familiar to me than the Welsh countryside. Mark, who worked for the development company, who was dealing with the 'Your Band' venture was a Liverpudlian and wanted to go to Holland for the match. He was buzzing when I said I'd go with him and I could sort us tickets out from Carra, so he booked the flights and I provided the tickets.

On Monday 11th September, Mark turned up at my house in Blundellsands mid-morning, so we could catch a flight to Amsterdam that afternoon. The weather was unusually hot for that time of year, so I only took one pair of combat shorts, a pair of trainers, a fleece, a few T-shirts and my flip flops. I threw them in my navy blue Berghaus rucksack that had somehow found its way into my possession, along with £400. That was all I needed as I was only there for two nights, plus I wasn't really drinking, so that was one less thing to worry about.

The flight was on time; Amsterdam and the Scouse Red Army that would be passing through on the way to Eindhoven were calling my name. After a couple of beers with Mark and a few other lads, we headed off back to our hotel which was overlooking the Rembrandtplein in the centre of Amsterdam. The usual head-out-of-the-window routine to scour your new location was on the cards; Mark and I obviously obliged; only this time the smell of skunk, takeaway food and the singing Scouse voices made me feel like I wasn't far away from home.

The next morning I was woken by my phone ringing early. I was having one of those dreams when a phone actually rings in your sleep and you have to wake up to answer it. I fumbled around the hotel bedside cabinet to grab my mobile. Once I'd got hold of it, I tried to focus on who was calling me this early; as it was about 7'ish and that meant it was 6 am at home. My neighbour's number was flashing.

'That's fucking weird', I thought, 'there must be something wrong for him to be calling this early'. I guessed it might be my house alarm going off when I answered the call. "Hello?" I said, in a croaky, early-morning type of voice. I couldn't really hear what my neighbour was saying, as the noise of sirens rang out in the background.

"The Police have raided your house," said Alan, my overly-polite neighbour.

"What?"

"There's about four riot vans, three cars, 20 police officers with dogs and they've busted your door off its hinges," he shouted.

The commotion in the background made my whole body freeze and total shock engulfed my soul and mind and sent nerves I never knew I had, jangling.

"Okay, Alan, I'll call you back", I said, as fright turned into pure terror. I tried to call Lisa but her phone was engaged. 'What the fuck is going on here?' I thought, while I went through my phonebook to find my graft pals' personal numbers.

The next person I called was my pal who went away to the World Cup, he was home now. I dialled and waited….it rang.

"Hello," I said quietly. There was no reply. I never said another word, but I could hear voices in the background and then a strange voice said,

"Hello, who's this?"

I put the phone down sharply, knowing that it was the Police who'd answered, so I quickly picked up another pal's number who I grafted with and called him, whilst I sat on the end of my hotel bed with the feeling of impending doom gathering overhead.

The ringtone came and I waited again for it to be answered, hopefully by a friendly voice.

'Hello', I said tentatively.

"Is that you, Paul?" It was Gary's girlfriend.

"Is everything okay?" I asked

"No, it's not...the Police have raided our house and are still here now, where are you?" She sounded panicked.

"Look, I'll call you back later". I hung up the phone, pronto and hung my head in disbelief. My world had just caved in, big time. I called Lisa back and this time she answered.

"Look, I'll call you back as soon as I can, I can't talk now cos I'm with the Police," she said nervously.

"What have they said? Are they looking for me?" I asked quickly, rubbing my now-sweaty right palm.

"Drugs and YOU", she whispered down the phone, just before she hung up. As I brought the phone away from my ear, the floor seemed to open up and all the wondrous moments in my life were flushed away in one big swirl. My kids, family and friends all flashed by in a millisecond in HD widescreen. Oh my God, the hole swallowed me up, too - my entire body went numb. I could only hear my inner soul which felt like the inside of an under-threat beehive.

With my head in my hands for what seemed like forever, my true senses and feelings started to return to normal. Well, if you can call the feeling of impending doom normal, that is. WHAT THE FUCK WAS I GONNA DO? That's all that was rolling about in my half-empty brain now, as the other half of my brain's contents had been wiped away in one clean sweep. Somehow the delete button had been activated minutes earlier and I couldn't get away from feeling absolutely empty. I had to kick my arse into stop feeling sorry for myself and start to deal with this naughty, naughty situation I found myself in.

Mark was in the next room, so I woke him at about 8 o'clock and I told him I'd be going out for the morning but I'd be back at midday to catch the train to Eindhoven. He was none the wiser to my situation and I wasn't going to tell him, so he scratched his head and headed back to bed. I had a few pals who lived in Amsterdam, so I bolted out of the hotel door in pursuit of help. I was properly fucked here, with only €350, shorts, flip flops and a borrowed rucksack to my name.

My head never stopped spinning as I walked across the cobbled roads, tramlines and cycle tracks of central Amsterdam. En route to find one of my old buddies, I dismantled my mobile phone and smashed it into as many pieces as I could. I knew the Police would have my numbers if they'd raided my house, as I'd read an article in the Liverpool Echo a few weeks earlier; the main thrust of it was that if SOCA came knocking at your door, you were in deep shit as they don't make mistakes.

That's what was rushing around my head as I walked around the sun-drenched, narrow streets of Amsterdam. After an hour of door-to-door pleading, I eventually got hold of someone who sorted my head out. It was the shot in the arm I needed and I arranged to plod on as normal. A short taxi ride across town and I bumped into Mark who was enjoying the sunshine in Rembrandtplein outside the coffee shop next to our hotel. After something to eat and a coffee,

Mark and I left to catch the train to Eindhoven. I didn't want to call Lisa as I knew the Police would be questioning her, so I called a friend from the train station to explain my situation. He immediately got on it for me and went to get hold of Lisa.

The train journey was a quiet one for me as I couldn't get the thoughts of my kids, Lisa and my family out of my head. I was mulling over that I might not see them again. I didn't know what was going to happen but I was picturing the absolutely worst scenario and I just couldn't stop thinking about it. Mark was talking to me but I couldn't hear a single word as pure fear was so loud in my head; his mouth was moving and I just nodded as I travelled to Eindhoven, numb.

We headed to the usual big square when we arrived to find a few of my pals who'd also made the journey. I made my way to the first payphone I could find to call my pal who'd gone to pass on the message to Lisa. When I got through, he was with Lisa and my kids.

"E r lad, I'll put Lisa on," he said, as soon as he answered. There was no greeting of friends as we both knew the severity of the situation; formalities went out the window.

"Are you ok, Luv?" I asked, apologetically.

"Yeah, I'm sound, the front door has seen better days like, but they said as soon as I speak to you, I've to tell you to come and speak to them."

"What? Why do they wanna see me?" I stammered.

"They're saying you're involved in a major drug gang. They've nicked 14 of your mates and they want you. Paul, what are you gonna do?

"Fuck knows just yet, babe, but don't worry, I'll make sure you're looked after. I don't wanna say too much on the phone so I'll get Phil to keep in touch with you." Phil was one of the lads who I'd met during my Blue Ruby band days; he was staunch as fuck and I knew he wouldn't blabber stuff around. I needed people like that around me especially now.

By the time we reached the stadium around 7pm, I was worried about maybe getting nicked there. There was always a small group of local Police who travelled to away games and I thought I'd be on their radar. I reluctantly mingled with the Liverpool fans entering the stadium with Mark, who was still unaware of my serious dilemma.

Once we entered the stadium, I bumped into a few lads who'd travelled over only a few hours earlier and they couldn't wait to let me know that the raids were all over the local news. One told me 20 had been nicked and three and a half million pounds' worth of drugs seized. Another told me a slightly different version of the first story. Every grafter who travelled to that match seemed to know that my house had been raided; news travels super-fast in those circles; especially bad news.

The match was insignificant to me, as my head still spun around ploughing chasms of doubt, doom and damage. It ended up 0-0 and I couldn't have given a flying fuck. I've had bad experiences connected to football matches before, but this one stood alone, and

I mean alone. That's exactly how I felt: lonely, scared, vulnerable and also slightly excited about what was round the corner.

When I told Mark I was staying in Holland to meet up with a friend, he still had no idea I was in deep shit. So there I was with roughly €300, clothes for a two-day trip and the weight of the world on my shoulders.

Waving Mark off in the taxi as he began his return journey to Liverpool, I headed in a totally different direction filled with emptiness. My kids, Lisa, my mum, brothers and sisters, my music pals, my graft pals, my existence and everything I treasured, I more-or-less waved off in Mark's taxi.

My brothers now lived in Perth, Australia, so I called them both to let them know my situation. I was trying to hold myself together while I explained my dilemma,

"Look Ste, I'm fucked, proper fucked like ze Germans." I was trying to make a joke of my situation.

"What's happened, Kidda?"

"My door's gone in yesterday and 11 of my mates have been nicked, they're looking for me but I'm still in Holland, I don't know what to do."

Obviously I knew he couldn't really help me but I just needed to get it off my chest. I'd not said a word to anyone in my immediate family and I knew he would contact them and more importantly, say the right things. After another brief conversation with my eldest brother,

Robert, to sketch him up, it was time to locate my pal who said he'd find me a place to stay. Two hours later, I was on my way to start a new life as a wanted fugitive.

Hiding Out

Seven flights of narrow wooden stairs led to my top-floor bedsit on the outskirts of central Amsterdam. Everyone knows the story of Anne Frank hiding from the Germans in a loft in Amsterdam during World War II, well, I was now re-enacting the whole story.

After scanning my new surroundings and looking out over the rooftops, it was time for a few more phone calls home. It was two days since we'd passed the point of no return and I'd had a bit of time to think clearly. A pal had given me the name and number of one of the solicitors dealing with two of the lads who'd been charged. My pal had sketched him up as much as he could, but he didn't know it was me who was calling.

I waited patiently as his secretary put me through. After the initial pleasantries with no names being mentioned, we got down to chatting about the case.

"I'm gonna read out a list of names and then I'll ask you some questions, but I must say now, for legal reasons, if you're on the list, you need to contact the Police and arrange surrender, okay?" the solicitor said, in a matter of fact way.

He began to read the names and I was second on the list of 13. The solicitor continued,

"Now if you're in the top few, then you've got serious problems."

"What do you mean by serious?" My heart was beating furiously and louder than ever.

"Well, if you are in the top four and you've got plans in the next seven or eight years, I'd advise you not to come back home, that's only if you can stay away. But again, for legal reasons, if you're wanted, you need to contact the Police to arrange surrender," he said knowingly.

My heart sank as I asked him to 'read the list of names again, please.' Then it sank deeper and deeper until there was nowhere else it could go. I thanked him for his help and hung up in slow motion. I was properly fucked.

I called my pal, Phil, and arranged to speak to Lisa to let her know that I was going on the run. Now I'd never, ever imagined this scenario happening to me, so I wasn't prepared in any way. No way was I handing myself into the Police for them to line me up with 11 others and start to mudsling, not a chance.

A month in to my 'Anne Frank revisited' tour, I'd risen to become Britain's most-wanted criminal. My face was plastered all over websites, TV news, local and national press in connection with a three and a half million pounds' drug conspiracy. They even plastered my picture on a huge advertising lorry that was driven around Liverpool and its neighbouring suburbs for everyone interested to gawp at. Things were closing in on me fast, I was beyond paranoid.

A few of the lads I knew who lived in Holland had a whip-round and got me enough money to look after myself for a few months.

"It's not cheap when you're on the run, you'll have to get out grafting, lad", said one of my pals, who had lived in Amsterdam for the past 10 years. Advice was flooding in from all the graft lads now. I filtered the advice and took on board what was relevant, while I started to rebuild my entire life from scratch.

A couple of months of not moving out of my lofty bedsit and being looked after by the lads, and it was time to make a move. Where would I go? Is it safe outside? Would anyone recognise me? What should I do about my family? Who can I ask for help?

Questions and more questions went round my head as I pondered my next move. The most important thing was that I had a chance to start a new life; my pals sitting in solid-brick cells in Liverpool's Victorian Walton prison never had that option.

I really wanted them here with me, but that was wishful thinking. I felt for every single one of them and their families as I packed my borrowed, blue rucksack and headed down the seven narrow flights of wooden stairs.

On The Move

Zurich was the first step on the new path I'd been forced to take. I'd heard stories about Needle Park and the beautiful lakes; I also had a friend living there who I knew would be buzzing to see me.

After an overnight-trip on the train, I arrived at Zurich's central station three days before Christmas 2006, greeted by freezing, heavy winds. It took my breath away and reduced my eyes to slits the second I got off the train.

My clothes were not stopping this severe weather cutting through. My four layers of inefficient cover surrendered to the weather as I made my way up the steps of the train station.

I headed to the nearest phone and called my friend, Frank, who answered quickly and was overjoyed once he'd realised I was only three miles from his apartment. It was 8am as I waited in the kiosk bar café shop on the main floor of this huge, stunning train station, waiting for Frank to come and pick me up.

He arrived, with his Estonian girlfriend holding his hand; that really took me by surprise as Frank had never come across as the 'holding-hands' type. He was a terrific guitarist whom I'd known for 20 years, who also knew his way around security systems.

He'd decided Liverpool had seen better days after Thatcher got a grip on it and legged it to Holland first, before heading to Switzerland. Basel was his first city, but he eventually settled in Zurich and he hosted many of the travelling grafters who needed shelter or help along the way. His nature was that way, a decent, no-nonsense lad who liked a bit of undercover skulduggery. When I explained my predicament, he was more than welcoming and said I could stay as long as I wanted; that was if I could cook.

"Result! I'm a belting cook, Frank." I said, as he began to introduce me to his girlfriend, Janka.

Thirty minutes later, Frank and Janka were showing me round my new home for Christmas and New Year; obviously the kitchen was on Frank's agenda and our glorious Christmas dinner I'd talked myself into making on the journey from the station to his apartment. The conversation turned to proper gravy, which led us to a discussion about two Irish bars in Zurich which had access to Oxo or Bisto granules. With a quick nudge and a wink, I found myself heading back across town with Frank.

The Irish Bar was our destination in the hunt for some English creature comforts; Oxo, Yorkshire puddings, Christmas pudding, and of course, the black stuff, Guinness. Four hours later, Frank and I were having our own in-house concert in Kennedy's Irish bar in the centre of Zurich.

The honky-tonk piano and old acoustic guitar hanging up behind the bar found their way into our hands and there ensued the day's musical entertainment. Frank didn't know I'd learnt to play guitar and was stunned when I busted out some Beatles' tunes, in full Scouse voice too.

"Fuck me lad, you can deffo knock a tune out, lad, giz the guitar here; I'll play, you sing," said half-pissed Frank, as he grabbed the guitar and busted out tunes from Pink Floyd's 'The Wall'.

Who'd have thought that I was Britain's Most Wanted as I sang full pelt, openly in an Irish bar in Zurich to 30 unsuspecting drinkers. I'd been stressing for nearly four months now so this was literally music to my ears; good ale, good company and nobody had a clue who I was.

Another six weeks in Zurich with Frank and Janka and I'd decided to head back to Amsterdam…but not before I'd taken a train ride up the Swiss Alps to Gstaad to enjoy some snow scenery and filthy-rich antics from some of the most beautiful women I've ever seen in one place in my whole life.

The Palace Hotel was the playground for some of the world's richest people, which therefore attracted the most beautiful women. Frank had given me a guitar and I was strumming along on my veranda, when I was approached by the resident pianist to join her in the bar later on for a sing-song. I accepted the invitation and carried on with strumming away.

Two hours later, I was propping the plush bar up with Bella the Bulgarian pianist, singing my little head off. The funny thing about it was Tina Turner and Roger Moore (007) were applauding Bella and myself, as they were both regulars over the Christmas period at the Palace Hotel. I'm on Britain's most wanted list and now I'm singing to some of the world's A List celebs. It still didn't change the fact that I was missing Lisa and the kids like mad, but it did give me a hint of respite from my head having a wobble over my situation.

Back to the Dam – Keep Moving

It took nearly a full day travelling on trains to arrive back at my lofty bedsit on the outskirts of Amsterdam. Once I'd had a good night's sleep, it was time to get my arse into gear and find out how my pals were getting on back in Walton Jail, Liverpool.

Contact was made and it wasn't good news at all. It was looking like a possible 12 to 16 years on a guilty plea, or even worse, a 24 year sentence if I went 'not guilty' and was found guilty. My heart sunk even deeper and the impending doom rushed through my veins at warp speed again. It's mad how you can be feeling full of the joys of spring one minute and one sentence, pardon the pun, can reset your body into near cardiac arrest. Whoever coined the phrase 'The war of words' was spot on, because I was seriously wounded.

I called Phil, to arrange a chat with the brief (solicitor), who managed to sort it out rapidly. The words out of the solicitor's mouth made my decision making clear as ice-cold spring water. He said, confidently,

"Look, here's how it is now, the music is that loud, it's nearly deafening, but in five or six years, it won't be as loud, do you catch my drift?" That was it for me now, my mind was set on keeping moving, as a moving target was harder to hit.

The plan was to move from the bedsit, start grafting again (I had no choice) and keep out of the sight and minds of the Police. I still had a few quid that would last me for a while, but it was in English pounds and needed changing. That wasn't a huge problem, but most of the money-exchange bureaux wanted some form of ID, which wasn't good for my situation.

One of the lads put me on to a bureau that asked no questions and also gave you a great rate; the only problem was that it was on the main street in the centre of Amsterdam and I wanted to stay on the quiet side of things.

It was around the end of March 2007 when I was coming out of the bureau. It was about 10am on a freezing morning, with bitter wind which hurt your skin when it hit you. My coat was fastened right up and I had a hat and scarf to keep the wind off my face as much as possible, as well as it hiding it, when I noticed two fellas heading my way. I quickly turned and walked briskly in the opposite direction and took a sharp left down a narrow side street off the Damtrak.

I jumped into the nearest coffee shop and stood where there was no light at the side of the front door, waiting to see if the two fellas headed my way. My heart began to beat like a techno baseline track as I peered out of the corner of my eye for these two fellas to appear, or not, preferably. The woman who worked in the coffee shop was staring at me while she dried glasses and cups with a tea-towel from behind the counter.

"Can I have a coffee verkert, please?" I said quietly, pulling the scarf away from my face. I glanced out of the door again and noticed the two fellas, with heavy black jackets on and both wearing Russian Cossack hats walking up the narrow street. I didn't notice their faces as I didn't want to catch their eye in any way. 'Thump,

thump, thump' was my heartbeat as I leant back and watched the two fellas walk past the coffee shop and glance in.

"He's not in here," I heard one of them say in a Cockney accent.

I was convinced they were English police and somehow they'd stumbled across me. I started to look for another way out of the coffee shop, scanning the area rapidly. Then I heard another voice - in Scouse,

"He'll be around here somewhere, lad." Now the use of the word 'lad' at the end of the Scouser's speech definitely meant he wasn't plod; he could have been anyone else though.

My brain was in overdrive as I tried to make myself look invisible, standing by the coat rack behind the door. As the waitress handed the coffee verkert over the bar, I had to step out of the shadows. I glanced out of the huge window and noticed one of the fellas who was on my tail; my anguish immediately turned to relief as it was a proper pal of mine from Liverpool.

"Now then, Toffee!" I shouted through the window as loud as I could, while I headed to the door. Now, every grafter got a nickname or two and the Scouse big fella's nickname just happened to be after his beloved Everton; Toffee.

"Fuckin hell lad, I've been looking all over da place for ya. Are you ok?" Toffee asked as he greeted me with a massive hug in the coffee shop doorway.

He was a huge man, 6ft 3", but his personality was even bigger than that, so when he hugged me, I vanished in his huge, black, winter coat.

"This is my pal, Terry," Toffee said, as he introduced me to his Cockney pal.

"Fuck me lad, I shit myself when I first saw ya, I thought you were with the other mob," I said, with a huge grin, as Terry shook my freezing-cold hand.

We moved towards the table that in the far corner of the coffee shop and sat down with beaming faces.

"What's goin on lad?" Toffee asked, concerned, as he turned to the waitress and ordered three bottles of Heineken. "When in Rome, hey lad, ah fuck it, we'll just get on it all day!" Toffee chuckled across the table to Terry and me. We all nodded in agreement and I braced myself for the day's morale-boosting Slalom drinking session.

"Well, I'm on my toes lad, my door's been kicked in and my brief's saying to stay out the way for seven years or so, but besides that, I'm laughin'!" I said in a jokey manner, as we all toasted to the shout of, 'Well, life on ya toes it is, lad'.

"Cheers!" We said simultaneously.

Toffee had travelled from Spain to find me as he knew I'd be in need of help. I was over the fucking moon when he explained he'd jumped on a flight as soon as he'd heard my plight. 'That's a proper mate', I thought, as Toffee carried on trying to persuade me to get my arse over to sunny Spain.

To be fair, I wasn't interested in going to Spain as most lads who were on their toes legged it to the *'Costa del Crime'*, I had my own plans though. We ended up on the ale for two solid days, with the occasional break for Gaucho's steaks.

Toffee still tried to persuade to move to Spain, but in the end he respected my decision and decided to return with Terry, empty-handed. He made sure I was looked after by lads who he knew and lived in Amsterdam, so I didn't have to want for anything. What a true friend he was, he was a proper buzz too and I respected him wholeheartedly.

Once Toffee and Terry left, I was also about to bolt as I'd made plans to go to Poland, Belgium and Germany for a big payday. It didn't take me long, did it, to find my feet and get back to graft; I had no option. I was backed into a foreign corner and survival was my mission now.

Off I went with the guitar Frank had given me in Zurich to mooch around Europe and build a foundation to prop my life back up. I just couldn't escape this fucking life, could I?

My Greek Reunion

The most appropriate sign I could find in Athens

 Returning to Amsterdam after mooching around Europe, I had to find another place to stay. One of my pals, Peter, had asked me to move in with him as his missus had had enough of his antics; in other words, she scarpered on him. It suited me as much as it suited him, so I now had to traipse up 14 flights of stairs to my new abode overlooking a huge lake on the outskirts of Amsterdam.

 Once again, I was in control of everything food wise, as Peter didn't have the patience to shop, prepare and then cook; he was more of a social animal. That didn't bother me as I was now well and truly in graft mode and Peter helped out now and again. To be fair, he worked his socks off with me to swell our kitty to a tidy sum, we didn't want for anything now.

The semi-finals of the Champions League were upon us and would you fucking believe it, Liverpool v Chelsea again. The only differences this time were firstly, I wasn't there and secondly, it went to penalties to decide the tie at Anfield, a place in the final in Athens was on the line.

On the night of the second leg at Anfield, Peter and I were walking around our apartment like caged lions, with anxiety written all over our faces. Peter was an Evertonian, but surprisingly, not a bitter one, so he wanted us to win. In fact, I'd given him plenty of stick as I remembered when he was a kid on the streets of Norris Green wearing a Liverpool kit. He never denied it; he knew the truth.

All I thought about was my son Paul, and nephew, Alex, who I knew were sitting on the Kop sweating and praying for a victory. Dirk Kuyt had the responsibility of taking the possible match-winning kick as Pepe Reiner had made some superb stops to put us in a winning situation.

"He'll score dis, Paul," Peter said, as he put his hands on my shoulders while I crouched down, two inches from the huge, flat-screen TV.

"Come on Dirk, come on Dirk, Rafa's got his Dirk out, Rafa's got his Dirk out!" I shouted at the TV, while Kuyt put the ball on the penalty spot at the Anfield Road end of the stadium. He walked back, spun round and then ran to strike the ball. "GOOAAALLL, get in you fuckin' beauty, go ed lad!" I screamed, while falling on my back doing the dying fly, while Peter spun me round like a child.

"I told you lad, I told ya, didn't I? I fucking knew you would beat Mourinho's Chelsea, lad," Peter gulped, while he bent over to pick me up off the floor.

"Right, we're going to the final lad, let's get on it now," I said, as I went to see how much money we actually had stashed in our apartment.

The night before, we'd watched AC Milan's Kaka weave his magic to knock out Manchester United and give AC Milan their place in the final in Athens in May 2007. That meant a repeat of the Istanbul final in 2005, which brought back the brilliant memories of that night.

Phil, my pal who was keeping an eye on Lisa and the kids without her knowledge, filled me in that Paul and Alex were going to the final. Philly Carra had dropped two tickets off at Lisa's house, which was an unexpected bonus and boost for her and Paul. I was buzzing when Phil gave me the news, this gave me a chance to bump into them while they were in Athens.

Phone calls to my brothers in Australia were next on the cards; I let them know that I'd be going the final and it would be nice if they could get over to Athens from Perth. I told them I'd look after the ticket side of things and urged them to bring their sons. I was shocked when, a few days later, they all took me up on my offer. My chance to see family members was a positive turn of events for me, I couldn't contain my excitement.

It had been nearly nine months since I'd seen any of my family or close friends, as I prepared for the journey to Athens via Germany. Two trains and a plane journey and I'd arrived to glorious sunshine. It was Sunday teatime and I had two full days to get myself sorted as Paul and Alex weren't due to arrive until Tuesday morning.

Tickets were now an issue as my brothers and their three sons were due to land on Monday evening. For one reason or another, tickets were scarce, the touts didn't have many and they were asking for two grand a pair. They were buying pairs of tickets for €2000 from the locals who'd managed to purchase them from UEFA. My work was definitely cut out for me now as I had to quickly find six tickets.

By Monday morning, Peter had arrived in Athens to join me in pursuit of elusive match tickets. There was a local park not far from Syntagma Square, which was the place for the Champions League Fan Zone in the centre of Athens. I had to cut through a narrow wooded park to meet up with Peter, a stone's throw from the centre of Athens.

As I walked, I was approached by two local lads who had tickets for sale. I was wary to begin with, but they seemed genuine enough and only wanted €400; which was cheap, considering. There were plenty of forgeries going around, but I'd seen a few real ones and I knew what to look for. These two were 100% real; I bit their hands off and arranged to meet them in an hour as they said they had more.

Four hours later and I'd managed to get six tickets for the match for €2,400 in total. I'd turned up in Athens with 10 grand, so in the scheme of things I was still flush and looking forward to bumping into my family. As I'd bought these tickets from random strangers; they trusted me now and kept bringing me more to sell on.

My luck had been touched by something beautiful as I ended up with another 10 and sold them for €12,000 to a Scouse tout I'd known ages. Over the years, I'd spent fortunes on tickets from touts, so it was about time that I made some of that money back. More and more tickets seemed to be popping up in this park as word got out to the locals and I was the only Scouser there. By the time I left the park to meet up with my brothers and nephews, I had €24,000 in my pocket. Now it was time to meet my family.

As I spied from distance, I could see my brothers and their sons across the bar I'd arranged to meet them in. I'd sent Peter ahead to make sure they weren't getting followed. This wasn't the time to let my guard down; there was always a glance over my shoulder, no matter where I was.

"Now then, Kiddas!" I shouted across the bar, as Peter gave me the thumbs up to approach them.

"Yeah, how have you been keepin', Paul?" Asked my eldest brother, Bob, as we hugged. He was always the serious one of the bunch.

"Wow, look at the size of these fuckers," I said, as I looked over Bob's shoulder at my grown-up nephews. Their smiles were genuine and like a heaven-sent gift to lift my spirits.

"How are you, Kid?" Ste asked, as he hugged me and shook my shoulders. Loads of hugs and laughs later, I took my brothers to one side and let them know my plight and to tell them that this trip is on me as I'd had a proper touch with selling a few tickets.

A lovely meal, a few beers and it was time for bed as an early rise was on the cards. Alex didn't have a clue that I'd arranged for Phil to shadow them across Europe and I'd had a text to confirm everything was good. I couldn't sleep as I was really nervous about meeting up with Paul. The thought of the Police somehow following him rolled from eye to eye, as I tried to get some rest. Let me tell you it was a very uncomfortable night, not just with the situation but the temperature too.

The Tuesday morning brought glorious sunshine mixed with a huge dose of anxiety, as I sipped my coffee in my hotel room. Phil sent a text to confirm they had landed and would be heading to the Fan Zone once they'd checked into their hotels.

Meticulous planning and several phone calls to friends who'd offered help was all I needed to take the plan to the final stage. One more coffee and some jam on toast to take the edge off my anticipation, and I headed towards Syntagma Square in the centre of Athens.

Seven of my pals had turned up in the sunken park facing the Government buildings in Syntagma Square to create a ring of protection in case it went tits up. My brothers had arranged to meet Paul and Alex in the Fan Zone so they could spend the day together.

I was tense and vigilant as I wandered around the Fan Zone with a hat, glasses and Liverpool scarf to blend in with the thousands of Liverpudlians who gathered there. It looked all clear as I received the text from Phil to let me know they were all together by the fountain in the centre of the park. One of my pals, Terry, was there with his son, Dean, who knew Paul so it was his responsibility to bring Paul and Alex to the Fan Zone bar where I'd plotted up. There were about 12 to 14 people now involved in making sure that the coast was clear and I wasn't in any danger. I hid behind a large Champions League logo until I got the final text to say it was 100% okay (*bleep bleep* - ALL GOOD) the text read.

I took one step out and noticed Alex first and then Paul who was right behind him. Alex didn't recognise me as obviously I'd grown a beard of sorts and lost plenty of weight. "Paul!" I shouted, as I knelt down on one knee. He looked up and his facial expression changed and he ran at me like a whippet, shouting,

"Dad, Dad, Dad, DAAAD!"

My arms flung open to catch him and lift him up, while spinning him round a couple of times. Paul clung on to me like his life depended on it and I had to hold back tears; good job I had my sunglasses on.

"I knew you'd turn up, Dad, I knew ya know," Paul said, as he hugged me tightly with his smile brimming with love, joy and excitement. Alex was laughing as he wasn't expecting to see me; he was in total shock as he cuddled me apprehensively. I could understand that, as Alex was a level-headed lad who never knew what I'd really done in the past.

"What are you doing here?" Alex said, as he hugged me and Paul together; Paul was *not* letting go of me at all. He clung on for dear life and tears of joy now rolled down his left cheek on to my shoulder.

"What happened with the police?" Alex whispered in my ear.

"That's just a misunderstanding that, that's nothing to do with me." I replied. I just tried to brush it aside as a non-starter so as not to worry Alex or panic him in any way.

"So you're not wanted then?" He was surprised.

"No, that's all forgotten about, don't worry lad; let's have a buzz for a few days, hey?" I reassured him.

"Oh, okay." Alex replied, as I turned round to thank the lads who'd helped me to reunite with my son. My pal, John, came over to me with tears rolling down his cheeks and said,

"That's just brought about 10 of us to tears, fuck me - that was priceless; the look on your Paul's face was unreal." Then he grabbed my arm and said,

"Lad, you've just reduced some real Scouse tough-nuts to blubbering wrecks, that was emotional that."

The relief that coursed through my body was visible on my face once I'd had a few hours with my son, brothers and nephews.

I was stressed to fuck wondering whether the police had put two and two together and somehow followed my family but that was the chance I took, obviously not without caution either. The only thing bugging me now was that I needed to see Lisa and Elizabeth, I had to somehow sort something out while I had my friends and family around me.

Terry and his son, Dean, were sitting next to me and Paul outside McDonald's in Syntagma Square as thousands of Liverpool and AC Milan fans converged on the Fan Zone to enjoy the glorious sunshine and soak up the atmosphere. I'd known Terry since I was a kid and he'd helped me out a few times along the way, as I'd helped him too, you know the way proper mates do without question.

An idea popped up in my head there and then as I turned to Terry and nodded at him for him to come a touch closer while I spoke in private.

"Terry, would you mind doing me a favour?"

"Yeah, no worries mate, what is it?" Terry replied without hesitation.

"Would you take my kids on holiday and I'll sort it out to meet you so I can see Elizabeth and Paul? Lisa might wanna come too but that's not a problem, just don't let her know anything, okay mate?" I said to Terry, while peering round, still looking for the police as they could have been anywhere at any given moment.

"Where and when, mate?" he replied, nodding his head in agreement. I reached into my zip pocket in the front of my combat shorts and peeled off six, purple €500 notes, folded them neatly while looking around, so no-one noticed and palmed them into Terry's hand in the blend of a handshake.

"There's three grand, take them to Euro Disney in two weeks' time, Friday to Monday, I'll get Phil to keep in touch with you. Is that enough money?" I asked, looking in Terry's eyes.

"Not a problem mate, me missus will be buzzin' lad, nice one!" he replied, with a massive grin as he put the notes in his passport and zipped shut his man-bag. Even more relief oozed out of my body as I turned to Paul and gave him a high five, while he sipped on his coca cola. Two more weeks and God willing, I'd see all of them together.

Paul stayed with me that night in my hotel; I couldn't stop staring at him while he slept and now and again my heart would plummet to new depths knowing that I'd fucked up again as a father. The only positive spin on things was I had time with him now to enjoy and that's what I intended to do.

Chaos

Wednesday was match day and I found out where the team hotel was. At some point, I would be heading in that direction, you could bet on that as Paul would be over the moon to see his idols before the game. Blue skies and glorious sunshine beat down on the lemon and orange trees that daubed every square in Athens, as Paul, my brothers and nephews made our way back to Syntagma Square to join the swelling number of Scouse and Italian fans.

Within five minutes of getting out of our taxi, I'd bumped into about 20 lads who I knew. They all seemed shocked to see me; that didn't bother me though as I was buzzing just to be with my family and friends.

The Coral and James from Starsailor were gathered under a cluster of lemon trees, as a freak sun-shower rained down like arrows on Syntagma Square. As the rain continued, there seemed to be more and more people heading for cover under the lemon trees.

Within five minutes, the steam from our body-heat rose like a cloud due to the sheer number of people seeking shelter. The shower lasted about 30 minutes, but the aftermath of mud, piss and ale lasted a whole lot longer. Wow, it stank as we all tried to dry off in the Athens' afternoon sunshine.

Some of the players' families were in the Square enjoying the atmosphere, too. It wasn't long before we were talking. I'd met a few of them when I was at the *'Champions League Istanbul Relived'* experience at Anfield, so they recognised me from there.

I bumped into David Grant, who was with Howard from the Halifax Building Society adverts. He was none the wiser about my situation but was inquisitive about my sudden disappearance. I told him I'd split from my missus and I was working for a tour management company across Europe; what else could I say? I had to make something up on the spot quickly as the truth was life-changing to me, imagine the look on his face if I told him I was on the run. 'Not good' would have been an understatement.

I was surrounded by famous band members, TV celebs and wags and their families, while I stood with my family, enjoying the buzz. A few Scouse lads I knew from Amsterdam came over and asked how I knew all of these people and one of them asked whether I would introduce him. Now, this lad was off his barnet on whatever, so I did introduce him to certain people, but reluctantly.

"Who's dat?" Del said, while pointing to Bruce Crouch.

"That's Crouchie's dad, Bruce," I replied.

"Can you introduce me to him, lad?" Del asked, quickly.

I turned round and shouted,

"Bruce, can you come over here when you get a mo?" He was talking to someone so I didn't want to seem rude or pushy, but within 30 seconds he made his way over. Bruce was as tall as his son but much wider; he was a huge man.

"Hiya Bruce, this is my pal, Del. Del, this is Bruce." I said, introducing the pair of them. I knew Del was a funny fucker, especially when he was off his barnet - there were no boundaries to his conversations.

"Hiya Bruce", Del said, as he held his hand out to shake Bruce's huge hand. "So you're Crouchie's dad?"

"Yeah, yeah," Bruce replied, with a smile on his face.

"I just wanna ask one question, Bruce."

"Fire away, Del."

Del turned to his right-hand side to put his drink down on the floor and pointed to the lemon tree high above Bruce's head and said,

"You couldn't get me a lemon off that tree, could ya?"

I couldn't stop laughing and neither could anybody else who'd heard it too, even Bruce found it funny. Del then decided to go on the rampage with a barrage of quick quips to all the people standing within a 10 foot diameter. It didn't take long for him to burn a few celebrity bridges and that uncomfortable feeling was making everyone scarper. At least Bruce saw the funny side of the lemon tree gag and stayed giggling endlessly.

Two hours later, Bruce Crouch was in a taxi with Paul and myself heading to the team hotel, on the outskirts of Athens. Earlier on, Bruce hinted at going back to the hotel, so after he'd had several more beers, I persuaded him to take us to meet Peter and the rest of the players.

Paul was over the moon when we were allowed into the heavily-guarded hotel. It was packed with cameras, journalists, officials and everything concerning Liverpool Football Club. After the usual photo-shoot opportunities and a chat with some of the players, it was time to meet up with my brothers and nephews, who by now were heading towards the recently-built Olympic Stadium.

The scenes outside the stadium were of absolute, badly-organised chaos. We had to build a wall of adult bodies around the kids to protect them from the crushing crowds. This was getting out of order and panic was setting in all around us, as fears of another Hillsborough were running through the veins of all who attended that fateful day. This time though, we took our fate into our own hands and forged a mass of bodies to help us move; ring fencing to protect the children.

By now, Paul was hysterical and was screaming,

"I'm gonna die, I'm gonna die, Dad help!"

"Stop panicking son, don't worry, we'll be okay, I *swear*, Paul." I said, trying to help calm him down as we pleaded with police to stop the bottleneck of crowd control that was being used.

"Move these barriers out of the fucking way NOW! There are kids here, some of them are being crushed!" I shouted at the Greek police, who were not interested at all. They just seemed to want to threaten you with their batons and CS gas.

The situation was becoming more and more threatening by the second as the build-up of crowds behind us was increasing. One of the Greek police noticed Paul crying and rushed past the barrier of armed police and started to rip the metal fence apart at its weakest point. Two minutes later, the Police Officer helped us to safety and we were inside the grounds, but we still had to get through our turnstiles. It took us 20 minutes to calm down to a level of normality and figure out our next move.

As I'd purchased the tickets from different sources, the seats were scattered around the stadium. Ste, Rob, myself and our sons walked around the inside concourse to rendezvous with Alex, who was with his mate at the opposite end of the stadium. Once we'd met up, I decided we'd make our way into the same turnstile, so we'd all be together. That seemed the only sensible thing to do as they had travelled halfway across the world to be with me.

The chaos on the turnstile allowed about 10 of us to walk into the stadium without showing our tickets once; it was ridiculous but I wasn't going to complain about it now, although it had cost me nearly €2,500 Euros for these tickets and they were still in my front zip pocket in my combat shorts.

The stadium was awash with red, white and black and this time the Italian fans had turned up in numbers. On paper, Liverpool's team was a lot stronger than our 2005 Istanbul team, so with an air of confidence, the Red Army sang their hearts out to welcome our beloved team onto the pitch for the kick-off; the 2007 Champions League Final was about to begin.

Stories were rife amongst fans that the chaos had got totally out of hand and thousands were locked outside the stadium who had tickets. I still had mine in my pocket, untouched by anybody, but at least I was in the stadium.

Paul was singing his little head off non-stop, which I totally buzzed off, so too did a dozen AC Milan fans who were directly behind us. They kept tapping me on my shoulder and congratulating me on Paul's fanatical support. Now Paul knew every song concerning Liverpool FC and had an undying attitude due to our Istanbul experience, never give up, ever.

The Italian fans, who were all in their mid-thirties, could not understand how someone that young had so much passion, fight and belief. There's a life lesson there for us all to take something from. I was just happy to be with all my family and the match was an added bonus, as I clung on to Paul with my head on his chest, and I helped him stand up higher on his seat.

The match was a bit of a tactical affair that never went our way, as Inzaghi scored twice to give AC Milan the lead. It wasn't until the last 10 minutes of the match that we got our shit together and caused AC Milan problems.

Dirk Kuyt scored a late goal, but it just wasn't enough and AC Milan ended up victorious. That didn't stop Paul from singing all the way back to Syntagma Square. To be fair, the match was playing second fiddle to my feelings as my family's reunion was upmost on my mind. That feeling of emptiness was increasing now, as I knew I only had one night left with Paul. Ste and Rob were staying until Friday, so at least I had family for company once Paul had gone.

Syntagma Square was full of jubilant AC Milan and dejected Liverpool fans, but nobody told Paul he was supposed to be feeling down. He was relentless in his non-stop singing as he found the highest point on the central fountain and proceeded to out-sing the Milan fans single-handed. Cameras clicked and flashed as Paul danced and sang in the face of defeat. It was absolutely wonderful, I couldn't stop smiling. All my fears of him growing up without me around had eased, as I knew from that moment that he'd be okay in life; he was eight years old and taking on every jubilant AC Milan fan and winning. Victory in defeat belonged to Paul and myself that night.

Night-time was spent finalising the plans with Terry and Phil so that I could see Elizabeth and Lisa in a few weeks' time. Paul had one more night with me as he was leaving for the airport at midday on Thursday. I made sure he was okay and there was no mention of our possible encounter in Paris as I cuddled him on the hotel bed for one last night. The disappointment of the match wasn't even bothering me; but the impending departure of Paul was.

The following morning was another empty moment as I watched Paul and Alex wave to me from the rear of the coach taking them to the airport. As it vanished into the distance, I sat down on the half-built brick wall outside their hotel, put my head in my hands and sobbed. The feeling of numbness was overwhelming, driving a dagger of emotion through the furthest reaches of my soul. What have I done? WHAT HAVE I DONE?

Two days with my brothers and nephews seeing the historical sites of ancient Athens and a few beers along the way gradually eased my emptiness. Peter had decided to make his own way back to Amsterdam, so once I'd seen Ste, Rob and my nephews Ste, John and young Robert off, it was time to make my way back across Europe to Amsterdam via Frankfurt, Germany.

A few weeks earlier, I'd arranged a meet with one of my graft pals in Frankfurt, as he wanted me to do some running about for him. I was still flush with dough, so I thought, 'What the fuck, it's got to be first class all the way.' It was time to start enjoying money now, it was the only way.

Back to You, Fuckers

Two weeks passed in a flash as I'd been travelling to Germany, Italy and Holland and now I was plotted up in a hotel on the Euro Disney site on the outskirts of Paris. I'd had the 'all clear' that Terry had arrived with his family and mine too. I was walking around the hotel room staring at and checking my mobile every 30 seconds waiting for the text.

'BEEP BEEP' went my phone. "Which room number?" I skipped a heartbeat with excitement, drama and love. I couldn't wait to see Lisa and Elizabeth; I'd missed them big time and I wanted to make sure they were okay.

I texted my room number pronto and waited by the door while I poked my head out to catch a glimpse. I could hear the lift bell ring as the door opened. I stepped out of the doorway to make myself fully visible and Elizabeth came hurtling towards me with her arms out.

"Daddy, daddy!" she shouted, as I ran to her, picked her up and swung her round while cuddling her. Lisa was two feet behind Paul, who was dragging his bag, dressed in his Liverpool kit with his name on the back. I gently put Elizabeth down, grabbed Lisa and hugged her with all my might.

"I'm sorry, luv," I said quietly, as I kissed her gently. "I'm really sorry, babe…" I helped them bring their luggage into the hotel room.

Elizabeth was a really funny child; her sense of humour was wicked and she always knew how to play her parents. I could tell from the second the door was closed that Elizabeth had something to say, as she was looking at Lisa with a certain glint in her eye.

Lisa was shaking her head at Elizabeth as if to say, 'Shush, don't you say anything yet.'

"What's wrong?" I whispered to Lisa.

"Some of the kids in school have been saying. *'Your dad's on the run and he's a drug dealer'*. She's been coming home from school crying." Lisa replied, as she took me towards the open window where it was a bit noisier.

"Aaargh, no way, luv, should I say something to her?"

"No, I'll sort it out, you know kids can be cruel at times. Anyway, the papers are saying you've been involved in cocaine, heroin, weed and firearms…have ya?" she demanded.

"Look luv, I'm not too sure what this is all about, but I'm sure it will all blow over." I replied.

"Fuckin blow over? Are you mad, they've raided the house twice and wrecked it, they're saying they're gonna take the house off us." Lisa fumed.

There was a knock on the door. 'It's only Terry', came a voice from the other side, as he brought one more suitcase. The tension was a bit tight as Lisa wasn't too happy about what she was left to deal with back home. Terry could sense the atmosphere and gave me a look of, 'I'm on it, kid', and scarpered swiftly, to leave Lisa, me and the kids to catch up.

I managed to ease the tension and we had a great night in Euro Disney. I'd asked Lisa whether she would she mind staying a bit longer as it might be a while before I saw them again. That was no problem and we decided to make a week out of our reunion.

Elizabeth was coming out with her usual one-liners that ruined me; she certainly knew how to put me down and in my place. I shouldn't have really laughed, but she was always on the money when it came to comedy timing.

We watched the move *Bruce Almighty* with Jim Carrey early one evening, and that night, we all cuddled on the bed in darkness. Elizabeth came out with,

"Dad, can I say something?"

"Of course, luv." I replied.

"It's got a swear word in it", she sniggered.

"That's alright, as long as you don't repeat it on the street, okay?" It went silent for a few seconds and then Elizabeth said in a grown-up American accent,

"Back to yooouuu....FUCKERS" We all roared laughing and rolling around the bed, as that was the funniest line out of the film. Elizabeth's laugh was even funnier and it triggered one of those uncontrollable fits of all-round giggling for about 10 minutes. She certainly knew how to make us all laugh. I'd really missed that the previous eight months.

The trip was going well until Paul went over on his ankle playing football with me. To be honest, I just thought it was just a sprain, so we put him on the couch with plenty of ice on it. He was in severe pain and before too long, the swelling was increasing rapidly. Lisa decided he needed to go home as it was not looking good, so the trip had to be cut short. Terry helped Lisa and Paul to get everything together, as I spent the last hour with Elizabeth walking around Euro Disney.

Well, that was the end of that then, they had to leave and I was left with even more emptiness than ever before. The highs and lows of my life kept coming; no wonder they wanted to fit a pacemaker years earlier; the stressful, wondrous life of a drug dealer, now on the run, just got worse and worse.

A week had passed when Phil got in touch to tell me that Paul was in plaster up to his knee, as he'd broken his ankle. I was gutted for him as I knew he loved his footy. I was gutted for Elizabeth too as she'd be pissed off with the attention a plaster cast brought to her brother; her eyes would have definitely rolled a few times along the way at Paul milking it. Life at home was carrying on now without me, so it was decision time again. I had to leave my family alone for a while, so I could settle down somewhere on mainland Europe.

Where Do I Go?

With Mum, Emilly, Paul, Lizzie and my sister, Kathy

July 2007 and my 38th birthday. I'm sitting in glorious sunshine in Rembrandtplein having a few beers with some of the lads who were still around. Most of the graft lads would leg it back home for the summer with their families, but there were plenty who couldn't.

Phil had been in touch and told me that my sister, mum and niece were heading to Spain for a two-week holiday. *That's it; I'm heading to Spain to see my mum.* I knew she'd be quietly worried and I'd have a chance to reassure her.

Another train, plane and taxi journey and I was heading towards Salou, just outside Barcelona, to meet up with my mum and sister.

The hotel they were booked into was familiar to me, as I'd stayed there a few times. There was a bar which always had a naff, seaside, foreign-entertainment feel to it, but you always had a good laugh after a few beers. That's where I headed to as I knew mum liked that kind of vibe.

When I arrived, I peered through the window and noticed mum sitting at the back of the bar with my sister, Pat, and Deana, my niece. It was karaoke night and full to the brim with holidaymakers; I sneaked in and persuaded the karaoke fella to let me sing 'Blueberry Hill'; one of my dad's favourite songs.

I jumped up on the small stage at the front of the bar and began to sing along with the music. I could see mum looking, but she couldn't recognise me with my beard, hat and glasses covering my face. Pat didn't even recognise me until I took my glasses off.

I heard Pat shout, "It's Paul!" as she grabbed hold of mum and ushered her to the front of the stage to get a better look. Mum's eyes aren't the best, but as she got closer it sunk in and she was crying. I cut the song short as by now mum, Pat and Deane had smothered me with hugs and kisses.

"Are you okay, Son? I've been worried sick about you… and how did you know we were here?" she asked, jubilantly.

Mum's relief at seeing me was instantly visible. I didn't want to stay around for too long as it was full of English tourists, so after three glorious days, I decided to head off to Southern Spain, to meet up with Toffee.

Two weeks had passed by now and I was looking well with my newly-acquired tan, as I lay on an inflatable chair in Toffee's pool overlooking a beautiful hillside in Marbella. I'd bounced all over Europe for the past 10 months trying to earn some money, stay out of trouble and not get nicked, and this was the only place I'd felt safe. There was a life there if I wanted it bad enough; needless to say, once I'd mentioned it to Toffee and his missus, they encouraged me even more.

I couldn't get back to Amsterdam quickly enough to pack my cases and make my way back across Europe to settle down and start to try and build a new life, obviously on the quiet. By the end of July 2007, I was settling into my new, fully-furnished, top-of-the-range penthouse apartment in Marbella.

I'd always told myself I'd never move to Spain as it was 'on top to fuck' - full of criminals who were on the run, so why would I want to put myself into that melting pot? You know why? 90 degrees heat, flip flops and shorts and a party-time lifestyle. Not to mention it was like a rabbit warren; loads of hills with thousands of apartments everywhere you turned. That meant you could hide and not be detected when necessary.

Toffee was an absolute no-nonsense type of fella who knew I'd had a bad 10 months, that's why he pulled out all the stops to introduce me to some proper old-time fellas.

Before too long, I was ingrained in everything criminal that was evolving on the sunshine Hooky Coast. I tried to keep my head down, but you just can't do that there, it was 100mph every time I ventured out, even if I just went to the shops for some provisions, some sort of mission would ensue. Unpredictable madness 24/7.

Marbella was a far cry from the windy, cobbled, tram-lined streets of Amsterdam, where 10 months earlier I hid out in a lofty bedsit. There was a smile on my face now, although I had to keep the contact with home to a bare minimum; that meant Lisa and the kids had no contact from me for the next year which gave me time to swell my kitty and make plans for a possible family reunion.

Nobody knew where I was and that's how I wanted to keep it. If I got the creeps any time, I'd up sticks and move to another location pronto, obviously that's an expensive chore, as well as stressful.

Life in the sunshine didn't soothe my stress levels, it just made me look better; my tan was a belter but I missed my family more and more daily. I had to try and pull all the stops out to get my family to see me somehow.

With the summer of 2008 approaching fast, I tried frantically to contact Phil through third and fourth parties. I hardly spoke on phones and especially in the UK, so it was proving difficult.

I tried with caution and eventually got hold of him and persuaded him to travel alone so I could chat to him face to face. My fingers were crossed in anticipation every single day, waiting for Phil to show up. This was a big ask and rejection could lead to me heading in a new direction.

Who knows, maybe another adventure was about to unfold. I just hoped it was the one I wanted; my family together again.

Family Time

Another military-precision pickup had to be arranged to collect Lisa and the kids from Malaga Airport; she'd decided to move to the Hooky Coast.

I stayed out of the way for two weeks as she settled into her new apartment in the hills on the outskirts of Marbella. My pals kept an eagle-eyed lookout on all her movements as she and the kids enjoyed the glorious weather. They gave me regular updates and all seemed clear of any signs of police activity; for now anyway.

Toffee and a few other lads kept me company while I awaited the eventual reunion with my family. The kids were none the wiser that I was about to drop in on them and I knew they'd be thrilled once I'd surprised them. That proved to be another dramatic affair for everyone involved.

I was staying in a villa, which Toffee had somehow been left in charge of. It was huge and the gardens and pool were perfect and outrageous. As Toffee knew Lisa, I left it down to him to pick them up and keep schtum about the real reason he was taking them all out for the day. Eventually, I received a text from him; 'OPEN THE GATES'.

Now this villa had a long driveway, lined with huge palm and pine trees and the massive, metal, electric gates were remotely operated. I rushed to the kitchen where the remote was kept, pointed the small, grey fob towards the drive and pushed the red button to open. Toffee's silver VW Golf appeared as the gates opened inwards and I hid behind the half-open kitchen door at the end of the driveway. I could hear the kids laughing at Lisa and Toffee as the car pulled up.

"Oh, this is lovely, who lives here?" I heard Lisa ask.

"Look at the pool, look at the pool!" Lizzie shouted to Paul, as they rushed out of the back seats and headed towards the inviting water.

"Can we get in, can we?" Paul and Lizzie asked simultaneously, as they stood by the water's edge. That was my cue to make myself known, I stepped out of the doorway and shouted,

"Go 'ed kids, it's our pool for now."

"Dad! Dad!" they both shouted, as they ran with arms flapping towards me.

"Paul, ha ha ha! What are you doing here?" Lisa asked, as I knelt down to cuddle the kids.

"I'm living here", I said, as I snuggled into my children's arms.

"No way, Dad", said Lizzie, with her eyes nearly popping out of her head.

"You're living here?" Lisa repeated, as she knelt down to join in with the group-hugging session. "You're not kidding me are ya? Are you really staying here?" Lisa said again, with a massive grin on her freshly-tanned face.

"Yeah babe, I'm staying here for a few months, so you and the kids can move in, if you want."

"Paul, we're moving in here," Lizzie shouted, their eyes now enlarged and they started to run towards the pool. The kids were over the moon with the villa and especially the massive pool. By the time Toffee left, Lisa was asking all sorts of questions about what had happened, where I'd been and more importantly, who I'd been with. It was non-stop and intense, but after the initial onslaught, she simmered down and became more reasonable to talk to. I told her that the Police were no longer looking for me but I couldn't go home for at least five years - obviously that was a slight exaggeration. I knew that she still had the thoughts of where and who I'd been with, running around her head.

After a wonderful summer reunited with Lisa and the kids, I had to head off to Barcelona for a while and Lisa prepared the kids for a new Spanish school adventure. By the time I arrived back in Marbella in early October, the kids were tackling the Spanish language head on and Lisa had made some friends through the kids' out-of-school activities. Little did Lisa know, but she was friends with children of the 'Great Train Robbers' and other well know gangsters' wives, girlfriends and general hangers-on. I wasn't going to burst her bubble and tell her, to be fair, Lisa was a good judge of character and most of the women she'd become friends with were decent, friendly people. They'd settled into life on the Hooky Coast, but I still couldn't be 100% comfortable and relaxed as I was still a 'wanted' man.

Liverpool were drawn in the same group as Athletico Madrid, which gave me the perfect opportunity to go and watch another European tie with Paul. Lisa and Lizzie were left to shop until they dropped back in Marbella as Paul and I headed to the Vincent de Cauldron Stadium in Madrid.

It didn't take us too long to find the customary, fan-filled square in the centre of Madrid and meet up with a few old friends who were shocked and happy to bump into me. Every bar we seemed to go into had old friends scattered about singing the legendary football anthems. We even bumped into my old pal, Gary, who I last saw back in Istanbul in May 2005 with his head in his hands in the airport the day after the final which he'd left at half-time. This chance meeting had a lot more conversation and Gary was pissed as a fart as he hugged me every chance he got.

"Fuck me, Pee, I thought I'd never see you again", he said repeatedly, as he grabbed me in a drunken manner.

"Ya lad's the spit of ya, Pee, I can't believe it mate, I'm buzzin that you're okay", he slurred, over and over again. By this time, Paul was looking at me to let me know he'd had enough of the drunken chit-chat, so we made a sharp exit and headed towards the stadium.

We arrived about an hour before kick-off and of course, Paul wanted to get in early, but I didn't. The reason was, I didn't want to chance it early as I knew there would be Liverpool police outside the stadium having a nose about, so I wasted a bit of time buying some scarves, hats and a banner for Paul from the stalls on the approach to the stadium. As we got closer, there was a line of Spanish National Police wearing jack-boots, berets and carrying machine guns. 'Oh shit', I thought instantly, as my hand grasped

Paul's hand tightly. I looked at my son and could see his face change. He knew my predicament and it showed itself at that instant.

"Are we gonna be okay, Dad?"

"Yeah, don't worry son, just hold my hand and keep walking", I replied calmly, to ease his fears.

We were within spitting distance of the heavily-armed Spanish National Police and before we opened our mouths, they'd noticed we were Liverpool fans and ushered us down a corridor of National Police officers, to be greeted by three Scouse coppers with high-vis vests over their jackets.

"This way, lads", one of the coppers said, as he pushed two Spanish coppers to one side to reveal a gap in some fence. I looked at Paul and noticed he was crying and he'd started to pull on my coat.

"Dad, no, no", he said, as tears rolled down his face. The Scouse copper looked back and noticed Paul was crying.

"What's up, son?" he asked in a concerned voice.

"He's a bit wary of crowds after the Athens final, it was a bad experience for him", I replied quickly, as I knew Paul was terrified of me getting nicked. Paul definitely thought I was being taken away, but they were just showing us the way to the Away supporters' end of the stadium. To be honest, I shat myself for a few seconds and it wasn't until the copper sounded concerned about Paul's wellbeing that the penny finally dropped. That was a close call. It wasn't until I looked back and noticed the coppers checking everyone's passports that I realised I'd had a walkover due to Paul's tears. Phew!

The match wasn't a European classic by any standards and finished 1-1, after we'd taken an early Robbie Keane lead. The two-hour, sing-song and the total respect of the Athletico Madrid fans after the match was worth the earlier risk but the incident did start to sow seeds of doubt about how I was dealing with my situation. The train journey back to Malaga the next morning was no smooth ride either, as it was laced with plain-clothes Spanish coppers, so I was buzzing when I finally arrived back at my new, hillside hideout in Marbella.

Every three months or so, I'd move to a new home, as I was always hearing stories of English police nicking wanted criminals on the 'Costa del Crime'. There were thousands of wanted people in and around Marbella from all over the world; South Americans, Africans, Russians, Bulgarians, Irish, Jocks, Scousers and Cockneys. You name it, every country was represented in some way, shape or form.

Christmas with the kids in the sunshine was a buzz, as a few of my pals from back home had arrived with their kids. I hired a few inflatable water slides for our pool and that kept the kids entertained, and most of the adults too after a few cold beers. The kids were now fully integrated into the Spanish lifestyle, as was

Lisa; good job really as I had to make my way to Barcelona once the New Year had passed and the kids were back at school.

I was back on the road at the start of 2009, 1000 kilometres to Barcelona, fully loaded with a car full of cash. I'm not going to say it wasn't stressful, because it was, as I'd been pulled over on a toll stop just outside Valencia. With my fake ID and booking confirmation letters, I waited patiently for the Guarda Civil to eyeball me several times; a war of nerves broke out.

I sat with an air of calm oozing out of my pores, but inside my brain, I was being pulled over hot coals, naked. As I reached over to the passenger seat to grab the bottle of water that sat next to the half-eaten, dodgy sandwich, I heard a knock on the side window. A Guarda Civil officer was indicating with his index finger to lower the window. I complied straightaway, which sucked out all the cool, conditioned air out immediately and replaced it with something scorching and bitter. My throat dried up instantly as the Officer babbled some rapid Spanish dialect to me, which I couldn't understand.

"Habla Inglés," I said in my corny, Spanish way.

"Uno momento", he replied, as he walked towards another officer and whispered into his ear. The two of them looked and walked towards me with their hands firmly on their machine guns, which were pointing towards the ground.

"You're English?" the second officer said, in perfect English.

"Yes", I replied, in a Cockney accent, as my fake ID was from that area. I couldn't afford to take any chances.

"Passport, driving licence and insurance, please", he said, as he bent down and peered into the car to look around. He moved towards the back door and opened it, as I passed my fake ID out of the front window, which the first officer took from me and started to look through my paperwork. I'd been stopped by police in Marbella a few months earlier and the ID passed with flying colours, so I was feeling confident.

The second officer picked up my black guitar flight case, spun it around on the back seat and began to unlock the four catches. He flipped the lid up and tapped me on the shoulder.

"Is this yours?"

"Yes", I replied, in a matter of fact way.

"So, you play now for me", he said, while pointing to my beautiful Takamine acoustic guitar on the back seat of the cash-filled car.

"Yeah, no problem." I reached back, grabbed the guitar and pushed my seat back to give myself some space to manoeuvre.

'Well, I don't know why I came here tonight, I've got the feeling that something ain't right, I'm so scared I nearly fell off my chair....' I sang out with gusto, as I strummed the chord sequence of the Steeler's Wheel tune.

The two officers smiled and passed my paperwork to each other and then started to nod their heads in time to the music.

"Good, good, bueno, bueno" they replied, once I'd finished the chorus. I was just hoping they wouldn't continue with their search as I'd heard stories of thorough searches that took over two hours sometimes.

Somehow these two officers had bought my act and put me through to the next round of survival.

"You can go now, drive carefully", the second officer said, as I packed the guitar back into the flight case on the back seat. Once I'd returned to the driver's seat, he passed me the paperwork and passport and I knew I'd had a right touch.

Pulling the seatbelt across my chest, I could feel my heart beating so hard, it was visible on my now sweaty T-shirt. I pulled away from the toll and glanced in my rear-view mirror, my foot began to shake on the clutch, as the flashing lights of the stationary police cars faded into the distance. Another near-miss, but it wasn't over yet as there were still 300 kilometres or so left to travel. I never went more than 10 kilometres per hour over the speed limit for the remainder of the journey and arrived at my destination safe and sound, with the second leg of my task still to complete.

Three weeks later, the job was done, and I was driving back towards Marbella with my foot to the floor on the accelerator buzzing with the news that Liverpool had been drawn against Real Madrid in the Champions League later stages. Another Madrid trip was being planned in my head, with the knowledge that Paul would be over the moon with the Bernabeu experience. Once I'd seen the lads and de-briefed about my Barcelona trip, I was making arrangements to travel to Madrid with Paul and Toffee. Although Toffee was a proper Evertonian, he still loved the crack of a Scouse get-together; it was standard procedure, really.

I didn't want a repeat of the last trip to Madrid, so arrangements were made to meet up with some of my pals back home to take Paul into the match.

The journey to Madrid on the morning of the game was like any normal European away trip in the way that I bumped into loads of lads I knew from home. That was standard too. Malaga train station was awash with red-and-white-clad Scousers, half pissed having a laugh and a joke.

The arrival of our train was greeted by armed Police, but they were just as show and not specifically for any wanted criminals. There must have been about 10 lads who I knew on the train who were wanted by one Police force or another, you could feel the tension as we all tried to blend into normality on the station platform. We'd glanced over at each other and acknowledged the common factor; balls and cheek.

Two hours later and I'd managed to dodge my way through Madrid's National Police a few times to get to Paul and my pals in a hotel a short distance from the Bernabeu.

Within the next hour, Toffee, James from Starsailor, The Coral lads and many other pals from the UK had joined us in the hotel bar for a proper get-together. Many other pals had joined us in the hotel bar for a proper reunion. It was just like the good old days and a full blown sing-song ensued until we all left for the stadium an hour before kick-off.

Up high in the top tier behind the goal, about four to five thousand Liverpool fans were herded into a tight-seated section with Paul and myself somewhere in the middle of it singing our heads off.

Watching Paul shout, sing and scream out at every single incident brought back loads of memories; it was nerve-tingling at times. The match was a pretty even affair considering Real were at home. Liverpool grew stronger as the seconds, minutes and hour passed by, so when Yossi Benayoun popped up with a late headed winner, the atmosphere went through the roof in our top tier position.

Johnny Cash's 'Ring of Fire' was sung for about 20 minutes solid as scarves were tossed around while we waited to leave the Bernabeu. It was a glorious night and it continued back at the hotel until the early hours. Paul was over the moon and to be fair, I was too, what a result, 1-0 to the mighty Reds. The return leg back at Anfield a week later even more unbelievable as we crushed them 4-0, wow, a 5-0 aggregate score-line sure looked good to me and every other diehard Liverpool fan.

As most things concerned with Liverpool Football Club and Europe had that 'standard' stag, it was no surprise when we ended up reaching the quarter-final against, who, yes, Chelsea; only this time, the game was no one-goal, tense drama of a penalty shootout as they beat us at Anfield 3-1 and looked red-hot favourites to go through to the final in Rome in May.

The second leg at Stamford Bridge was an unbelievable match and was settled by divine intervention in the end as Frank Lampard edged Chelsea ever so nearer, after we'd pulled it back earlier on. I ended up watching the game in a bar in Barcelona as Toffee and myself had to go and meet with some colourful overseas characters who we'd been working with. They thought I was nuts as I was up and down like a yo-yo on crack cocaine during the match, but that's Liverpool Football Club for you, with the mighty highs and unbelievable lows that now and again mirrored my life. At least I didn't have to traipse back across Europe to Rome; that was left to the Mancs and Barcelona to fight out.

Charity on Your Toes

Lizzie got herself into a children's choir that had its foundations in charity work connected to the Philippines. This happened in school as she was overheard singing, and to be fair, she does have a beautiful tone to her voice, so someone picked up on it and before too long, it became a twice-weekly thing.

The Smokey Mountain Children's' Choir performed at high-end Marbella fundraising events and she loved it. It wasn't long before I was roped into helping out as Lizzie had told the organiser and patron of the charity about my musical connections. Before long, Anna-Metta, who was Danish by birth and married to a very wealthy half Spanish/Filipino fella, was on the phone asking for help.

I agreed to meet up and before long, I was Head of Events Management for the Smokey Mountain Appeal. I just couldn't say no but I was actually good at this type of work, it seemed to come naturally. Lizzie was contented too as she now saw a lot more of me, that made us both happier. Once Lisa found out I was helping, she questioned me about the security side of things; for example, was it wise to be a figurehead of a charity with a criminal background, so on and so forth. I loved helping out though and that was that.

Two months in and we'd raised nearly €14,000 for the Smokey Mountain Appeal. This helped build a day-care centre on the bottom of the Smokey Mountain rubbish tip, where really young kids are exposed to severe hardship and disease. The satisfaction it gave both Anna-Meta and myself once the funds were sent to the

Philippines was tremendous. I'd pulled out all the stops and had various signed football shirts, boots, albums, CDs, T-shirts and VIP guest passes for the V-Festival sent over.

I could see Lisa's earlier point earlier more clearly now, as I was putting myself on offer. She was still uncertain of my predicament, as I was, and bouncing around Marbella like some high-profile Events Coordinator was not the most sensible thing to do as there were stories of people being nicked every couple of weeks.

We decided to take the kids to Barcelona for a week then head to the Benicassim Music Festival on the way back. I'd spoken to my pal, Neil, who was a top-end tour manager and I'd wangled a few artists' wristbands for us. Toffee and a few of the other lads from Marbella joined us for the three-day music festival. Lizzie had a few of her friends there too and were over the moon at the prospect of seeing or maybe meeting Lily Allen. She was headlining on the first night, as were the Kings of Leon on the second night.

We all began to settle down with our artist wristbands on, backstage in the hospitality food tent when a freak hurricane and storm swept through the site. Rigging was being flung from the main stage and somehow fires had started on the adjoining campsite, which turned the whole site into a disaster zone. Lizzie and Paul were terrified and with that, we made a sharp exit to our hotel, about six kilometres from Benicassim. Lizzie and her friends were gutted when they realised that Lilly Allen wouldn't be playing and the following day, the Kings of Leon also pulled out for one reason or another.

Neil was looking after a North-East band called Maximo Park and they had been offered the top slot on the second night due to the Kings of Leon no-show. This worked out perfectly as I'd managed to obtain more artist bands for Toffee and his pals. I even managed to blag Lizzy's friends access to every backstage area.

The bands from the UK had their work cut out for them as five Scouse kids wandered unrestricted from dressing room to dressing room. Elbow, The View, Franz Ferdinand and Pete Docherty were all terrorised (in the nicest possible way) by Lizzie and her face-painted friends. They were even on the main stage in front of 60,000 spectators when Maximo Park took to the stage, and kids being kids, they were not happy being in the best possible place to watch a live gig on stage, they wanted to be in the crowd, in fact they wanted to be in the front – in the mosh pit.

It was a brilliant few days in the end all thanks to Neil and Maximo Park for really looking after us. The pictures ingrained into our souls and emotional hard-drives will always be with us. Time spent with the kids was precious, especially when they loved it; more Lizzie really, as Paul's not that much into music, but it was still enjoyable for all.

The remainder of the summer was spent with the kids enjoying the sunshine as much as I possibly could. A few of my music pals arrived and that turned into a proper, week-long bender. I was king of karaoke for that week along the sunshine drenched Hooky Coast. Every opportunity I got I was up on the mic singing my heart out. There were a few dodgy people in one bar who I thought were moody and gave me the horrors of sorts. They started to film me on their mobiles a bit more than you'd usually film someone singing in a holiday resort bar and we decided to cut that night short. I even moved apartment again; this was becoming unbearable. I felt like a fucking pikey having to move every time I felt insecure and vulnerable.

Sky News

September 2009 and the kids were starting their second year in Spanish school. I was busy running around meeting different groups of like-minded people. I knew I had to earn a living somehow, but in the back of my mind was the notion that something would save me and my family from looking over our shoulders.

It was 6.55am on the 9th of September when my phone rang as I lay in my new apartment. It was another one of those dream-woven phone calls that turned out to be real. I reached for my cheap, Nokia throwaway phone and fumbled until I'd pressed the answer button.

"Yeah?" I said in a half-asleep soft voice.

"Put Sky News on," said a voice, whose tone was urgent. I looked at the number and noticed it was one of my graft pals.

"Why?" I was still half asleep.

"Just put it on now, will ya?" he shouted down the phone.

"Fuck me kid, keep ya hair on, what is it?" I reached for the Sky remote on the bedside table.

"Never mind keep ya hair on, you might have none left by the time you see this."

My head was spinning with all sorts of shit, but I wasn't expecting what I heard next.

'We'll be going live to Malaga Crown Court where they're having a Press Conference about Britain's Most Wanted criminals. The three most wanted are Paul Walmsley ...

I never heard the other two names as my head filled with impending doom. This was serious again.

"Are you still there, lad?" I could hear as I looked down at my phone in my right hand. I'd forgotten about my pal calling as I was engrossed in my own deep, dark thoughts. I put the phone to my ear and replied,

"Yea, I'm still here but I'll be legging it soon."

"Wait there lad, I'll come and get ya."

I never even replied, I just put the phone down and stared at the TV as a huge picture of me was now live on Sky News. This was properly fucked up as my kids and Lisa lay sleeping not too far away, what was I going to say to them this time?

For the next hour, my phones were red hot with all and sundry calling as they awoke to the pictures of me not only on live TV, but in every national paper; both UK and Spanish.

Every 15 minutes this news segment popped up with my huge photograph being flashed as they told the world that I'd been seen in Marbella and I was wanted for involvement in a £3.5 million drugs conspiracy. Fuck me, the ground could have opened up at that particular moment, I wouldn't have batted an eye lid either as I was numb. My only concerns were for Lisa and the kids now. How was I going to handle this messy situation that wasn't fading into the distance? It had been three years of running, dodging, hiding, sweating, looking and hoping I wouldn't get caught, now that meant nothing. I was officially in the top three of Britain's Most Wanted fugitives and they were letting me know that I wasn't going to have an easy ride.

By the time my pal arrived at my apartment, I was 100% adamant what I was going to do next; nothing. I'd decided to stay put for a week, at least until proper arrangements had been made to look after Lisa and the kids anyway. Advice was coming at me from all angles, but I knew what I wanted to do and that's all that mattered.

There were 10 people on the Wanted List and I actually knew three of them personally. It was bizarre looking at the roll-call of outlaws and reading the different stories that came out with the pictures.

One of them was a proper pal of mine who I'd had plenty of late nights with in a particular area of Marbella for the past two years. The Pirate was about 60 years of age and hailed from London. He was an absolute gent, who was also wanted on drug charges. Not only did we have a few watering holes in common, we now had the infamous 'fugitive' tag that was going to follow us around.

I got a message to him through the Hookyvine; letting him know what my plans were and gave him details and phone numbers. He knew he was more than welcome to join me at my remote new hideaway.

Gone Fishing

After another military-style operation involving several people, I was safely tucked away in a riverside caravan. It was powered by way of generators and solar power and its finest feature was its 700 kilometre distance from Marbella. This was my 11th home since I landed in Span 26 months earlier. It was becoming normality to me by now, although the kids, and especially Lisa, were at their wits' end, as I kept contact with them to a bare minimum through a third party.

Stocking up on creature comforts and living essentials was pretty difficult as I was secluded and relying on help from others. Luckily enough, there was a bar in the village that catered for the foreign fishermen who travelled there and their array of curry house dishes was right up my street.

After a week or so I received a text saying The Pirate was on his way to see me. Later that night, he arrived with his car packed with supplies that were truly welcomed and dispensed of immediately. Wine, vodka, beer, whiskey, Canadian club, rum, and oh yeah, there was some food too.

The outside freezer and fridge were stocked and now I had company to pass the time, not just any old company either. The Pirate was an absolutely great fella who never had a bad word to say about anyone; that's a rare quality in our game and I loved him for it. We got on like a house on fire and spent most of our time fishing on the riverbank until midnight. We both felt safe living like this at that particular time, as no-one was ever going to find us here.

The Pirate had brought a car with him and that was needed to get the diesel for the generators once a week. We had about 20 Jerry cans that would usually last us for about 7 to 10 days, well, that's until we decided to fit Sky TV to our isolated caravan. Fuck knows why we needed TV really, as the scenery was spectacular and we spent most of our time on the riverbank. It did come in handy when the car was trashed by a rogue wild boar one night, which left us caravan bound for a week until one of our pals turned up; plus we both liked our footy so the live games became our priority and took our minds off the situation.

Three months spent fishing was now coming to an end as Christmas and 2010 approached. It was time to head back to Marbella to see Lisa and the kids; that's if they were still there. I'd received messages that she was properly unhappy and considering going back to Liverpool. I couldn't blame her really as she'd had to put up with some serious shit where I was concerned. That gave me a kick up the arse to get back to her pronto and find out how she was doing.

One windy Tuesday morning in mid-December, The Pirate and I said our goodbyes and went our separate ways. We were both heading back to Marbella, but I was travelling by rail and he was picked up and driven by a friend.

The Final Goodbye

The kids were thrilled to see me when they arrived home from school on the Tuesday night, a week before Christmas. Lisa looked stressed and was at the end of her tether with the lies and shit that obviously came with life on the run. It didn't help matters when somehow a Liverpool Echo had found its way to her via some busybody, with even more pictures of me with a Santa hat on and the headline, *'The Festive Fugitive'.* They even blue-toothed my picture to everyone leaving Liverpool's John Lennon Airport for Malaga; this was becoming relentless. After spending Christmas and New Year with the kids, it was time to move on again and this time Morocco was my destination.

Returning from Morocco a couple of months later, I discovered that Lisa and the kids were heading back home. She'd finally had enough of the constant bollocks that surrounded me. Once I'd caught up with her and she told me exactly how she felt, it was obvious to me that our relationship had reached breaking point. It was then that I made the most heart-wrenching decision of my entire life.

I made arrangements to meet up with her in a Tapas bar off the beaten track. I was fashionably late, but for a good reason, I was checking out the area for any sign of SOCA or their Spanish counterparts. She was sitting at the back of the terracotta-painted bar with her back to the door sipping a chilled glass of white wine. As I walked up to her, still looking at every nook and cranny with my over-cautious 360 vision, I tapped her on the shoulder and kissed her on the cheek.

"Hiya luv, have ya been here long?" I asked quietly.

"About 15 minutes, this is my second glass of vino," she replied, her blue eyes glistening in the second-hand sunlight beaming through the side window.

"Well, I'd best get a beer and try and catch you up. "Una cerveza grander San Miguel, por favour." I said, in my poor Spanish to the middle-aged barmaid who was leaning on the end of the bar holding her head up with both hands under her chin, watching the TV.

After the initial couple of minutes chatting about the kids, I plucked up courage and said,

"Look luv, I think it's time for us to split up." I paused for about five seconds to gauge her reaction. "I mean, you've had a dog's life for the past five years, your mother is on your case, not to mention the entire British Police Force, so I wanna give you the chance to get your life back."

I was dying inside as every word came out of my mouth. Lisa's expression was stunned and her eyes started to fill up. It didn't take long for tears to stream down her cheeks and on to the tiled, table top.

"I know luv, I know it sounds like the right thing to do, but I picture see life without you in it, plus if anything happens, like getting nicked, I'll feel like I've deserted you; you know I won't do that, I'll never desert you, but I know it's for the best." By now she was sobbing and wiping her tears away.

"I haven't ruled out going back home and handing myself in, I mean, if I do get 16 years, I don't want you waiting round for me, you need to be free, babe." I spoke reassuringly and with a certain calm, while I took her hand and squeezed it tightly. I looked at her intensely, "I know you'll always be there for me, I know that wholeheartedly, I just need to be alone to do what I've gotta do, I don't wanna put you through any more shit."

"I know, I know it sounds right, but it's gonna be hard, especially on the kids," she replied.

"We'll not tell no-one luv, not a soul, so for the time being, they don't have to know, okay luv, promise me that…please?" I pleaded.

She agreed and it was time to let Lisa go and end our 15 year relationship. It wasn't easy for either of us, but it was the only thing I could do to set her free. I did have other reasons, but I was keeping them close to my chest, very close.

The emotional farewell in July 2010 left me empty and with the certain knowledge I had some serious life-changing decisions to encounter. I was back in Marbella but I couldn't really move over my front door as the Police net was closing in day by day.

My pal, Phil, came to stay with me. The news that Lisa had been in a bad way due to the split was a bitter pill to swallow, so I wasn't in good spirits; Phil knew it too.

Toffee was also popping in to see me and tried his best to lift my spirits, he even dragged Phil and myself out a few times on the ale. I had to be super careful now as the SOCA squad had been raiding bars and fingerprinting everyone in there. I was forever hearing stories of them rushing into some of my local bars wearing balaclavas and taunting the local barflies about who they were looking for. If I was to keep my destiny in my own hands, I had to stop frequenting these bars; it was only a matter of time if I didn't.

The Pirate, wasn't so lucky. One evening as he drank in one of our local haunts, it was too late for him to react to the oncoming Spanish/UK joint raid on the sun-drenched Hooky Coast bar. I was gutted when I heard the news and it only made me look deeper into my situation. I didn't fancy the idea of the shock and surprise of being nicked on foreign soil. His situation was worse than mine as he was looking at a life sentence. He was in his 60s and a life sentence would have taken the wind totally out of his sails and soul. The poor fucker, I couldn't stop thinking about him as I sat alone in my apartment in the hills of Marbella pondering my next move.

Decision time

It was March 2011 and I'd called Toffee, Phil and another pal round for tea; obviously I was cooking. I'd become a decent cook during the time I was on my toes in Holland and that was due to me being asked by one of my pals in Spain to help him out a few years earlier. To be fair I was a reasonable cook any way, but only of the standard roast dinners, chicken curries and spaghetti Bolognese dishes. Anyhow, I was asked to pick a fella by the name of Ivan up from Schiphol airport in Amsterdam. Obviously no questions were asked and I obliged without hesitation.

I met this fella in the arrivals hall and noticed his spotless, polished black shoes. He was dressed in an outstanding fashion and his firm hand shake gave me the feeling he wouldn't take bollocks from anybody.

We proceeded to drive and chat on the way back to the farmhouse on the outskirts of Amsterdam. Ivan explained he was a good cook while telling me he was staying with me for three months. Obviously this was news to me but I wouldn't question my pal as he'd done me loads of favours over the years.

The next morning Ivan explained I needed to take him to the local shops, markets and coffee shops so he could teach me how to cook properly. He told me it was all about the ingredients and timing. A good lesson in life, to be fair, but I'd not learnt that yet.

After a day of getting to know each other and shopping for food, he cooked the finest pasta dish I've ever tasted - not to mention the desert he knocked up from bananas, cinnamon and brown sugar. It was first class and I made sure I watched and took it all in so I could replicate it in future.

So the months passed and Ivan left me a far better person and chef than he found me. He was half Italian, half Serbian. I never really asked any questions as he gave the impression he wouldn't have answered then anyway. It wasn't until I was watching Sky News a month or so later that his face came up in regard to him being wanted for war crimes in Serbia years earlier. This fella was a general in the military with a genocide charge hanging over his head and he was living and eating with me for months. That's how I became a more-experienced cook – strange but true.

In the meantime, I'd not been over my door for three months' solid. I was smoking weed again and I'd set up a mini recording studio in my spare room as I'd dived back into music. The solitude, weed and music combo had helped me reach a decision regarding my life. As all my pals sat down to lemon chorizo sausage, pitta bread and feta salad, I asked them to raise their freezing bottles of Heineken for a toast.

"Well, lads, here's to me going back home to hand myself in, I said, with a smile-cum-smirk on my face.

"Fuck off, ya daft cunt!" Toffee retorted.

"No lads, I've made my mind up and I'm going next week." I replied quickly, sipping on my cold beer.

"Things aren't that bad, mate, just give it some more time or go to Australia and see your kid." Toffee said sternly. Phil looked at me and raised his glass and said,

"I think he made his mind up months ago and that's why he split up with Lisa. So firstly, let's give him some credit for having the balls to set his loved one free and secondly, giving his arse up to big Benny on B-Wing," he said as the lads all roared laughing and swigged their cold beers.

For the next hour, Toffee tried to talk me out of handing myself in, but it was fruitless as my mind was totally made up. I had kids who looked up to me, what sort of example was I setting? How could I hold my head high and honestly talk to my children about right and wrong, when I was clearly in no position to do that.

My decision to hand myself in was also done made the thought of me possibly starting a new life; once I'd taken my medicine and served whatever sentence was awaiting me, this was going to be a massive challenge, but I was up for it 100%.

Making the decision to go back home was only a small part of the equation; I had to get back to Blighty in one piece too. Another plan had to be made and executed perfectly, before I could even think about handing myself in. You'd think it would be easy handing yourself in, wouldn't you? Oh no. Everything seemed to need some sort of plan, so that was my next set of moves.

I made my plans and told no-one the whole strategy as I wanted this to be a safe and low-key affair. Toffee was in Barcelona and that suited me as I knew he'd try to talk me out of going home, so after a brief-but-heartfelt conversation with him, he treated me with the utmost respect and I started to make my return.

The journey encountered four borders, but I was used to this by now as I'd had five years' plus experience of being undetected. That's not to say I wasn't feeling apprehensive as I crossed into the UK which was by far the most nerve-tingling phase of my journey and also the most dangerous. I wanted my destiny in my own hands, plus I wanted to say my goodbyes to my family and friends who'd stood by me through all of this.

My utter relief as I walked through Border Control was palpable and gave me a buzz. No matter what was around the corner, there was no denying the thrill from being undetected. I could have stayed hot-footing my way across borders, but I'd made my decision and it wasn't just about me.

Two hotels, two train rides and three taxis and I was outside an old pal, Alan's, house in Warrington. He was shocked to see me and he had to do a double-take just to make sure it was me.

"Fuck me lid, what the fuck are you doin' here?" he said, as he grabbed my shoulders and hugged me.

"Well, I'm hoping you can put me up for a while until I hand myself in," I said, with a smile on my face.

"What? You're handing yourself in? You best come in then lid, and yeah, you can stay here mate, no problem," he said, as he helped me with my luggage and guitar case.

We headed straight into his kitchen where he began to make a pot of fresh coffee. He stacked my luggage, lit a cigarette and said,

"Wow, I didn't expect to see you turn up on my doorstep, the on-ya-toes doorstep challenge, hey?" he said jokingly, as he puffed on his ciggie. Alan kept laughing and shaking his head in disbelief at me actually sitting in his living room with him having a coffee as if nothing had changed. I hadn't seen him since 2004 and I'd taken a chance on him still living in the same place and luckily for me he'd stayed put. Once we'd had a proper chat about my plans, he began to run around for me and contact my family, friends and solicitor.

Final Bender

Enjoying my last night of freedom with Alex and Dave McCabe before handing myself in to the police

Within a week, I'd contacted everyone and was happy to find out Lisa and the kids were settled in their own home. I was a bit nervous to see them as I'd not been in touch for a while and they didn't know I'd come home to hand myself in. I knew she took the dogs for a walk every Sunday morning in a local park with the kids, so that was a perfect place to bump into them, undetected and away from prying eyes.

My park rendezvous was another emotional affair. Once I'd told them my plans, it seemed to release hidden pressure and make the get-together meaningful and heartfelt. I'd told them I'd expect to get anything from a 10 to 16 year sentence, going on what I'd heard on the grapevine and from my solicitor. There was no going back for me now as I'd instructed my solicitor to contact the Police to arrange surrender.

I contacted all the lads from my music days and explained my impending situation. I'd also arranged a sort of last supper party in a friend's pub so I could say goodbye to everyone who cared.

A trip to my dad's grave was emotional too as I'd not been for a while. I even had time to visit my beloved Anfield and watch Liverpool beat Valencia 2-0 in a pre-season friendly. The pre-match build-up with 'You'll Never Walk Alone' brought me to tears as Paul was sitting next to me, aged 13. I couldn't stop thinking of how long it would be before I sat next to Paul at a football match or how long Lizzie and Emilly would be taking the piss out of me for being a typical dad. They were questions that would be answered soon enough as my solicitor had been in touch to say the Police had given me an appointment to attend Copy Lane Police Station in five days' time. That gave me enough time to have a proper drink with the lads and spend some precious, quality time with the kids.

The party went on for two days solid; with Dave McCabe, Nick Power, Tom from Maximo and Tony Grant all coming out at various stages to have a farewell drink and chat. Lisa showed up last of all with the kids and that proved to be the most heart-wrenching experience of the two-day bender.

I wasn't pissed as the impending situation sobered me up every time I thought about it. I even phoned Toffee to let him know it was my last night of freedom; he still tried to talk me out of handing myself in. As I laid my head on my pillow for the last time a free man, I was anxious but also relieved that I was going ahead with it. Needless to say, I didn't sleep much that night and was up at 6'ish getting ready and waiting patiently for my pal, Jay, to come and take me to McDonald's next to Copy Lane Police Station in North Liverpool.

It was 10 o'clock on the morning of 27th September 2011, an unexpected heatwave covered most of Britain. I sat having a Maccies' breakfast with Jay waiting for my solicitor to arrive.

Shahid Chowdhury from Middleweeks Solicitors in central Manchester, a stone's throw from Strangeways Prison, arrived at 10.30am and sat with a coffee discussing what might happen. Because I had a European Arrest Warrant out for me, he explained that I wouldn't be interviewed, but I would be charged and sent to court for a hearing. I trusted him completely and knew I was in good hands; in fact, I was in the best possible hands at that moment.

I didn't arrive at the Police Station until 11.30am and the two plain-clothes, female detectives awaiting my arrival were shocked that I'd arrived at all.

I was cuffed, charged and cell-bound within 30 minutes, while I waited for a sweatbox to take me to Liverpool Magistrate's Court. Every 10 minutes or so, the flap would open and some SOCA detective would peer through and make some comment about me not looking so happy now and how they'd seen videos of me in Spain.

After a brief interview with my solicitor, I was cuffed and put into a sweatbox heading for Liverpool Magistrate's Court.

The Court Process

The Desk Sergeant was trying to make small talk with me,

"You'll be going home by tea-time, Paul. We've got you down as an ODC."

I asked him what that was and he told me it was an Ordinary Decent Criminal.

Peering through the darkened window on the police-escorted, court-bound bus, I watched my city go by at the rate of roughly 40 miles an hour. As the van drove down Cheapside, I noticed Elevator Studios where I'd spent many long days as we waited for the electric shutters to open at the back of the courts. I looked up to the third floor and saw the window of Ruby Studios, I'd so often looked out of, smoking a joint with a tasty coffee in my hand. This felt a million miles away from those not-too-distant memories.

Thirty minutes in a massive holding cell with nicknames and messages daubed on the miserable walls felt like a lifetime, while I waited to be taken up to court. My hearing lasted all of five minutes. I was remanded and sent to Liverpool's old Victorian, Category B local prison in Walton, until my next Crown Court appearance.

Arriving outside Walton prison, I was feeling a bit anxious as I'd never been there before. I knew plenty of people who were in Walton at that time, but they weren't expecting to see me. Once I'd been booked in and given my food pack, bed pack and induction information, it was off to the Remand Wing.

Walking through empty, cream-painted corridors and up a flight of blue stairs, we ended up outside a thick metal door with 'B Wing' stencilled on it. It was strangely tranquil and the three other lads behind me were quiet as the jailers' keys jangled and clunked into the old, worn keyhole. The door opened and the noise from behind was seriously loud. It reminded me of the swimming baths when I was a kid; shouts, bangs, laughter and keys jangled into a cacophony to make the atmosphere real and electric. You could feel the tension in the air as we walked through B Wing in mid-association time.

It didn't take long for someone to notice me from the landing above and within seconds, everyone was letting everyone else know there was a familiar face on the wing.

A lad who I'd known for about 20 years shouted out; his name was Bogie,

"Do you need anything, Pee?"

"Yeah, I've come empty-handed Bogie, get what you can." I replied with a smile on my face, knowing that I'd be properly looked after now.

About 10 steps into the walk to the office, I heard another shout from behind me. I dropped my bag of bedding and bits on the gleaming floor and spun round to spot my old pal, Matty M, peering through a half opened cell door.

"Fuck me Pee, what are you doin' here?" he said, with a broad, welcoming smile.

"I handed myself in this morning and it looks like I'm here for a bit, lad," I replied, as I walked into his cell to shake his hand.

Now I'd known Matty for a time too, so it wasn't long before I had three pillowcases full of food, sweets, toiletries, clothes, proper bedding and reading material. By the time I'd reached the Screws' office, there were at least 10 lads who I knew well, offering help and letting me know where their cells were; Jamio, Richo, Nige and Sean all made themselves known by hanging over landings and sending me some prison essentials as I made my way up to the first-night-induction landing on the 5's.

The view overlooking the skyline of Bootle, Seaforth and the River Mersey from my fifth-floor, brick cell was spectacular, especially as it was a glorious, balmy, heatwave-drenched day. Kicking back and looking at the thick, arched ceiling, the thoughts of my kids, Lisa, family and friends raced round my now incarcerated brain at warp speed. For the first time (but not the last), I put pen to paper and composed my first poem. I called it 'Luck'

Luck

I kick back and lie in my bunk
Looking at the arched ceiling
I'm a boy again

I peer through the gap in my door
Whilst I tie my shoelaces, not for the first time
I'm a boy again

I discover I'm colour blind in a panoramic style
As I stare through walls as thick as elder oaks
I'm a boy again

The ink meanders through reflective thoughts
Pleased, but without a smile
I'm a boy again

Mistaken youth now addressed
As walls tumble like crumbling ruins
I'm a boy again

I'm a boy again
But now I can look up to the stars

I could hear a fella crying in the next cell while I sat on the toilet. It seemed to go on for 20 minutes or so. I knocked on the blue, painted pipe that went directly into his cell and waited.

'Knock, knock.' His reply came back on the pipes.

"Can you hear me?" I shouted down a tiny hole at the base of the pipe.

"Yeah, mate," he replied in a morose voice.

"Are you okay, lad?"

"Not really," he blubbered again.

"Listen mate, don't worry, I'll come and see you when we're unlocked in the morning and I'll look after ya, I've got loads of goodies here, okay?" I said, to try and ease his situation.

"Thanks mate." Came the reply with a bit more life and positivity in his voice.

"How come you're upset?" I asked him, as he'd seemed to have perked up.

"I've just been sentenced today."

I automatically thought he'd had a big sentence rammed down his throat due to his crying and my heart went out to him.

"What did ya get?"

"28 days."

"What? 28 days, so you'll only do 14 days in here, then you'll be going home?" I said sarcastically.

"Yeah."

Now here's me looking at a time, helping a fella out who's going home in two fucking weeks; just my luck. I obviously told him to have a big pan of 'get ya shit together soup' and stop blubbering as there's plenty worse off in here than himself right now.

Welcome to HMP Liverpool.

Prison Life

Dates had been set for January 2012 for court, so I settled into HMP Liverpool (Walton) for the Christmas period. I'd been given a cleaner's job and moved into a cell on the 2s with a kid from Wigan called Johnny.

We'd been given the number one job on the wing and that came with a few extra privileges along the way. Johnny was a great fella who loved a giggle and knocked out the meanest, smelliest shits on B Wing; you'd always know when he'd been on the toilet.

Matty M was in the next cell and he even knew when Johnny had been for a shite, it was unbelievably smelly to say the least. We'd have to scatter and make a sort of semi-circle exclusion zone outside our cells and wait for Johnny to appear with his load lightened.

"It's official lads, shite stinks, deal with it!" Johnny would shout in his broad Wigan accent in the doorway of our cell every morning.

Lisa and the kids came up to visit, as did all my proper pals: Dave McCabe, Gary Murphy, Philly Carra, Tony Grant, Scotty, Tom, Jay and Ste G were all popping in to see me when they could. To be fair, I was never short on visitors as my sister, Kim, organised family members into some sort of rota to let me know that they were all there for me. The overwhelming feeling of being loved was starting to make inroads into my soul as Kathy, Sue, Pat, Shirley and my mum came to visit.

I received all my legal documents and the charge sheets from the CPS; I was being charged with two counts of conspiracy to supply and import Class A drugs. If I went not guilty and unsuccessfully challenged these charges, I was looking at 24 years. Now, obviously I'd only do half of that, but that's not the point, 24 fucking years was sounding heavy.

The depositions contained 22,000 pages of surveillance, interviews, statements, pleas, evidence logs and summaries from the Dutch Police and SOCA. I sat up until the early hours going through all the paperwork meticulously and I left no stone unturned. Day and night for eight weeks I read, made notes and quadruple checked every piece of paperwork and in the end I'd found a few points that made me sit up and think, 'I've got a chance with this'.

I phoned my solicitor and told him I'd found flaws in my charges and within 24 hours he was at the jail with the Barrister, Oliver Jarvis. The main evidence was a bug in a car where the fella spoke openly in a telephone number fashion about deals here, there and everywhere. I didn't know this fella at all - I did know a friend of his, but not that well, really. Anyway, I sifted through the recordings and there was not one mention of me on the bugged evidence. My hard work had paid off. With this news, my solicitor and barrister headed off to make representations to the CPS.

I was up early on 19th January for a plea hearing at Liverpool Crown Court and was informed that I was heading to Warrington Crown instead; my Judge had moved circuits. I was wounded as that meant I'd head to HMP Altcourse after court, instead of coming back to Walton. I didn't even have time to say goodbye to the lads as I only properly found out on leaving Walton. So after another brief appearance in Warrington Crown Court, I was taken to HMP Altcourse, not without me trying my utmost to head back to Walton. Another date was set for a plea and mention due to my diligent and thorough research of the evidence.

Driving to HMP Altcourse, which was built on the area that was my playground as child, was surreal. I passed all my childhood memory landmarks and family homes. My school, shops, roads I skipped across, fields I played footy on and the cemetery I was in a few months earlier to say goodbye to my dad, all passed by. This had a real feeling of irony running through it.

I went through the same procedure that happened on arrival at Walton, but with a big difference. I knew some of the staff on Reception and was greeted with smiles. This was weird. As I walked up to the Reception booth, the screw, who was a woman, was smiling at me.

"You don't look like your photo in the paper, Paul," she said in a familiar way. I looked at her beaming smile and grinned and said,

"Which photo?"

"The photograph that has been in every paper for the past five years," she said, still smiling and filling in some information into her computer. She looked up from her keyboard and said very calmly and friendly.

"How's your mum and ya sisters?"

"Do I know you?" I asked quietly, trying not to let the other two screws behind me hear.

"I'm Jane's sister, you know, from over Scargreen Avenue, we used to go out to town with you in 89/90. The good old days of the State," she said quickly and knowingly. It jogged my memory instantly and I said,

"Fuck me, don't you owe me £40 for some weed and tablets?"

"Shhussh, will ya!" Her face changed and began to look worried.

"Don't panic, I'm only buzzin' with ya. By the way, I remember who you are and my mum's sound, so are my sisters."

I was ushered through to a sterile area, where I was greeted by a nurse who interviewed me and then I was taken to be interviewed by the CARATS Team (Drugs Unit). As I sat in the chair, I heard a voice.

"Fuckin ell, is that you, Paul?" I looked over my shoulder and another woman stared at me laughing. I recognised her straightaway, it was a girl who I went right through school with, Dawn.

"Don't tell me you work here too, I've just spoke to some other screw who knows me as well. How many more do you think I'll know in here?"

"There's loads of staff from our crowd, Paul, you'll bump into them all over the place. What are you in for? I always thought you were clever at school?"

"Well, obviously I'm not as clever as I thought I was." I replied, tongue-in-cheek.

Once the interview was over, it was time for me to be escorted to my new cell. Obviously we'd all gotten older, but I was a prisoner in their place of work now and no longer that straight 'A' cute kid from school back in the early 80s.

Out of Place

HMP Altcourse was a Welsh-based circuit jail and therefore full of lads from Mold, Wrexham, Caernarvon, Chester and even as far as Cardiff. It felt like a stable for thick, Welsh idiots as most of the lads seemed to be educationally challenged in some way.

I was in a single cell for the first two weeks, which suited me perfectly, but that changed once the prison was filling up. I ended up moving into a cell with a kid from Wrexham who was labelled as a bit of a tough nut and a bully.

Frank was a former bodybuilder who didn't suffer fools at all, so within five minutes of our first chat, some ground rules were laid down by Big Frank.

"Go fuck yerself" was my reply to Frank's insistence at me taking the top bunk. "Not a chance mate, I'm in the bottom bunk and don't enforce any of ya pad rules on me as there's two of us in here mate, compromise maybe, no one-way-traffic on the rules, that stops now." I said firmly, but with a smile on my face as Frank stood towering over me.

"Okay lad that seems fair." Frank replied, in his broad Welsh accent. Within 10 minutes, Frank and I had hit it off and became mates. I was utterly surprised when I delved deeper into Frank's personality and realised that he was no idiot, no bully, but a super-intelligent fella. He was well read and had formed some great traits along the way, which made him an unusual breed, especially in prison.

I was given a job as an educational mentor on my wing and was part of the drama and radio class at HMP Altcourse and enjoyed the extra bonus of having Sky TV in my cell. It was a well-run prison that actually gave you a chance of getting your shit together; if you wanted to.

Frank and I often sat in our cell waiting for some unfortunate fucker to ask for help with some kind of prison paperwork. The number of problems that occurred through lads not being able to read or write on the wing was unbelievable and really sad at times. I often sat and felt sorry for some of these lads, they never had a chance to succeed in life and now they even struggled in jail.

Back to Court

On the morning of 27th February, I was woken at six o'clock to be told I was on my way to court for my plea and mention. I'd known a few days earlier due to my solicitor coming to see me, so I'd packed all my stuff and legal documents into the clear-plastic, prison-issue bags. It took to 14 bags to carry all my belongings. The Reception staff had their work cut out when I turned up at 7.30am ready for my Liverpool Crown Court hearing.

Three hours later and I was in a holding cell in the depths of Liverpool Crown Court. The Screws had informed me that I was up at 11.30 am and my legal team were on their way down to speak to me.

The door opened up at 11 o'clock and I was cuffed and escorted into a legal area, where my team sat talking to each other. I was led in by a tall, fat Screw, un-cuffed and told to sit down.

"Right, Paul, there have been some developments, but we haven't got much time, so they want this dealt with today", said my Barrister, Oliver Jarvis.

I looked at Shahid, my solicitor, "Today?"

"They're prepared to drop one of the conspiracy charges if you plead guilty to the other one, which will get you no more than 12 years." he said in a straight, serious tone. My heart stopped beating, or that's how it felt, as I began to digest the life-changing information.

"Now there's a sound and legitimate reason why I'm trying to get this done today. The new drug sentencing guidelines have been introduced today and you could be given a 10 year sentence with the premise of being a 'significant' member of your organisation or gang', so to speak."

I paused, took a deep breath and looked at Shahid whom I totally trusted and asked for his advice.

"Well, you know I'd run a trial, Paul, but if it goes wrong, you're looking at a possible 20 year plus sentence, so the 10 to 12 on offer doesn't seem that bad on balance, but that decision is yours to make in the next 10 minutes".

My life seemed to come down to a 10-minute period sitting in a legal area in the depths of Liverpool Crown Court.

I didn't need the time to decide my fate as I'd had the past five years to run every possible scenario around my head.

"Let's deal up, take it, let's do this today." I said positively and quickly, while looking at Shahid and nodding constantly, indicating my mind was made up. "Come on then, I'm absolutely sure. Enough is enough and by the sound of it, I'll only serve six which is appealing to me right now." I said, as I stood up and indicated to the Screw that he could take me back to the holding cells. After shaking both their hands, I was cuffed and escorted back to the cells.

While I sat alone in my pad, I heard noise outside the door and jumped up to look out the small, round, window. There were loads of fellas coming in cuffed and being put into the cell next to me. I peered through and noticed my old pad mate, Johnny from Wigan.

"Johnny, Johnny!" I shouted, knocking on the window.

"Now then, Pee, what you doin' here, lad?" Johnny said in his broad Wigan accent as soon as he noticed me.

"I'm getting dealt with today, Johnny, I'll try and speak to ya when I'm done and dusted." My face was pressed firmly against the glass, getting the last glimpse as he went out of sight into the cell next door. When his door was slammed, mine was opened and I was cuffed and escorted to a lift, which took me to Court Number Two. I was taken to a small ante-room where I was met by my solicitor and barrister, who informed me that the Prosecution were happy with the deal and I was briefed about which charges I would plead 'Guilty' and 'Not Guilty' to.

Five minutes later, I was brought up the small flight of stairs, cuffed to two Screws and seated into the glass-surrounded dock. As I looked around, I noticed my pals, Tom the Spark and Ste G were in the gallery at the back of the court directly behind me. I'd told my family I didn't want anyone to attend the court as I didn't want them to get emotional; my sisters would have definitely cried. There were also three SOCA detectives seated at the side of the court who kept on glaring at me while I spoke to Tom and Ste at the back of the court.

The usher told us all to rise in his deep, firm voice. The Judge came in, sat down and peered over his gold-rimmed glasses in my direction and indicated for us to be seated. My Barrister spoke first and then the Prosecution spoke briefly about the description of the offences I was being accused of. Once they'd finished with all their summing up, the Judge read out the two charges and asked me what my pleas were.

"Guilty to Charge One and Not Guilty to Charge Two." I answered, nervously.

The three SOCA detectives started to move about and shake their heads as the Prosecution stood up and said they were happy to take my pleas and drop the second charge. I was nervous and grasping my sweaty hands as the Judge and my Barrister sifted through papers and discussed the sentencing structure my offence warranted. The Judge looked at me and said,

"Well, it's to my knowledge that it shall be no more than 10 years as Mr. Walmsley was a significant member of this organisation that dealt in any illegal drugs," he paused and asked for the usher to approach me.

"Can you stand up?" the usher asked, as he gesticulated. My name was announced and the Judge took a sip of water and said,

"Mr. Walmsley, you have been found guilty of conspiracy to supply Class A drugs and for that you'll be given a custodial sentence. Ten years will be the length of the sentence, but for your courage to hand yourself in and take your medicine, today I'm going to knock six months off. You are sentenced to nine and a half years, Mr. Walmsley. Take him down."

With that, the two Screws ushered me out of the court, but not before I had time to turn back and talk briefly to Tom, Ste G and look at the not-so-happy SOCA detectives. I shouted to Tom and Ste,

"Thanks for coming, I'm sound, lads, I'll be in touch soon as I can." The door was closed to the ante-room and I was led towards the lift feeling relieved and surprisingly happy about the final outcome. It could have been a lot worse.

I never had time to think about what happened as I was taken to another holding cell, but this one contained Johnny and Tangy, who was his co-accused.

"Yo Pee, what happened, lad?" Johnny screeched.

"I've got nine and a half and I'm happy with that." I said, with a smile on my face. Now Johnny had been in the cell when I had paperwork scattered all over the place until the early hours, so he knew the case inside out, as I did his. We'd helped each other out at times as sounding boards are an essential part of reading through your depositions. Johnny and I did that regularly back in HMP Liverpool a few months previously.

After the initial boisterous 10 minutes, we settled down in the holding cells and the usual wind-ups and banter started to fly about. I'd joked about going back to HMP Altcourse where I had Sky TV, snooker tables, two canteens a week and was left unlocked until 9 o'clock most nights. These luxuries were a million miles away from the stern regime that was in place at Walton nick. I suppose we were both just trying to deflect the impending seriousness of our sentencing as Johnny was also looking at a big one.

During one of our wind-ups, the Screws unlocked the holding cell and told me I was heading back to Altcourse. I said my goodbyes and wished Johnny and Tangy luck, and left them with the thought that I had Sky TV in my cell; they were both wounded at that but nevertheless, buzzed off the brief encounter.

As I waited in the depths of the court in the sweatbox to go to Altcourse, one of the screws came on board and informed me I was heading back to the cells.

"Why, what for?" I was confused.

"You're going to Leeds," the screw laughed. "There's no Sky TV there," he said, as he led me back to the holding cell with Johnny and Tangy.

"What are you doing back?" Johnny shouted, as I walked through the cell door. "They're fuckin sending me to fuckin Leeds," I said, as I turned and looked at the Screw, who was smiling at me.

Johnny and Tangy couldn't contain their laughter and roared, rolling about on the wooden benches which edged the holding cells.

"You're fuckin fumin', aren't ya, lad?" Tangy said, as he held back his laughter. Johnny just giggled away for about 10 minutes and eventually I even had a chuckle. It was funny but I was not looking forward to going to HMP Leeds as its reputation was one of worst jails in the country along with Walton.

Johnny and Tangy's trial continued and they left at 5'ish, but I was still there for another two hours in the massive holding cell at the end of the court's inner depths corridors.

At 10.30pm I was sitting in a sweatbox outside this huge castle-type jail in Leeds as the rain beat down on the bus, giving the impression that someone's fingers tapped away on the roof. In the darkness, the shape of the jail looked daunting and somewhat weird, as there was no noise at all as I was escorted of handcuffed into the Reception area.

The atmosphere of this place was not welcoming at all as this Victorian jail's staff went through the reception process quickly and on to the first night induction wing. That's when the day's events began to sink in. Oh shit ... I've got to do four years and nine months behind bars, and that's if it all went well.

Get On With It

The next morning I was moved to F Wing, the biggest block in the jail. There were 170 inmates and the majority were of Muslim faith. There was only one Scouser, a kid called Wrighty from Anfield, who was awaiting trial for drugs. When I popped my head in to my new cell, it absolutely stunk of a death. A head appeared from the bottom bunk and smiled to reveal two full teeth; the rest looked like a burnt fence.

He introduced himself as Mick from Leeds and he had the craziest, clacking lisp I'd ever heard. I couldn't look at him in case I burst out laughing, and when he'd jumped up out of bed, his cock was hanging out of his prison-issue boxer shorts. I backed out of the cell and began to load my bags of clothes, bedding, food and court paperwork, as Mick fixed himself then helped me to move in.

My 22,000 pages of paperwork was raising eyebrows on the Wing as it was left outside my cell door until I'd made room for it in my cell, as the Prison refused to store it due to Fire Regulations. The funny thing was, two hours later when I'd met the lads in the cells either side of me, they both informed me that they were in for arson; that works well with 22,000 pieces of paper taunting their desires stacked at the bottom of my bed.

I'd settled into HMP Leeds and Mick turned out to be my real-life, victim-awareness project as I talked at length about his raving drug habit and problems. Through his constant injecting into his thigh, he had an open flesh wound that wouldn't heal. The stale smell would not leave our cell and every morning I'd wake up with it wallpapered to the back of my throat. His body was breaking down, organ by organ and the smell got worse by the day. No matter how many times he showered or we cleaned the cell up, the smell would reappear rapidly. This was karma for me, this is the by-product of what I'd been doing for years and now I was dealing with it first-hand. Poor Mick, he was on that much medication in the end, he would nod off standing up.

A few months later, the Governor, Paul Baker, was on the Wing and I was playing a prison-owned guitar. After a 10 minute mini concert, he signed my application for books and my guitar to be handed in. As it happened, he turned out to be a hands-on Governor who treated you fairly and with respect.

There was another fella from Middlesbrough on the wing who played guitar; his name was Andy Lindo, who was in for murder. I didn't find out his story until later on, but on first impressions he was a nice enough fella. I didn't 100% know what his circumstances were, all I knew was that he played the guitar really well. We often sat on the wing having a jam session to pass the time; in fact, I totally got the music bug back.

On the morning of 11 May 2012, I was woken up to the news that I was being moved to a Cat C jail near Doncaster. HMP Lindholme was an hour's drive in another sweatbox on a scorching Friday morning. Another Reception check-in and rummage through my belongings and I was on my way to L Wing. It was a weird building; only a periscope short of being a submerged submarine and full of weirdos.

Within a few days, all the Scousers had made their way to the fence on L Wing knowing there was a fellow Scouser in the jail. It didn't take long before lads who I knew from back in the day showed their faces through the metal fence.

Ste, The Wasp, and his younger brother, Jay, Big Butch, Tricky, who I knew from Marbella, Robbie, who was one of my co-accused and Gary G from Norris Green all turned up at the fence to meet and greet.

I was allowed on E wing, which was separated into eight spurs. Each spur had eight inmates with their own cells, and a social area at the end with TV, fridge, toaster and a seated area. It was like a mini version of *Big Brother* but for convicted male criminals. I ended up on Ste, The Wasp's and Tricky's spur. There was a lad from Salford called Baskey, who I was padded up with. I landed right on my feet as Baskey was the funniest, kindest and most-popular lad in the jail. God help anyone who tried to take the piss out of him as he had a knack of cutting people into small pieces with his ultra-fast banter.

HMP Lindholme was a working jail, so you either went on courses or you educated yourself. My mind was made up from the beginning as I'd always wanted a proper education. I'd been an A-grade student at school and the thought of getting a second chance in life jumped out for me. When I told all the lads I'd turned my back on my previous life, I was looked upon with a certain, 'Oh yeah, I bet you have', sort of attitude.

There was a reason I knew everyone when I first bounced onto B Wing in Walton Jail in my hometown, Liverpool. Most of the lads were around my age and had been grafting just like me; getting a second chance in life thrilled me.

I'd received news that my old pal, The Pirate, had passed away in HMP Rye Hill in Oxfordshire. I'd been writing to him every month and was looking forward to meeting up one day. It rattled me to my core and it spurred me on even more to get out of this rat-race lifestyle. I didn't want to end up dying in jail. I wondered what his family were going through, as he was a proper family man.

Rest in peace, Ste Pittman.

Moving On

After being encouraged to enter a poetry writing competition by Miss T, who was an Officer on our Wing, I set my new-life ball rolling. I enrolled on Open University courses and was mentored by a published author named Andy Croft, who constantly encouraged me and others who were interested, in putting our thoughts and feelings down on paper. So I did.

Growing up in Norris Green, Liverpool, was like growing up on any Council estate in the late 70s and early 80s. There were no computers, iPads, Smartphones or social networking sites to keep us locked away in our bedrooms. This gave us the opportunity to venture out to our reachable surroundings; when we got there we did what was any youngster would do; had fun.

The thing is though, that fun would come at a price later on. Everyone always thought I had a chance when I was a kid. They thought I'd become a footy player or some kind of academic; but the endemic nature of the surroundings, mixed with certain unforeseen circumstances put an end to those aspirations.

Situations spiralled out of control once my dad died, I thought I knew best, I knew it all, no-one could tell me anything. Boy, how badly informed I was as an enthusiastic teenager. If anyone close to me who I had respect for would have told me, I wouldn't fully mature until I was in my early 40s, I would have told them to 'leg it', but no-one ever did. I had to find that out the hard way. But it's true, you don't grow up until you're in your early forties. Deal with it, men.

The Truth

There's a TV series called *Location Location Location* which is about finding a house to live in; the title of the show suggests it's all about the locality. Well, from the late 80s to the present day, Liverpool should take a leaf out of the TV series' theme, but give it a twist; *Drugs, Drugs and More Drugs* with the follow-up series called *Gangs, Gangs and More Gangs With Guns.*

Things have changed in my home town; my generation are either on drugs, fucked up after drugs, looking for drugs or making their own drugs. If they're not doing any of the above, they're either in jail, visiting jail or waiting for the day when jail enters their lives in some fashion and have been doing so since they were teenagers.

It takes a while for the Police to build a file on you as the sheer number of people grafting is massive in Liverpool. By the time they've got enough info on you, you're in your early 30s, then it's down to misfortune or some lowlife grassing bellend who's got it in for you; either way, you're on their radar and the SOCA squad comes for you with the might and technology of the British Legal system firmly behind them. Watch out, Young 'uns.

These fellas are not messing about, oh no, they take everything you have; money, liberty, opinion, future and most of all, your family.

So this epidemic that's been running through the veins of our society since the 80s is no longer just a 'working class' problem. It has transcended into a cross-social background issue that had crushed human development in certain parts of the country and created a culture that's only just forming.

I know I haven't helped matters improve along the way, obviously due to my wrongdoings, but this problem has roots which have been around for centuries; it has circled back on itself now, you only need to check out the 'History Trail'. I only wish the 'powers that be' would not brush this problem under the carpet, they need to deal with this from the bottom up… Education and Parenting.

I missed plenty of chances when I was younger due to lack of both. That's my story and I'm sure you've got your own thoughts, ideas and experiences about some of the issues raised in this book. You might know somebody who's experienced some of the plights, flights and dramas of my life. I hope you do, then you'll have more of an insight into my journey, indirectly through them. If you don't have somebody you know who's had a similar rollercoaster journey, then don't panic, there's still time.

I've witnessed over 130 people lose their lives while watching football matches and somehow, by way of fate, luck or good fortune, I'm here today writing this book. To say it hasn't affected my choices, roads travelled or decisions is up for debate, especially in my head. What do you think?

It's Friday 21 June 2013 and I'm on another journey down another road, but not in a sweatbox. It's an emotional rollercoaster, but with me finally in control. The people who really do matter are on this rollercoaster with me until the end and I can't wait until it stops and I can cuddle my kids, family and friends with no baggage weighing me down.

'You'll Never Walk Alone'.

Epilogue

It's Friday 28th July 2017 and I'm sitting in my flat in North Liverpool contemplating the last 3½ year, as that's when I thought I'd completed this book. I've been released from HMP Kirkham and a free man for 13 months on licence in the community.
So what's happened?

In 2013 in the space of a couple of months, my sister, Lynn took her own life and to say that totally devastated our family is an understatement. While I was grieving, I heard the news that Lisa, the mother of my two youngest children, was marrying her childhood sweetheart. I didn't even know she had one. I thought I was her only sweetheart, oh boy was I wrong.

A month later I was informed that my mother had been diagnosed with dementia and two of her brothers, my uncles, has passed away and then my aunt, Aggie, my mum's youngest sister had also been given her last rites by the priest. I felt helpless and overwhelmed by the sheer lack of support I could give to my family at that time.

The only good thing to come from this was that my personal officer, Mr. Paul Evans, who was a gentleman and stand-up human being somehow pulled a few strings to get me closer to my family. He got me a transfer to HMP Kennet in North Liverpool, five miles away from my family home. I have to stress just how much of a nice fella he was. He treated all the inmates with the same respect he got from them, which was always first class. This restored my life with hope and helped me immensely.

On arrival at Kennet, I buried my head in books and enrolled on every course I humbly envisaged benefiting from:

- ITQ higher diploma
- Events Management diploma
- Coaching and Mentoring diploma
- Humanistic Counselling higher diploma
- Personal Fitness Trainer course
- Gym Instructor
- NLP Practitioner higher diploma
- Religious Correspondence higher diploma
- BTEC tutoring diploma (level 4)
- Psychology with Counselling BA degree
- Creative Writing – which lead to a Koestler Award Writing Scholarship.

The writing scholarship was borne from what you've just read. I met the Creative Writing tutor in HMP Kennet, Becky Tallentire and she gave me the confidence to express my creativity and opened me up to the knowledge that learning was knowing anything is possible.

I gave her my enormous hand-written paper folder and told her that it was my life story. It had taken me six months to write; spending three hours every night, from 7 to 10pm religiously scribbling down my past experiences; she reluctantly took it and said she would read it when she had breaks in her busy working day.

Two weeks passed and Becky sent a message over to the Induction Wing and summonsed me to her lair. She was intimidating as she was a bespectacled, six foot, slender woman and her tongue was razor sharp due to her vast vocabulary and acerbic, Evertonian wit. Yes, she was from the blue half of the city and uber proud of that fact. She was always at it with the banter and loved giving and taking stick, that's why I got on with her so well.

When I arrived at her chewing-gum-grey-walled classroom on the education wing. I was greeted with a huge smile and the words:

"Oh my God, Walmsley, this is amazing. We have to enter it into the Koestler Awards. We need to start typing it up, it's brilliant and I'll be astonished if it doesn't win the top prize."

She was so excited and this gave me instant goose bumps and we both made our way to the computer to begin making a hard copy. We only had six weeks for the deadline, so time was of the essence.

Over the next few weeks, Becky set about typing up my work. She told me my Liverpool Football Club stories made her skin crawl and unearthed bitter rivalry and forked-tongued, healthy banter.

Due to the time constraints and the fact that the folder couldn't leave the prison walls, it had to be done during work hours. Eventually, the first few chapters were typed up, proofread, altered, polished, edited and eventually sent off to the Koestler Trust on the final day of the deadline for entry.

So now it was in the hands of the professional judges to evaluate, critique and (hopefully) enjoy. Six weeks later I received a letter from the Koestler Trust stating my entry had been received along with 80,000 others and the results would be published online at the end of August, which was 10 weeks away.

Prison is governed by protocol, rules and regulations that are sometimes over the top, but set in stone. I suppose they have to be that way to protect the public. With that in mind, 11 weeks after receiving the Koestler letter, I was summoned to the Governor's office and naturally assumed I was in trouble.

I was shocked to find a welcoming handshake and pat on the back for being awarded the 'Platinum Award' for my writing. This was the top accolade and with 80,000 entries it meant mine had shone and been critically acclaimed by professional writers, publishers and the Koestler Trust. I was beaming with achievement, pride and emotion. Wow, this feeling was amazing and gave me hope to continue with my creative streak and to gain every ounce of knowledge I could absorb in the future.

A couple of months passed and I was allowed out on a Saturday to go see my family for a few hours and this was the start of my integration back into the community. It wasn't long before I was allowed outside the prison environment and given a position of trust working at the Brunswick Youth and Community Centre (Brunny) in Bootle, Liverpool. It was strange having a job in Liverpool as I'd bounced around the city with no constraints for years and now I was monitored daily by prison staff and probation. This was another massive step towards building a new life without being involved in crime.

There was a sports/football based academy in the Brunny and it wasn't long before I was seconded to them from the centre and became an integral part of 16-18-year-old education, lifestyle and finding pathways into a brighter future. I was helping the youth of today.

Life started to take on a different meaning for me. I was working in the community, helping young people, while working to create a better future for myself. I became the go-to guy for advice, sign posting and early intervention into gangs and crime-related behaviour. People began to respect my opinion and this gave me added hope and a sense of self-worth, which in turn helped build a reputation of being knowledgeable in regard of criminal behaviours or criminal behavioural patterns.

Within the space of a few months in 2015, I was moved to HMP Kirkham in Flyde, Lancashire and given a car by the sports' academy to travel to Liverpool on weekdays to continue with my community work at The Brunny. I received offers to speak at conferences, events and even an offer from the Sumo Guy, Paul McGee to attend a presentation master class, which obviously I did and made more connections into the private and public sector with my message of resilience. Over a period of 18 months whilst at the Sports Academy, I completed a Level 4 higher diploma in Teaching and Tutoring in the Lifelong Learning Sector.

I was constantly monitored by the Prison Service and staff at Merseyside Probation Service. The Chief Executive at the time was Annette Hennessy OBE. She constantly gave me her time and support and helped me to network into the Universities as a keynote speaker. For that, I'm eternally grateful and will always class her as a friend.

Over a period of 6 months, I was allowed to speak at four major conferences one being an EU symposium about reducing reoffending where I was one of the keynote speakers. I was escorted to this event by the Number-One Governor from HMP Kirkham. A week later I was allowed to travel to London to receive my writing scholarship from the Koestler Trust which was a measure of how far I'd come in such a short space of time. This gave me another creative lease of life which in turn encouraged me to write more songs and poetry.

Several of my poems were published in the Inside Time newspaper and the Kirkham prison band now turned into my own live kickass group. Colin, Flynn, Dave, Shand, Cliff and many others would religiously practice my songs and regularly perform them to the inmates. The band was originally called Kirkhamsized, but I had my own unofficial name, *'Me and Two Murderers'*. It was amazing having my own band playing songs I'd written whilst sitting in a cell.

Eventually, I was allowed home leave from Friday morning until Tuesday afternoon. Being set free into the public to see your loved ones might sound strange to some people but it comes with its own set of problems. You have to be aware that the prison still owns your arse on a daily basis.

One home leave was spent with my mother, I held her hand as she told me she was not afraid to die. We both sat in Fazakerley hospital where she was waiting to have an operation for lung cancer. She was having her left lung removed. I was strong for my 81-year-old, dementia-suffering mother who was still as funny as ever.

When she sat in the bed waiting for the nurse to come, I asked her how the hospital food was as I removed the plastic lid from the plate. I was surprised to find 95% of it still on the plate when my mother said:
"It looks better with the lid on, Son,"
Mum came through the operation fine and has recently celebrated her 83rd birthday. What a woman.

On 28th June 2016, I was released from prison and instead of heading home I went to the Echo Arena and spoke at the International Festival for Business speaking about what ex-offenders can offer employers. Becky Tallentire was in the audience, as proud as Punch, she gifted me my very own copy of a book I'd admired and borrowed from her in HMP Kennet called *Dear Me: A Letter to My Sixteen Year Old Self*. James Timpson and Claire McGregor also spoke and this raised my profile in the press when the story went viral. I didn't engineer this press attention, it was more of a shock and dealt me a few blows, not to mention more media attention, and now TV had raised its head.

Offers flooded in due to the nature of the story and the work which I'd now engaged in. I had to keep a low profile because I didn't want to live my life in the past, I wanted to live it in the future, although that being said, my past had shaped me into the person I am today, and I don't have too many regrets. So, I decided to stay out of sight for two months.

I was offered a job at the academy and was also given the role of Project Coordinator at The Brunny for a pilot scheme which I'd pitched to the local authorities. *'Dream to Achieve'* was launched and 40 young people from Bootle, North Liverpool, had: myself, Peter Riley (musician), Lorraine and James Riley from the GANGS project, down their ears about gangs, drugs and the consequences they'll have to face once they're entrenched into that lifestyle.

My own kids are finally proud of their dad who was once known as *Daddy Dickhead*, but now they know I have made many sacrifices to progress and they couldn't be happier or more proud of their father. My eldest, Dayne is a heating engineer, Emilly is in her third year of university training to become a registered nurse, Paul is in his second year of university studying sports science and Lizzie has just been accepted into LIPA (Liverpool Institute for Performing Arts). This fills me with even more pride and hope for the future.

My family who have supported me unconditionally are so proud and keep me on my toes daily. Kim, Shirley, Sue, Kathy and Pat have all been fantastic sisters while my brothers, Steven and Robert who still live in Perth, Australia have always been there for me when advice is needed.

In 2014, my world was rocked when Alan Wills, my dear friend and founder of Deltasonic was killed in a freak cycling accident in Liverpool. Alan was a true gentleman, inspiration and a loyal friend who kept in touch with me throughout my prison sentence and during my darkest days. His joie de vivre was legendary and he was a visionary on the music scene. I send my eternal love to his partner, Anne and want her to know Alan is never far from my thoughts.

The constant support from everyone at the academy (James, Stu, Wilko, Lippo, Dylan, Lewis, Karl and all the students) have lifted my spirits and given me a purpose. I've had the privilege to be the Pastoral Care Lead whilst tutoring and mentoring over 60 young people over the last two years, it's been an absolutely fantastic journey for us all. Throughout all of this I've had the support of Philly Carragher and the 23 Foundation which has helped me forge stronger links within the community.

To be fair, most of my students think I'm nuts, but in a good way. I'm unconventional and would like to think I teach them a lot more than just sports psychology. In fact, I tell all their parents and guardians that I won't make them a better footballer, I won't make them a better coach, but I will make them a better human being.

I also have to mention the group of girls from the *Dream to Achieve* project at The Brunny. There were 40 young people on the project but the 15 girls showed me total respect and gave me an insight into the exploitation of young people across the city. I thank them from the bottom of my heart for being so funny and honest and for trusting me. The whole group engaged with me, but there was one knife-wielding 13-year-old who was shaken by my presence. After some deliberation and clever communication skills, he became very polite and quickly turned and gave me a fist-pump in acknowledgement.

All of us are born good; circumstances over time change us and shape our mentality, so I know if I want people to change then I have to change, too. This particular 13-year-old however, will have to face up to difficult times if he continues with his lifestyle choices. But let me tell you, I'm not giving up on him.

Skunk seems to be smoked by so many young people today and without any due care or attention to future mental-health risks or issues. Back in the 80s, the drug of choice for the youth was heroin (smack, Nasty, Bobby, brown, etc.), as ignorance is and was bliss at times. Well, smack got a grip on most of the users and turned university prospects, future professional footballers and the good-looking council estate lads and girls into hunch-backed, scruffy, gaunt individuals who ended up with no future, no teeth and little hope in their prospects of a good healthy life. I witnessed this with my own eyes.

My job now is to document all of my life experiences and help young people who need to be pulled out of the flames. These flames are peer expectation and the pressure of the environment around them. It's not easy, but with the right choices, interventions and a pathway to achieve and hope, we can all help some of these young people.

One day they will shine like the brightest diamonds that have ever been excavated. Why do I know this? Because I was one of those kids and if I can obtain a resilience and a dream to achieve, then there is definitely a model to work from to deliver hope to these young people on the council estates around the country.

This book was written for my mother, Kathleen Walmsley; she gave me hope and has never stopped believing in me.

I hope this gives you hope.

Printed in Great Britain
by Amazon